Shakespeare

PETER ALEXANDER, F.B.A.

*formerly Regius Professor of English Language and
Literature in the University of Glasgow*

LONDON
OXFORD UNIVERSITY PRESS
NEW YORK   TORONTO
1964

Oxford University Press, Amen House, London E.C.4

GLASGOW NEW YORK TORONTO MELBOURNE WELLINGTON
BOMBAY CALCUTTA MADRAS KARACHI LAHORE DACCA
CAPE TOWN SALISBURY NAIROBI IBADAN ACCRA
KUALA LUMPUR HONG KONG

© Oxford University Press 1964

Printed in Great Britain by
Butler & Tanner Ltd, Frome and London

CONTENTS

INTRODUCTION

In a study that treats briefly of Shakespeare's family associations at Stratford and of his professional career as an actor and dramatist in London, it is impossible to do more than refer in passing to the very important contribution to our understanding of Shakespeare's work made by a long line of editors, and in recent years by the group of bibliographers who have given so searching a scrutiny to the circumstances in which the text of Shakespeare's plays has been transmitted to us. The labours of A. W. Pollard, W. W. Greg, and R. B. McKerrow have been continued in this country by Professor Dover Wilson and Dr Alice Walker, and in America by Professor Fredson Bowers and the contributors to his *Studies in Bibliography*, as well as by Professor Charlton Hinman who has so skilfully exploited the resources of the Folger Library in his thousand-page study of the printing of the First Folio. The findings of these scholars cannot be set aside as of no interest or value to readers in The Home University Library, but even in a university the work of the bibliographers is largely a post-graduate study. Enough, however, has been said in the following pages, it is hoped, to reassure readers that the findings of the bibliographers have fully justified the reliance that is here placed on the integrity and knowledge of 'a payre so carefull to show their gratitude both to the living and the dead' as Shakespeare's first editors, John Heminge and Henry Condell.

Chapter One

STRATFORD-ON-AVON

SHAKESPEARE was christened on 26 April 1564 and died on 23 April 1616. The inscription on his monument in the Church of the Holy Trinity at Stratford-on-Avon, which gives his age as 53, indicates that he was born on or before 23 April 1564. As he died on St George's Day it is convenient and appropriate to suppose that he was also born on the day of England's Patron Saint and to accept 23 April 1564 as his birthday.

He was the son of John Shakespeare, a glover and active member of the Common Council of Stratford, and Mary Arden, a daughter of one of the oldest families in Warwickshire. Some time in 1582 he married Anne Hathaway from Shottery, a hamlet less than a mile from Stratford; their first child Susanna was christened on 26 May 1583, as on 2 February 1585 were the twins Judith and Hamnet. Ten years later Shakespeare was one of the three principal sharers in the most successful company of actors in London.

None of Shakespeare's contemporaries thought it strange that a boy born in Stratford, who passed the first twenty or so years of his life there, should in the next thirty years of work in London give the stage a series of comedies and tragedies that place him among the great creative minds of the ages. Ben Jonson, in the lines which he wrote in 1623 for the volume in which Shakespeare's colleagues, John Heminge and Henry Condell, collected their friend's plays, does not think

it out of keeping to refer to the place of birth of the
dramatist whom he judges to have excelled even the
dramatists of antiquity, the men Jonson himself was
fain to call his masters. Yet Jonson could not conceal
entirely his loyalties as a scholar or refrain from wishing
that Shakespeare for all his genius had paid more
attention to classical forms and perfected himself in the
art of learned imitation that Jonson cultivated so resolutely. Here as elsewhere in his references to Shakespeare we can see the conflict in Jonson's mind between
his feelings and his theories that asserts itself, however
momentarily, in the phrase 'small Latine, and lesse
Greeke'. When he told Drummond that Shakespeare
wanted Art he was putting to his host one side only of
the debate about Shakespeare's judgement and genius
that occupies the characteristic note in his *Discoveries*
where he, in all fairness, claims the right to speak his
mind even about what he admires, 'for I loved the man,
and do honour his memory on this side idolatry as
much as any'.

The admiration that carries as an undertone the
doubt that finds expression in the phrase 'small Latine,
and lesse Greeke' is not without its echoes in later
times. Housman ventured to say that a more intensive
study of 'Virgil and the Greeks would have made
Shakespeare not merely a great genius, which he was
already, but a great artist which he is not'. And Housman here was following, however rashly, the critic
whom he admired, for Arnold made the point more dis-
creetly when he regretted that Shakespeare had not like
'those unapproached masters of the *grand style*' Sophocles and Homer 'sureness of perfect style'.

Jonson, Arnold, and Housman agree with many
other lovers of the classical poets in regretting that

Shakespeare was not more given to their study in his preparation for his own work; there is, however, a very important difference between the criticism of Jonson and the earlier commentators and that of later times. Jonson stressed the importance of certain formal features of classical drama that are now regarded as accidental rather than essential elements in its composition. The value Jonson attached to these formal elements can be studied in his tragedies of *Sejanus* and *Cataline*, and in the comments their unfavourable reception by the audience drew from him. *Sejanus* he admits is 'no true poem' in that it neglects the Unity of Time and lacks a proper chorus; *Cataline* he dares to call 'a legitimate *Poem*', although it lacks Unity of Place. It is, however, of such comedies as *Volpone* and *The Alchemist* that Jonson can say,

> The laws of time, place, persons, he observeth,
> From no needful rule he swerveth.

These 'laws' attributed to Aristotle and outlined by Horace had become through the commentaries of Italian scholars and especially of Scaliger part of the equipment of those with any pretensions to critical authority. It was natural for the scholarly Jonson to feel even as he admired the genius of his friend that as a dramatist Shakespeare had taken liberties with Time and Place that were not to be countenanced.

As Shakespeare generally ignored the Rules as understood by what was accepted as scholarly opinion and yet produced plays that were admired even by those who prided themselves on their learning, his success was attributed to Nature or

> Art without Art unparaleld as yet.

This explanation of Shakespeare's supremacy was taken up and enlarged on after the Restoration, when the criticism of Shakespeare became a topic for a succession of poets, scholars, and men of letters. Jonson had been careful to guard against uncritical appeals to Nature by insisting on the part that must be assigned to Art in Shakespeare's work,

> For a good Poet's made, as well as borne.
> And such wert thou.

Jonson did not, however, provide any terse comment on this aspect of Shakespeare's skill as easily adapted for quotation and comment as his remark on Shakespeare's Latin and Greek. Further this remark was given an exaggerated significance by the critical temper that prevailed after the Restoration.

The older Elizabethan and Jacobean stage traditions were weakened by the closing of the theatres in 1642. Many of the actors quitted the stage for the armed forces, and in spite of occasional efforts to defy the Puritan interdict, it was not till the Restoration that regular playing was again possible. With the return of the King, the Court, and other exiles, from the Continent, where the prestige of France was paramount, French influence gave a new colour to what came down from the native source.

On Shakespeare's stage the female parts had been taken by the boys or younger members of the troupe, but with the Restoration women became as in France members of the companies. The young spectator, as Macaulay put it, could now see 'with emotions unknown to the contemporaries of Shakespeare and Jonson tender and sprightly heroines personated by lovely women'. Whether Macaulay regarded such emotions as

germane to the matter of the play he does not say. Criticism now was often little more than an elaboration of French opinion. The views that Jonson had proclaimed in what he called 'these jig-given times' were already the accepted canons of the French stage on the eve of its giving room to Molière and Racine. The French Academy founded by Richelieu in 1637 was called on by its patron to condemn Corneille's *Cid* for failing to observe the Rules according to Aristotle; and the Unities and Decorum became necessary passwords even to general approval in France. In 1674 Thomas Rymer translated Rapin's *Reflections on Aristotle's Treatise of Poesie* and began his attack on what he considered the lack of form and propriety in the older English drama that culminated in his *Short View of Tragedy* (1694). This contains his examination of *Othello*, where Rymer's notions of Decorum and Poetical Justice are most clearly displayed. Poetical Justice, an expression coined by Rymer, requires the dramatist to let us see the wicked adequately punished and the good suitably rewarded; he must not leave the matter, as we have to do so regularly in life itself, to 'God Almighty and another World'. The murder of Desdemona, Rymer felt, could not but 'envenome and sour our spirits' and make us 'repine and grumble at Providence and the government of the World'. For if this is the reward of virtue, 'what boots it to be Vertuous?' The will and purposes of God Almighty may be beyond our comprehension, but this must not, Rymer argued, be admitted by the poet. As for Decorum it seems to Rymer entirely lacking in *Othello* which he finds 'plainly none other than a Bloody Farce, without salt or savour'.

That there is some rightness in Rymer's opinion one might be surprised into thinking by Mr T. S. Eliot's

remark, 'I have never seen a cogent refutation of Thomas Rymer's objections to *Othello*'. But Rymer's ideas on drama resemble those on art that Proust had in mind when he wrote, 'The arguments of M. de Norpois (in the matter of art) were unanswerable simply because they were without reality'. At one moment Rymer treats the drama as if it were to be judged by the criteria we apply to history, in the next he insists on its presenting us with characters cut to some abstract pattern that ignores the individual peculiarities of men; he examines the plot of *Othello* as if it were the account of some actual occurrence Shakespeare was reporting in a confused and contradictory manner, while Desdemona and Othello are condemned as unlike Rymer's idea of a typical Venetian lady and a typical Blackamoor soldier. Rymer's way of looking at art is repeated in every generation, and Chekhov in laughing at those of his own generation who would have a writer omit the warts from his portraits and describe only honest mayors, high-minded ladies, and virtuous railroad contractors, is dismissing as nonsense the categories Rymer and his kin would impose on the mind of the dramatist. The notions that in drama a king must never be shown as an accessory to a crime, that no woman is to kill a man except her social position is superior to his, that a subject must not kill a king, are like so many more of Rymer's assertions only less absurd than the indulgence he extends to Christians, however humble, who may kill a heathen sultan, or to Englishmen who may ignore all distinctions of rank in killing any foreigner, even a foreign king.

By the time of Johnson the unreasonable nature of Rymer's use of the Unities and Decorum in his critical tirades was becoming clear. In his *Preface* of 1765

Johnson in addition to his famous examination of the place of the Unities in drama observes, 'When Shakespeare's plan is understood, most of the criticisms of Rhymer and Voltaire vanish away'; and as the intrusion on the tragic scene of anything that might seem low and undignified was as offensive to Rymer as to his French preceptors, Johnson in contradiction of their authority signified his approval of the scene in *Hamlet* that had given special offence to sticklers for decorum by adding, 'and the Grave-diggers themselves may be heard with applause'.

It was unfortunate that the first account of Shakespeare to appear in print that was systematic enough to be accepted as a Life of the dramatist was written when the Rules of the drama had still behind them the full prestige of French fashion. This was published in 1709 when Nicholas Rowe (1674–1718) introduced his edition of Shakespeare's plays with *Some Account of the Life, etc.* of the dramatist.

It may seem strange today, when the affairs of living poets and writers are favourite topics for journalistic comment and frequently subjects for academic research, let alone matter for autobiography, that there is no *Life* of Shakespeare from a contemporary hand. Biography, however, had not yet become a regular feature of English letters. As Bacon observed, 'I do find it strange that these times have so little esteemed the virtues of the times, as that the writing of lives should be no more frequent'. Bacon was speaking as a historian and a man of affairs who wished to penetrate the façade of official business and discover the motives that prompted the principal actors in affairs of state; he was not concerned with poets who may prove the glory of their age, but as a rule only when they are in their graves. Clarendon

in his great history of the civil war was one of the first
to adopt Bacon's suggestion and introduce character
sketches of individuals on both sides; but while telling
us of many who might otherwise be forgotten he
nowhere in the history mentions Milton, although the
poet himself regarded his defence of Liberty as

> my noble task
> Of which all Europe rings from side to side.

Milton's life, however, did not pass unchronicled; he
tells us something about himself when he felt it necessary to justify his position in the great debate in which
he was involved, and the controversies of the time explain in part the accounts we have from younger men
who knew him. On the other side Walton's *Lives* of
Donne and other Anglican divines were a tribute from
a churchman and royalist not merely to men of genius
but to associates, as it were, in a great trial. But for the
earlier generation of poets and dramatists, for Spenser,
Shakespeare, Marlowe, and many others, there are no
contemporary accounts that can be called Lives, and
what is known for certain about their private and
family affairs is largely due to the patient research by
scholars, historians, and antiquaries, of later genera-
tions.

Rowe unhappily came too late to his task to hear at
first hand about the dramatist from anyone who might
have known him; he did not even visit Stratford but
merely transmits what Betterton the actor gathered
there on a visit about 1708. Rowe was, however, as a
dramatist himself interested in the plays. He had been
sent, after a good classical grounding as a King's
scholar at Westminster, to the Middle Temple in order
that he might follow his father's career as a lawyer.

The early death of his father left him in comfortable circumstances and he now turned to writing for the theatre, *The Fair Penitent* in 1703, which has as one of its characters the gay Lothario, and *Jane Shore* in 1714, being among his various productions. Like some other men of letters of that time he held a minor parliamentary appointment; after the accession of George I Rowe was in 1715 made poet-laureate; on his death in 1718 he was buried in Westminster Abbey. Although his edition of Shakespeare deserves the commendation Johnson gave it, Rowe did not engage in any historical research that would have enabled him to put his *Account* of Shakespeare's life on a sound basis. He contented himself with what Betterton picked up at Stratford, and recorded what stories circulated in his own day in London about the dramatist, binding all together by what his reading of the plays suggested to him. Some seventy years later Edmund Malone (1741–1812), the friend and helper of Boswell, set himself to order or augment 'such particulars as accident has preserved, or the most sedulous industry has been able to collect'. This industrious enquirer felt that 'The negligence and inattention of our English writers, after the Restoration, to the history of the celebrated men who preceded them, can never be mentioned without surprise or indignation'. That Rowe's *Life* should have continued to be the accepted account was to Malone a matter not to be contemplated without astonishment.

Rowe not unnaturally looked at the plays in the light provided by the critical prepossessions of his time. So insistent was learned opinion on the dramatist's observing the Unities of Time and Place in his productions that Rowe felt bound to suppose, with others of his age, that Shakespeare's neglect of these Rules could be

explained only by his never having heard of them. Speaking of the plays Rowe observed:

If one undertook to examine the greatest part of these by those rules which are established by *Aristotle*, and taken from the model of the *Grecian* stage, it would be no very hard task to find a great many faults: But as *Shakespeare* liv'd under a kind of mere light of nature, and had never been made acquainted with the regularity of those written precepts, so it would be hard to judge him by a law he knew nothing of. We are to consider him as a man that liv'd in a state of almost universal licence and ignorance.

Here the conflict between that instinctive appreciation of Shakespeare's genius and lack of understanding of his technical skill, so obvious in Jonson's comments on Shakespeare, enters a new phase. Jonson it is true felt that Shakespeare did not share the enthusiasm for the imitation of the ancient writers that he himself regarded as a requisite in a complete poet or maker; Rowe now attributes this failure on Shakespeare's part not merely to his small Latin and less Greek but to his downright ignorance of the practice of the classical dramatists.

Rowe's interpretation of the evidence afforded by the plays allows him to represent Shakespeare as lacking a regular education and goes half-way to the extreme view that Shakespeare was a vulgar or unlettered man, who could not therefore have written the works attributed to him by his colleagues and contemporaries.

To assume, however, as some do, that Ben Jonson and the many others who treat the plays published under Shakespeare's name as indeed Shakespeare's were shameless liars, and the public who believed them simple gulls, and that those who erected the monument in the church at Stratford with an inscription com-

memorating his genius were placing a lie in the very sanctuary itself, is to enlarge on that part of Rowe's account which is demonstrably false and to use Rowe's ignorance here to discredit the remainder of his account as the elaboration of a popular but false tradition.

Three considerations show that Shakespeare's failure, as Rowe regarded it, to shape his plays in accordance with the Rules provides no support whatever to the conviction that Shakespeare lived in a state of licence and ignorance. Shakespeare's contemporary Marlowe and the other university men who wrote for the public stage at that time took even less care to observe the Unities than Shakespeare; yet Rowe would hardly have ventured to assert that Marlowe, Greene, and Nashe had been living at Cambridge in a state of licence and ignorance and had turned to the drama with no better guidance than that provided by the mere light of Nature. Nor did Rowe himself, though not a university man, leave school uninstructed in the Rules of the drama, for he was brought up under the rod of the great Richard Busby 'who suffered none of his scholars to let their powers lie useless'. Yet the very evidence Rowe cites as proof of Shakespeare's ignorance is found in his own pieces for the stage. As Dr Johnson observed: 'In the construction of Rowe's dramas there is not much art; he is not a nice observer of the unities. He extends time and varies place as his convenience requires.' Rowe, like so many other critics, preached what he did not practise. Perhaps Rowe may be excused for not being as sufficiently informed about the Elizabethan drama as later commentators, and for failing to see that the form adopted by Shakespeare is no more attributable to ignorance than is the treatment of time and place in the plays of Marlowe or in those he wrote himself. Nor perhaps

is it surprising that the pupil of a headmaster who had given some sixteen bishops to the church did not know that Latin and the usages of the Roman stage had been taught at Stratford long before Elizabeth's foundation of Westminster. Rowe, however, did observe that in *The Tempest* the Unities are kept 'with an exactness uncommon to the liberties of his writing'. And Rowe, had he possessed any knowledge of the chronology of Shakespeare's works, might have added that in *The Comedy of Errors* Shakespeare demonstrated in his early years as a dramatist his perfect command not merely of the Unities but of the stage procedure generally of Latin comedy. Rowe admits that he cannot square his own assertion that 'It is without controversie, that Shakespeare had no knowledge of the writings of the antient poets' with Shakespeare's authorship of *The Comedy of Errors*. Rowe's hesitation here does not, however, prevent some later commentators from hastening to assure us that Shakespeare is not the author of this play—although his authorship is clearly attested by contemporary authority—thus cutting down the evidence on which Rowe's generalization is founded till it fits his conclusion.

Rowe's insistence that Shakespeare cannot have known the Rules also ignores the many opportunities Shakespeare had to read and to hear, for Ben Jonson was not likely to be silent, about their importance. Again Shakespeare had read Sidney's *Apologie for Poetrie* where the neo-classical view is put with the utmost clarity, as well as Florio who was equally emphatic on the correct form for Comedy and Tragedy; nor could Shakespeare have been ignorant of the references in the Prologues to Jonson's plays at the Globe. It is clear that, contrary to Rowe's opinion, Shakespeare

was familiar with the Unities; as he shaped his plays on a different principle, the question of the adequacy of their form will be treated in the examination of the plays themselves. Unfortunately Ben Jonson's feeling that Shakespeare's judgement was not equal to his genius has had the support of many later critics; yet with the waning of neo-classic prepossessions it was possible for Coleridge to insist that Shakespeare's judgement was equal to his genius, and for Wordsworth in his Essay of 1815 to wonder how long it would be before the misconception that Shakespeare was a wild and irregular genius passes away and

it becomes universally acknowledged that the judgement of Shakespeare in the selection of his materials, and in the manner in which he has made them, heterogeneous as they often are, constitute a unity of their own, and contribute all to one great end, is no less admirable than his imagination, his invention, and his intuitive knowledge of human nature.

That the absence of the Unities in no way impairs the Unity of Shakespeare's plays can be shown only in the later discussion of the individual pieces; meantime it is necessary to free what is known of Shakespeare's years at Stratford and his earliest years in London from the misunderstandings and misrepresentations with which the notion that he was a man living in a state of universal licence and ignorance has inevitably confused the record.

Shakespeare's parents were not natives of Stratford. His father John Shakespeare was the son of Richard Shakespeare who farmed land at Snitterfield which lies on the higher ground some four miles north of Stratford. His land and farm Richard Shakespeare held on

lease from Robert Arden, a gentleman in comfortable circumstances who had other properties some four miles to the west at Wilmcote where he himself lived and where his house still stands.

John Shakespeare left Snitterfield for Stratford at an early age to serve his apprenticeship to a craft, for by 1552, when he was fined a shilling for making an unauthorized muckhill in Henley Street, he must have been in business for himself and a householder. He is later described in official documents as a glover; as the freedom of the craft of glovers and whitetawers required a seven-year apprenticeship John Shakespeare would leave Snitterfield not later than 1545.

This affair of the muckhill has sometimes been cited as evidence of the licence and ignorance prevailing in Stratford and of the contribution of the poet's father to its unhappy state. That would be, however, to judge the past by what is common practice today, a most misleading and unhistorical procedure. Seen in its proper context the fine is evidence of the care exercised by the authorities of Stratford in enforcing their sanitary regulations, for however primitive these arrangements may seem today they were those in operation in London and elsewhere in England and Europe. Milton's description of the contrast between the stench of the populous city, 'where houses thick and sewers annoy the air' and 'the smell of grain, or tedded grass, or kine' may remind us that sewers were open ditches and that when Prince Hal refers to 'the melancholy of Moor Ditch' the audience would almost sense the noisome sewer just outside the city wall. Nor was John Shakespeare a careless offender against cleanliness; associated with him in this affair were two other respectable citizens, Humphrey Reynolds and Adrian Quiney, who

were also fined twelve pence each; for these householders were endeavouring to change the pattern of
refuse-heaps prescribed by the authorities. This deliberate exercise of private enterprise, however, was
unacceptable to authority, whose vigilance in this and
other matters affecting the cleanliness of Stratford is
adequately demonstrated by the many fines inflicted,
without respect of person, on the inhabitants of the
borough.

In 1552 John Shakespeare was occupying the western
of the two houses in Henley Street now preserved
by the Shakespeare Birthplace Trustees. This house
Shakespeare held on lease till he purchased it for £40
in 1575. Meantime, however, in 1556 he purchased the
eastern house, later called, but on slender evidence, the
Woolshop; the western house being regarded as the
birthplace of the poet. In adding in 1556 the eastern
house to that already occupied John Shakespeare was
preparing for his marriage to Mary Arden that followed
in 1557.

Mary Arden was the youngest of Robert Arden's
eight daughters. At his death in 1556 Robert Arden
made suitable provision for his daughters and his second
wife, who was childless; to Mary he left, as well as the
conventional dowry, a valuable estate called Asbies,
containing some sixty acres and a house. Although no
one has succeeded in tracing John Shakespeare's ancestors beyond his father Richard Shakespeare, Mary
Arden's forebears, it is now clear, belonged to the
family descended from the Saxon nobleman Turchill
whose large possessions in Warwickshire are recorded in
Domesday Book. He adopted in the Norman fashion the
surname Arden from his estate that included the forest
of Arden. The main branch of the Ardens occupied

Park Hall; but Robert Arden was the son of a younger
son Thomas Arden, who was the second son of Walter
Arden of Park Hall, and it was in 1501 that Thomas
settled at Wilmcote. That Thomas of Wilmcote
moved in the same social circle as Walter of Park
Hall is manifest from their relying each in turn on such
prominent figures as Sir Thomas Throckmorton and
Thomas Trussell as trustees in their private settlements.
The younger branch was as entitled as the elder to regard themselves as descended from Guy of Warwick,
King Athelstan, and Alfred the Great.

For the son of a younger son Robert Arden was un-
usually well provided for, and in spite of his having to
make provision for his eight daughters, Mary's portion
was a valuable one. Rowe describes John Shakespeare
as a dealer in wool; no doubt his wife's estate Asbies
provided grazing for sheep, and there would be wool to
dispose of; his business, however, was that of a glover.
Not only is John Shakespeare described in legal documents as a glover; in some jottings made about 1660,
Thomas Plume, Archdeacon of Rochester, notes of
Shakespeare: 'He was a glover's son; Sir John Mennis
saw once his old father in his shop, a merry cheeked
old man, that said, Will was a good honest fellow, but
he durst have crackt a jeast with him at any time.' It
has been pointed out that the Archdeacon must have
been mistaken in attributing this report to Sir John
Mennis who was born too late to have seen John
Shakespeare; yet in 1660 John Shakespeare's occupation could have been known only to his fellow citizens
and those encountering him in some way similar to that
recorded by Plume. That the jotting preserves for us a
glimpse of the poet's father in his later years seems very
probable.

Between John Shakespeare's coming to Stratford to serve his apprenticeship and his marriage to Mary Arden, the local government of Stratford had passed out of the control of the old manorial court into the hands of the new corporate body established by Royal Charter in 1553.

For centuries Stratford-on-Avon had been under the jurisdiction of the Bishops of Worcester whose stewards presided over the Court Leet held twice yearly in Stratford. The Leet, to which freeholders and residents were bound to present themselves or incur a fine, elected the Bailiff and borough officers. The preservation of order and the regulation of the social and economic life of the borough were among the concerns of the Leet. It was at such a Leet that John Shakespeare and his two friends were fined for breaking the sanitary regulations.

There had, however, grown up in Stratford an organization that was to have a powerful influence on the life of the community. This was the Guild of the Holy Cross. Like all medieval guilds its original care was for the souls of the departed brothers and sisters; to that end it built its own chapel and maintained its own priests. It did not, however, ignore the needs of the living; it provided for the poor and aged by building the row of alms-houses that stretch along Church Street from the Chapel, and the Guildhall.

The school at Stratford had originally been attached to the Church of the Holy Trinity. The church itself had been enlarged by John de Stratford, once Rector of Stratford and later Archbishop of Canterbury from 1333 to 1349; he also attached to it a College of Priests. The Guild, however, took over the school, and the building erected for that purpose in 1427 still stands to

the east of the Guildhall and is now known as the Pedagogue's House. After 1553 the school was moved to the upper floor of the Guildhall. In 1482 an endowment set aside earlier by John Jolyf, a member of the Guild, to provide free education became operative; Stratford thus early felt the benefit of that enthusiasm for education which throughout the next 150 years prompted men of means to provide their country with a system of education that has been described as more competent and comprehensive than the nation was to possess again till late in the nineteenth century. There were thus opened to the young who were able or ambitious opportunities that the history of the period proves were not neglected.

Nor was the economic position of Stratford forgotten. Sir Hugh Clopton, a native member of the Guild, who was Lord Mayor of London in 1492, replaced the wooden bridge that carried the road to the south across the Avon by the stone structure of fourteen arches that has withstood the floods that frequently damaged the previous structure and interrupted traffic on what was an important route for trade.

John Shakespeare's entry into this well-organized community cannot have preceded by any considerable time the important change in the local organization that followed on the passing of the second Chantries Act in 1547. A chantry was an endowment to provide prayers for the souls of the founders of the fund; even in the fourteenth century Chaucer could contrast the active life of his Poor Parson with the idleness of chantry priests. Many priests, however, who were technically chantry priests were like the schoolmaster at Stratford engaged in important and regular duties. The Act, however, dissolved collegiate churches, such as that

founded by John de Stratford, chantries, and social
guilds like that of the Holy Cross at Stratford, which
maintained priests to pray for the departed brothers
and sisters; provision, however, was made for the support of priests engaged in teaching or preaching. The
other endowments meantime passed into the hands of
the Crown.

Deprived of their funds the inhabitants of Stratford
petitioned Edward VI for incorporation as a borough
and the return of the properties formerly belonging to
the Guild. The Charter of Incorporation was granted
on 28 June 1553, a few days before the death of
Edward VI. The Charter named the Bailiff who was to
preside over the Common Council, as it did the fourteen Aldermen who were to be the senior councillors.
Those so named were to choose fourteen Capital Burgesses; so that the Council would consist of a Bailiff
and twenty-eight members. Vacancies in the Council
were to be filled by the choice of the Council itself; the
Council was also to elect annually from its numbers the
Bailiff and its other officers.

Continuity with the old order was secured by the
Crown's nomination to the Council of those who had
already held office in the Guild. To the Council was
transferred the Guild estate, the annual value of which
was some £46, and that portion of the estate of the
former College of Priests worth £34 a year. From these
funds the Council were to pay the vicar and the schoolmaster £20 each, and £10 to a chaplain to assist the
vicar; the vicar and the schoolmaster were each to be
provided with a house. The Council were also to be responsible for the maintenance of the school, now named
The King's New School of Stratford-on-Avon, though
the school was neither new nor endowed by the Crown.

In addition the alms-houses and the bridge were to be
their charge.

The energy of the inhabitants of Stratford that had
secured for them the standing of a corporate borough,
and the careful provision of an earlier generation in laying the foundations on which the social life and education of the community were now firmly based, in no
way suggest the licence and ignorance amidst which
Rowe fancied Shakespeare was born.

Nor can Shakespeare's parents be considered as falling below the standard of conduct and responsibility
found in the burgesses of Stratford. Immediately
after his marriage John Shakespeare was co-opted as a
member of the Common Council and was during the
next twenty years one of its most active and devoted
members.

John and Mary Shakespeare had eight children, four
sons and four daughters: Joan (christened 15 September 1558), Margaret (c. 2 December 1562), William
(c. 26 April 1564), Gilbert (c. 13 October 1566), Joan
(c. 15 April 1569), Anne (c. 28 September 1571),
Richard (c. 11 March 1574), and Edmund (c. 3 May
1580).

William was the third child and first son. All the girls
except the second Joan died in infancy or early child-
hood. Gilbert and Richard were buried at Stratford in
1612 and 1613 respectively. Edmund died in London
in 1607 and was buried in what is now Southwark
Cathedral. Infant mortality in all classes of society in
that age was high, and one's expectation of life low;
simple troubles, quite apart from the major dangers like
plague, were regularly fatal, and internal lesions beyond the reach of surgery. That there was a tough strain
in the family is suggested by the younger Joan who, as

Mrs William Hart, lived till 1646, dying in her seventy-eighth year.

During his early years as a member of the Common Council John Shakespeare acted in such minor but important offices as ale-taster, constable, and affeeror, in the latter capacity determining the fine for offences where no recognized penalty was prescribed. In 1561 he became one of the two Chamberlains responsible for the borough accounts, his partner in office being John Taylor. The accounts were copied into the Council minutes by the Town Clerk, so that we have no specimen of John Shakespeare's penmanship; for although each member of the Council was expected to indicate that he had read the minutes by putting his signature or mark against his name in the list of councillors at the foot of the minutes lying on the Council table, John Shakespeare always makes a mark, generally what may be taken for a glover's dividers. This has given rise to the suggestion that John Shakespeare was so illiterate as to be unable to sign his name; and the question how he could in keeping a public account give and take receipts if he could neither read nor write naturally suggests itself. As John Taylor also uses a mark against his name the answer is still to seek. It has been suggested that he and Shakespeare may have used tallies, but tallies are no help in giving or accepting a receipt and are indeed of no service unless having written on them what they stand for. Tallies were used as being cheaper than paper, not because those who used them were unable to read and write. As Smart points out, the baker's wife in Scott's *Antiquary* made use of 'nick-sticks' or tallies in her business, but she was well able to read the private letters of other people which passed through her hands. Further Shakespeare and Taylor

were asked by the Council to continue as acting-Chamberlains for another two years, a most unusual request, and a strange one if the pair were illiterate. Why they should have been asked to act for the nominal chamberlains unless they had a special aptitude for the business and were known to be zealous and able in forwarding the affairs of the borough it is impossible to imagine. When they made their reckonings as acting-Chamberlains the Town Clerk made the following entries in the minutes of the Council:

March 21st. 1565. The accompt of William Tyler and William Smythe, Chamburlens, made by John Shakysper and John Tayler. . . .

The following year the making of the account is attributed to John Shakespeare alone:

Feb. 15th. 1566. The accompt of William Tylor and William Smythe, made by John Shaksper the XVth day of February. . . .

As Mr Oliver Baker has shown in his interesting study *In Shakespeare's Warwickshire* 'made by' means 'written by'; and he adds 'counters, without pen and ink, were quite incapable of recording anything'. Further Mr Baker has cited many instances in which men who sometimes contented themselves with signifying by a mark their approval of a document yet at other times signed their names. Shakespeare's special services in keeping the borough accounts is sufficient to rule out any suggestion that his mark in the Council minutes and elsewhere is proof of illiteracy.

In 1568 John Shakespeare became High Bailiff of the borough, an office that gave its occupant the standing of a gentleman, the right to his coat-of-arms, and

the dignity of being addressed on public occasions as Master. It was not, however, till 1596 that the College of Heralds made a formal grant of arms to John Shakespeare which is described as follows in the draft still preserved among the Heralds' papers: the shield 'in a field of gold, upon a bend sable, a spear of the first, the point upward headed argent'; the crest 'a falcon with his wings displayed, standing on a wreath of his colours, supporting a spear, armed, headed and steeled silver'; the motto 'Non sans droict'. A note that follows the draft indicates that John Shakespeare had many years before obtained from the Herald, who was responsible for heraldic grants in Warwickshire when John Shakespeare was Bailiff, a pattern for a proposed coat. The note adds that he had been Bailiff and the Queen's officer at Stratford, that he was a man of good standing, although the estimate that he was worth £500 may be an exaggeration, and that he had married the daughter and heir of Arden, a gentleman of worship. It is the coat granted in 1596 that is seen on Shakespeare's monument in Stratford church, and that was used by his daughter Susanna Hall as her seal. Why John Shakespeare did not follow up his earlier application to the Heralds, and matriculate the arms proposed for him by Robert Cook the Herald, is a question that admits only of the most speculative answer.

After his term as Bailiff John Shakespeare continued to take an active part in Council affairs. In 1571 he was chosen Head Alderman and deputy to the Bailiff, his friend Adrian Quiney. Nor was he in any financial difficulty as he purchased in 1575 for £40 the western house in Henley Street that he had so far held on lease. Yet in 1577 John Shakespeare after twenty years' active and regular service as a member of the Council suddenly

ceased to attend its meetings. The Council was prepared to fine members who declined to serve as directed,
and John Shakespeare himself had as Bailiff fined
Alderman Perrott, a former Bailiff, £20 for declining to
attend Council meetings. Yet the Council kept at John
Shakespeare's disposal his place as Alderman till 1586,
when it was noted that 'Mr Shakespeare doth not come
to the halls when they be warned, nor hath not done of
long time'; only then was his place filled. Meantime he
had been excused many of the levies made on Councillors or assessed at a lower rate. Whatever the reason for
Shakespeare's withdrawal from public service his colleagues obviously sympathized with him in his decision.

The earlier commentators naturally attributed
Shakespeare's retirement from public business to financial difficulties, caused perhaps by his too zealous attention to business other than his own private affairs. And
this seemed confirmed by the sale of his wife's estate
Asbies on 14 November 1578 to Edmund Lambert the
husband of Joan Arden, one of Mary Shakespeare's
seven sisters. The alienation of this valuable property
was, however, only meant to be of a temporary nature,
for it was clearly stipulated that John Shakespeare could
redeem the estate by repaying on or before 29 September 1580 the £40 he now received for it. This and other
transactions in 1578 and 1579 certainly indicate that
John Shakespeare was heavily committed financially in
various ways.

Some report, however distorted, of John Shakespeare's position at this time seems to have been gathered
by Betterton on his visit to Stratford, for Rowe says:

His father who was a considerable dealer in wool,
had so large a family, ten children in all, that altho' he

was his eldest son he could give him no better education than his own employment. He had bred him, 'tis true, for some time at a Free-school, where tis probable he aquired that little *Latin* he was master of: But the narrowness of his circumstances, and the want of his assistance at home, forced his father to withdraw him from thence, and unhappily prevented his further proficiency in that language. It is without controversy that he had no knowledge of the writings of the ancient poets.

John Shakespeare had eight children, of whom three died at a very early age; he had wool to sell no doubt from his wife's estate, but selling wool was not his trade. As we know, the inhabitants of Stratford whom Betterton encountered, and, as we shall see, those questioned at an earlier date by another enquirer there, had no proper information about John Shakespeare's business. That they would know about the details of his son's schooling and especially of his withdrawal from school, an event more than a hundred years old, when they knew nothing of the shop John Shakespeare kept long after his son had left for London, only the credulous will believe. Such a view of Shakespeare's schooling fits Rowe's opinion about Shakespeare's knowledge of Latin and is an accommodation to the notion then prevalent of Shakespeare as an uneducated lad from the provinces.

More light, however, has been obtained on this obscure period in John Shakespeare's relations with the Council from Mrs Charlotte Stopes's discovery that in 1580 John Shakespeare was summoned to appear before the Queen's Bench at Westminster and be bound over to keep the Queen's peace. Failing to appear he was fined £20, and his two securities John Audley of Nottingham and Thomas Cooley of Stoke were each fined

c

£10. John Shakespeare was fined on the same day in June another £20 as was Thomas Cooley, for they had stood as sureties for John Audley, who had been in his turn fined £40. This was a very considerable penalty to have to pay, and yet three months later on 29 September 1580 John Shakespeare presented himself at Edmund Lambert's house with £40 to redeem the estate of Asbies. Lambert made as an excuse for not accepting the money, and for still withholding the estate, the claim that certain other monies owed by Shakespeare were outstanding. Edmund Lambert professed to be holding the estate as security against these other debts; yet there was nothing in the original deed giving him temporary possession of the property that entitled him to decline the £40 Shakespeare now tendered. On Edmund Lambert's death in 1587 his son John refused to consider returning the property. Next year John Shakespeare brought a bill of complaint against John Lambert in the Queen's Bench, without success; for in 1597 the case was raised again by the Shakespeares in the Court of Chancery. Doubtless the delay was due in part to the expense of such a proceeding. By 1597 the dramatist was well able to regard the charges as no obstacle. John Shakespeare's delay, however, may have been in part almost dictated by his unwillingness at the earlier date to have the Court learn fully why he had entered into the original bargain with Edmund Lambert, a suggestion that arises from what seems the only possible explanation of the severe fine the Queen's Bench inflicted on John Shakespeare.

The Court in fining John Shakespeare £40 for failing to provide surety that he would keep the Queen's peace was not dealing with him because the lieges were in danger of their lives from his violence; the Court was

using this formula to enforce the conformity in religion required by the Queen, a conformity taken for granted in that age, more especially at a time when the emissaries of the Pope were encouraging Roman Catholics in England to deny their allegiance to the Queen. The sign of conformity required by the authorities was regular attendance at the established church. This was now being firmly enforced in the Midlands by John Whitgift, who had become Bishop of Worcester in the year John Shakespeare withdrew from the Council. Whitgift was the ecclesiastic on whom the Queen came to rely for the enforcement of her church policy, and in 1583 she made him Archbishop of Canterbury. As Master of Trinity College, Cambridge, he had already taken disciplinary action against Thomas Cartwright, the Lady Margaret Divinity Professor, whom he deprived of his chair and his fellowship; for Cartwright, like many of the Puritan persuasion, regarded the Church of England in its government by Bishops and its use of vestments and certain other forms as only half reformed. At Worcester the new Bishop set about enforcing church attendance, making lists of those who absented themselves and informing the Privy Council of what he judged these recusants to be worth, so that a fine in accordance with their means might be imposed. This allowed the government to have the offenders dealt with by the Queen's Bench. Whitgift had to admit that he found it hard to get witnesses against the Puritans, so prevalent was that form of disobedience in the Midlands; but Whitgift was not to be denied in his dealings with those he called contentious Protestants and stubborn Papists. That John Shakespeare was the victim of Whitgift's drive for conformity is the only explanation that seems to fit the circumstances in which

the fine was imposed. Anticipating this outcome John Shakespeare had temporarily dispossessed himself of a valuable estate, so that he might be reckoned a poorer man than he was and so suffer a less crippling penalty. That his brother-in-law took advantage of Shakespeare's somewhat equivocal position, and defeated his plan to recover his wife's property when the immediate trouble was over, is a fair inference from Lambert's very unhelpful attitude to a brother in difficulties. John Shakespeare, however, can never have been so poor or hard pressed that he had to give up his houses in Henley Street and his business there, for these properties were inherited by the dramatist, or so reduced that he had to deny his son the advantages of the education provided free of charge by Jolyf's generous endowment. Whitgift's assessors clearly considered John Shakespeare a man of good financial standing, for their report was no doubt reflected in the amount of the fine. That the investigators employed by Whitgift to enquire into the resources of those to be prosecuted would know how much Shakespeare was worth much more accurately than the inhabitants, who told Betterton more than a hundred years later that he was too poor to keep his son at a free school, is hardly open to dispute.

The question whether John Shakespeare was a Roman Catholic or a Puritan recusant inevitably presents itself. He was certainly on very bad terms, as Dr Hotson has shown, with the Bailiff who was his immediate predecessor, Ralph Cawdrey, one of the leading Roman Catholics in Stratford; for Dr Hotson has found an entry in the Rolls of the Queen's Bench indicating that Shakespeare took action that required Cawdrey to provide security that he would not assault Shakespeare. Moreover in the list of recusants drawn up in 1592 John

Shakespeare, for he persisted in his contumacy, is not grouped with those who were known Roman Catholics; he stands in a group of nine persons against whom the Commissioners for Recusancy write: 'It is sayd that these laste nine coom not to Churche for feare of processe of Debtte.' First on the list of nine is Mr John Wheeler, twice Bailiff of Stratford, a wealthy man who had clearly no need to fear arrest for debt on his way to church or to any other destination. Wheeler was struck off the list of Councillors at his own request on 6 September 1586, the same day as John Shakespeare. The conclusion that the nine that included Shakespeare and Wheeler were recusants not because of their being Roman Catholics but on account of some objection to Whitgift's discipline is supported by the excuse, clearly untrue in certain instances, reported by the Commissioners, for it bears out Whitgift's complaint that it was difficult to get witnesses to testify against the Puritan recusants.

Even had John Shakespeare at the time of his summons before the Queen's Bench been forced to take his son from school when he was fourteen or so, the boy would not have been without some Latin, for we can see in the Latin letter which young Richard Quiney in 1598 wrote to his father, then in London on borough business, what was expected in this way of an eleven-year-old schoolboy. The child's letter was preserved among the public papers left by his father Richard Quiney at his death, for he died in office as Bailiff in 1602. Among these papers is the letter dated 25 October 1598 that Richard Quiney himself wrote during his visit to London to Shakespeare, the only letter to the dramatist chance has preserved, now exhibited in the Birthplace museum. Quiney obviously could read Latin

easily, for his friend Abraham Sturley, Bailiff of Stratford at that time, also wrote to him at length in Latin.
There is every reason to suppose that the dramatist was
as familiar with Latin as Quiney, and however less his
Greek he must have progressed as far as the senior
forms at school, for it was only in the upper forms that
the study of Greek was added to that of the basic Latin.

Whatever John Shakespeare's difficulties they did not
prevent his giving his consent in 1582 to the marriage
of his eldest son to the eldest daughter of his old friend
Richard Hathaway. Without his consent, for his son
was still a minor, no licence for the marriage would have
been issued by the Registry at Worcester, now under
Whitgift's strict discipline. To obtain the common
licence to marry with one publication of banns the
parties or their guardians had to submit to the Episcopal Registry: (*a*) an *Allegation*—a sworn statement
by the applicant giving details of the position and connexions of the contracting parties; reasons for the
application, place of marriage—in short a statement that
could leave no ground for doubt about the legality of
the ceremony; (*b*) a *Bond* for £40, so that the Bishop
would be indemnified from any suit arising out of his
grant; the penalty was raised to £100 soon after 1592;
(*c*) a *Certificate* from some person whose word the
Bishop could take about the affairs of the contracting
parties. Then and then only could (*d*) a *Licence* be
issued to the clergyman where the ceremony was to be
performed. Naturally a fee was required for this privilege; in 1582 there were about a hundred licences of
this kind issued by the Registry. As a record of these
transactions (*e*) an *Entry* was made in the Bishop's
Register.

It is clear that the Allegations would be the most

revealing document; unfortunately none of that date have been preserved at Worcester. The Bonds being of a financial nature were, as is customary with the English, more carefully preserved, and that referring to Shakespeare's marriage is extant. Neither (c) nor (d) have been found, none from that date being preserved.

There exists, therefore, the *Bond* and the *Entry*. Two discrepancies between these documents have given rise to considerable speculation. The *Bond* is dated 28 November 1582, the *Entry* 27 November 1582. This has been explained by Joseph W. Gray's study of the procedure at the Registry. The *Entry* was not made till after the Licence was issued; the clerk making the *Entry* then took the date from the *Allegation*, although the *Bond*, without which there could be no Licence, may not have been completed for some days after the production of the *Allegation*. The other discrepancy is of a more notable kind: the *Bond* describes the bride as Anne Hathwey, the *Entry* as Anne Whateley. This has given rise to the assertion that on the 27 November Shakespeare tried to marry an Anne Whately, but on 28 November Anne Hathaway's friends arrived at the Registry and insisted on the bridegroom changing his bride. As the *Allegation* must have named the lady Shakespeare was about to marry, and as this would be repeated in the *Certificate*, the supposition that there was a change of bride would require us to suppose that a sworn application had to be changed as well as a certificate from a responsible party. There may have been registries where such changes could be made, but Whitgift's was not one; and the difference in date between the *Bond* and *Entry* is found in nearly fifty of the entries made in 1582–3, and simply explained. There remains the difference between Hathwey and

Whately; the clerk is not always accurate; he writes
Darby for Bradeley without our having to suppose the
bride was off with another man than that named in the
Bond. The clerk clearly did not make the *Entry* on
27 November as he had not yet seen the *Bond* and
issued the *Licence*; he back-dated the *Entry* to corres-
pond with the *Allegation*, but in the intervening days
the name Whately was a familiar one to registry
officials; on 27 November, the date assigned to the
Entry, a William Whateley was involved in a suit at the
Registry. The *Entry* was obviously made in haste, after
the formalities had been complied with, and the *Licence*
is described as similar to one already entered; the error
in the name in no way affected the *Licence* already
issued, for the *Entry* though carrying the early date was
obviously the last piece of documentation in the transaction.

No one would take Whately in the *Entry* for anything
but a clerical error were it not that the application for
the *Licence* was made on 27 November 1582 and
Susanna, the first child of the marriage, was christened
on 26 May 1583. This irregularity, as it seems by
modern standards, has given support to the suggestion
that the marriage was forced on Shakespeare. The facts,
however, do not justify such a conclusion. In Shakespeare's day, as in Scotland till 1939, 'two people could
conclude a perfectly valid and legitimate marriage
whenever and wherever they liked, without any witness
and independently of any ecclesiastical rite provided
that the essential condition of a "mutual consent expressed by words and actions" had been fulfilled'. The
words here quoted are from Professor Panofsky's
description of the Arnolfini portrait in the National
Gallery. The London portrait is both a portrait of two

individual persons and a representation of a sacramental rite; and the picture is signed by Jan van Eyck both as artist and witness to the marriage.

That marriages 'per fidem' were recognized in Stratford as in England, may be illustrated from various social circles: Mary Arden's sister Agnes was married to Thomas Stringer in the parish church on 15 October 1550, but her father's will made in July recognizes her as Stringer's legal wife; Thomas Russell, the overseer of Shakespeare's will, a scholar, soldier, and country gentleman, of unimpeachable standing, was living, as Dr Hotson has shown, with his second wife, and recognized as her husband, before the church marriage was solemnized.

It is true the Church exerted itself to persuade its members that marriages made on a *de praesenti* contract, as those described above were made, were sinful and dangerous. That they were lawful, however, is clear from the action of the Council of Trent in decreeing in 1563 that from that time a priest must be present, not to administer the sacrament, but as a witness of its solemnization. That decree was naturally enforced only in countries in obedience to Rome; but even in England in Shakespeare's own life the feeling was growing that a church ceremony should precede cohabitation, and Shakespeare himself in *Measure for Measure* exploits this ambiguity of feeling in his treatment of the position of Claudio and Juliet, who are, however, represented as inhabitants of Roman Catholic Vienna, where nuns and friars are not, as in Shakespeare's England, proscribed. Yet some ten years later in *The Tempest*, on an island not in submission to Rome, we have Prospero's admonition on the proper procedure in marriage. It may be said that we have no proof that Shakespeare and Anne

Hathaway were already married by pre-contract before the church ceremony; it is equally true to say that there is no justification for supposing that they were not so married. Both families obviously took their public duties and relationships seriously, and there is clear evidence that Anne's father, Richard Hathaway of Shottery, when making his will on 1 September 1581 expected his daughter's marriage to be in the very near future.

If the inscription on her grave is correct Anne was 25 when her father died. Yet although her sister Margaret, who was 9, was to have her portion when she reached 17, Anne was to have hers 'paid unto her at the day of her marriage', an arrangement that indicates she was already betrothed and soon to be married. On Richard Hathaway's death on 7 September 1581 his son Bartholomew and his father's second wife took over his fields in Shottery, while Anne may have moved to relatives at Temple Grafton, the locality indicated in the *Entry* in the Episcopal Register. At the time of her marriage Anne was 26, her husband 18, and this has added to the misgiving of those who have misinterpreted the documents preserved in the Bishop's Registry. This is not, however, evidence of irregularity. Samuel Johnson when he married Mrs Porter was 25, his bride 47, yet he described it as a love marriage upon both sides. The last matter connected with the marriage that has prompted speculation concerns the *Bond* which was signed by Fulke Sandells and John Richardson, both friends of Anne's father. Sandells had acted as the overseer of his will, and Richardson was a witness to it. Only occasionally did the father of the bridegroom figure as security in the Bonds at Worcester; and, as Gray has surmised, Whitgift may have indicated that normally he expected the bride's friends should, as an

additional measure of protection, appear in the Bonds
lodged at his Registry. As Shakespeare's father had only
recently been heavily fined, no doubt at Whitgift's
instance, he doubtless judged it imprudent to be drawing official attention to himself by offering surety for
another £40. Sandells had been entrusted with super-
vising the details of Richard Hathaway's bequests,
including Anne's marriage portion; that he should as a
consequence feel responsible for assisting in a marriage
Hathaway had indicated as imminent, and that Sandells
should take as an associate in the formalities another
friend of the Hathaways, can appear suspicious only to
those who feel they must find evidence of licence as
well as ignorance in Shakespeare's early years.

It was not Rowe, however, who set in motion the
many doubts and guesses that were later to distort the
evidence that relates to the dramatist's marriage. When
Betterton visited Stratford investigators had not yet
searched out the *Bond* and the *Entry*, which were
recovered only in the nineteenth century. Yet Betterton
heard that Shakespeare's wife was the daughter of 'one
Hathaway, said to have been a substantial yeoman
in the neighbourhood of *Stratford*'. The accuracy of
Betterton's report as thus transmitted by Rowe need not
surprise us, as there were Hathaways living in Stratford
at the time of Betterton's visit. Rowe just before his
reference to Hathaway describes Shakespeare's marriage as in accordance with his father's wishes. Yet
Rowe although he provides no help to those who wish
to regard Shakespeare's marriage as irregular, or as
evidence of his lack of responsibility, does immediately
follow his reference to the marriage with his report of
an affair that forced Shakespeare to abandon his wife
and family and seek refuge in London.

Perhaps the story that tells how Shakespeare's mis-
fortunes as a poacher made his fortune as a dramatist,
by forcing him to seek mean employment about some
London theatre where he suddenly discovered his
genius, is the most familiar episode in what E. K.
Chambers described as the Shakespeare Mythos.
Rowe's account of how Shakespeare had as it were his
greatness thrust upon him tells how he continued for
some time in the settled condition that followed his
marriage,

'till an extravagance that he was guilty of forc'd him
both out of his country and that way of living which he
had taken up; and tho' it seem'd at first to be a blemish
upon his good manners, and a misfortune to him, yet
it afterwards happily prov'd the occasion of exerting one
of the greatest *Genius's* that ever was known in dramatick
Poetry. He had, by a misfortune common enough to
young fellows, fallen into ill company; and amongst
them, some that made a frequent practice of Deer-stealing, engag'd him with them more than once in robbing
a Park that belong'd to *Sir Thomas Lucy* of *Cherlecot*,
near *Stratford*. For this he was prosecuted by that gentleman, as he thought, somewhat too severely; and in order
to revenge that ill usage, he made a ballad upon him.
And tho' this, probably the first essay of his Poetry, be
lost, yet it is said to have been so very bitter, that it
redoubled the prosecution against him to that degree,
that he was oblig'd to leave his business and family in
Warwickshire, for some time, and shelter himself in
London.

This story obviously cries out for a sequel that will tell
us how a man who, as Johnson puts it, arrived in
London 'a needy adventurer and lived for a time by
very mean employments' came to set up as a dramatist.

This continuation duly appeared in 1753 in Cibber's *Lives of the Poets of Great Britain and Ireland*:

Here I cannot forbear relating a story which Sir William Davenant told Mr Betterton, who communicated it to Mr Rowe; Rowe told it to Mr Pope, and Mr Pope told it to Dr Newton, the late editor of Milton, and from a gentleman who heard it from him, 'tis here related.

This is the story of how Shakespeare held horses at the theatre door and 'became eminent even in that profession', and of how he was 'of so fine a conversation' that he was given some mean employment in the theatre where he eventually made his reputation. As Smart observed the pedigree reminded him of Sir Benjamin Backbite's authenticating his story of the imaginary duel between Sir Peter Teazle and his nephew—'I tell you I had it from one, who had it from one, who had it from one'. Dr Johnson in his edition of 1765 gave the story its most ludicrous form; after describing how Shakespeare 'fled to London from the terrour of a criminal prosecution' and set up as a horse-holder, Johnson continues:

Shakespeare finding more horses put into his hand than he could hold, hired boys to wait under his inspection, who when *Will Shakespeare* was summoned, were immediately to present themselves, *I am* Shakespeare's *boy, Sir*.

For once Johnson failed to distinguish between history and folk-tale. No doubt in an age when an intelligent historian such as Hume could describe Shakespeare as a man 'born in a rude age and educated in the lowest manner, without any instruction from the world or from books' it was possible to believe that holding horses was a stage on the road to *Hamlet*. For Hume's

age, splendid as it was, did not know its place; it felt how much better it could have fashioned the plays given just a touch of dramatic genius, and often set about supplying the taste Shakespeare lacked by rewriting his plays. To refashion the pieces produced by a poacher and horse-holder, however skilful he showed himself in these capacities, did not seem beyond the intelligence and taste on which the later age prided itself.

It is not surprising that those who regarded the story of the fugitive poacher as history felt confirmed in the belief that the age was rude and licentious, and the poet in many ways a man of his age. Rowe had regarded Shakespeare's marriage as unexceptionable, but it was not unreasonable that the circumstances of Shakespeare's marriage, as they became more fully but yet very imperfectly known, should be interpreted in a context coloured by the irresponsibility that forced him to abandon his wife and family, to the care no doubt of his already sorely-tried father. Yet the deer-stealing story, so far from being proof of the licence and ignorance in which Shakespeare was living at Stratford, is an invention prompted by the assumption it was later supposed to support.

Sir Thomas Lucy had no deer-park for Shakespeare to rob. Malone could find no record of the royal licence that would have been required for such a park, for as William Harrison, who contributed his Description of England to Holinshed's *Chronicle* observes, 'It is trespass and against the law for any man to have or make a chase, park or free warren without good warranty of the King by his charter, or perfect title of prescription'. Smart, however, found that the grant for such a park at Charlecote was made to Sir Thomas Lucy's grandson

in 1618. Had this Sir Thomas, the third of that name
and title, inherited a park from his father or grand-
father, he would not have required to apply for such a
licence, as these licences once granted were passed on,
without any further formality, from the owner to his
heirs. To say, as E. K. Chambers does, that though
there was no park in the legal sense at Charlecote there
may have been a few deer running about in the grounds,
still leaves unexplained the treatment of Shakespeare
attributed to Sir Thomas Lucy. As Malone has explained such deer would have been unprotected by the
common law, 'every one having right to kill thereon all
beast of chase as *ferae naturae*'. To suppose that Sir
Thomas Lucy could have taken the law into his own
hands while himself guilty of trespass, and that against
the son of a former Bailiff of Stratford, amounts to an
admission that Rowe's story is a fabrication.

That the story is a fabrication may be seen from an
earlier version that still lacks the verisimilitude given
it by Rowe's easy narrative manner. Some time after
1688 the Rev. Richard Davies, Archdeacon of Coventry,
who was Rector of Sapperton, Gloucestershire, from
1696 to his death in 1708, made the following additions
about Shakespeare to manuscript notes that had passed
through his hands before being lodged in the library
of Corpus Christi College, Oxford:

much given to all unluckinesse in stealing venison and
Rabbits particularly from Sir   Lucy who had
him oft whipt and sometimes Imprisoned and at last
made Him fly his Native Country to his great Advance-
ment, but his reveng was so great that he is his Justice
Clodpate and calls him a great man and that in allusion
to his name bore three lowses rampant for his Arms.

It is clear that to Davies the dramatist was merely a

name; Justice Clodpate is not a character in Shakespeare's plays but in *Epsom Wells* produced in London
by Shadwell about 1672. E. K. Chambers insists that
the deer-stealing story is in origin a Stratford one, but
how a character from *Epsom Wells* found its way into
a Stratford tradition we are not told. Nor is it clear
why a Stratford tradition omits the familiar Christian
name of Lucy, unless it is the Rector's memory as well
as his knowledge of the plays that is sadly defective.

So far is this story from having the marks of a Stratford tradition that it is obviously a garbled account of
what someone had been telling the Archdeacon about
the significance of the opening scene of *The Merry
Wives of Windsor*. There Justice Shallow threatens to
make a Star Chamber matter of Sir John Falstaff's
trespass on his park: 'Knight, you have beaten my men,
kill'd my deer, and broke open my lodge.' 'But not',
Sir John replies, 'kiss'd your keeper's daughter.' To
emphasize the enormity of the offence Slender, Shallow's foolish cousin, dwells on the age and dignity of
Shallow's coat-of-arms: his 'successors (gone before
him)' and his 'ancestors (that come after him)' may
'give the dozen white luces in their coat'. To which
Shallow adds 'It is an old coat'. Shakespeare, as Johnson complained, was always ready to stoop to a quibble;
the luce was a fish of the pike family, but the old coat
provided an opportunity for punning on luce and louse.
'The dozen white louses', the Welsh parson observes,
'do become an old coat well', it is a 'familiar beast to
man'. The only possible connexion here between
Shallow and Sir Thomas Lucy is the luces, for the
Lucy arms showed *three luces hauriant*, that is as if
rising to the surface. No doubt this is the scene that
someone had tried to explain to Davies, for it is clear

he had never read it, and remembered most imperfectly what he had been told.

The reference, however garbled, in the Archdeacon's note to *The Merry Wives of Windsor* indicates the origin of the story and marks it as an early example of the many attempts to supplement the details of the poet's life by conjectures suggested by episodes in the plays. It is true Dr Hotson has shown that at the close of 1596 Shakespeare was a party to what was obviously a serious dispute with a Justice who displayed luces on his coat-of-arms. On 29 November 1596 a William Wayte deposed before a magistrate that he went in fear of his life from William Shakespeare, Francis Langley, Dorothy Soer, and Anne Lee. Wayte, as Dr Hotson proved, was the stepson and cat's-paw of Justice William Gardiner. His mother Frances Wayte was the daughter of Robert Lucy, and on the death of her first husband married William Gardiner, who impaled her arms, the three luces haurient Argent, with his own. If, as seems very probable, *The Merry Wives of Windsor* was written the following year, some time before the Garter Feast, 23 April 1597, Shakespeare may well have had this sinister Justice in his mind, and what could not be other than the interesting fact to a Stratford man that his coat recalled in one important feature the arms of Sir Thomas Lucy of Charlecote. But Justice Shallow of the play can hardly be regarded as a portrait or even a caricature of Sir Thomas or of the rapacious Gardiner. To suppose that Shakespeare was trying in the simple jesting of the opening scene to take a public revenge on one or other of these Justices is to attribute to Shakespeare a sad deficiency of gall, and to the audience an appreciation of Shakespeare's allusions rivalling that of later investigators.

D

We do not know whether the deer-stealing story was part of Betterton's gleanings at Stratford, for, though the version recorded by Davies indicates that the knowledge that there was by that time an authorized park there is an element in the story, there are other features that suggest not a tradition but an essay in exegesis. Certainly when John Aubrey visited Stratford some twenty years earlier he heard nothing about deer-stealing, and he welcomed traditional stories. What those he talked with there told him he recorded as follows:

his father was a Butcher, and I have been told heretofore by some of the neighbours, that when he was a boy he exercised his fathers Trade, but when he kill'd a Calfe, he would do it in a *high style*, and make a Speech. There was at that time another Butchers son in the Towne, that was held not at all inferior to him for a natural witt, his acquaintance and coetanean, but dyed young.

As Shakespeare's father was not a butcher and still maintained his glover's shop long after Shakespeare had gone to London, it is clear the neighbours Aubrey encountered did not know what they were talking about. Yet this story has been preferred even by scholars to what Aubrey heard from a man who was in a position to provide accurate information. Aubrey, having heard that there was still living in London a man who had begun his career as actor and manager of a company before the closing of the theatres in 1642, and who as the son of an actor and manager had so extensive a knowledge of theatrical affairs of the previous age that Dryden called him the chronicle of the stage, naturally sought him out. This was William Beeston, the son of Christopher Beeston.

The father Christopher Beeston had acted in the Chamberlain's company with Shakespeare between 1594 and 1602; they are both named as having played in Jonson's *Everyman in His Humour* in 1598, and must have appeared frequently together till 1602, when Beeston joined Worcester's men. This he did as his chances of promotion in the new company were obviously greater than with the Chamberlain's men, now a well established organization. The change can have provoked no ill feeling, for Augustine Phillips, one of the principal sharers in the Chamberlain's company, on his death in 1605, left 'my Servaunt Christopher Beeston thirty shillings in gould'. Beeston clearly had earlier been apprenticed to Phillips, and for that reason received from his old master the same legacy as Phillips gave Shakespeare. Beeston had been right in thinking he would make more rapid promotion in the new company, for he became a leading actor and finally manager of a company; as Professor Bentley observes, between 1617 and his death in 1638 Christopher Beeston was perhaps 'the most important theatrical figure in London'.

In 1638 his son William Beeston was well prepared to take over his father's part as manager, for as he explained in a case before the Courts in 1666, he had been 'bred up in the art of stage playing', and he was acknowledged to have been a skilled instructor, whose training produced many successful actors. As he was born not later than 1606, and perhaps even a few years earlier, he had the benefit of long training from a father who had in his youth served with the great men of the heroic age of the drama. William Beeston may even have seen Shakespeare with his own eyes and been old enough to understand the importance of the figure he

saw; for he cannot have been unfamiliar with his father's connexion with the dramatist.

Fortunately Aubrey heard of Beeston just in time to visit him in 1681, the year before the actor's death. They discussed, no doubt among other events of the earlier age, Jonson's reference to Shakespeare's 'small Latin and less Greek', for Aubrey concluded his account of Shakespeare with these words: 'Though as Ben: Johnson sayes of him, that he had but little Latine and lesse Greek, He understood Latine pretty well: for he had been in his younger years a Schoolmaster in the Country.' To leave no doubt about the source of this information Aubrey put against it in the margin: from Mr Beeston.

It would be hard to find a better authenticated tradition: a careful and industrious enquirer who not only obtains his information from one well informed about the subject but records the authority he relies on must always be heard with attention. Yet as not a few scholars have preferred the story that Shakespeare was a butcher, although this was the report of some nameless inhabitants of Stratford who were ludicrously mistaken about John Shakespeare's occupation, it is necessary to consider the reasons given for rejecting the better authenticated alternative.

In 1767 Richard Farmer, Master of Emmanuel College, Cambridge, published his *Essay on the Learning of Shakespeare*. As he was attempting to prove that Shakespeare had no real acquaintance with Latin, he rejected Beeston's information by arguing that 'it is not possible, according to Aubrey himself, that Shakespeare could have been some years a Schoolmaster in the Country', for Aubrey in the account, which he left in manuscript, had earlier noted the opinion held by

some that Shakespeare was a butcher. Farmer, realizing that he must explain why the schoolmaster story might not equally be cited to show that according to Aubrey himself Shakespeare could not have been a butcher, then tries to discredit Aubrey by quoting Anthony Wood's description of Aubrey as 'a pretender to Antiquities' and too credulous to be trusted.

Farmer's attitude to Aubrey is substantially that of E. K. Chambers who asks, 'Is the reporter likely to be reliable and well informed?' and answers, 'John Aubrey was industrious and full of interest and antiquity, but inaccurate and given to scandal'. Yet the only pertinent question for the moment is about the reliability of Aubrey's report. The further question about its giving a well-informed account of the matter must be decided by the authority we attach to Aubrey's source, provided we can trust Aubrey to report truthfully. When Aubrey tells us that Harvey informed him that his treatise on the circulation of the blood had lost him much of his practice, no medical man would think of dismissing Aubrey's statement by saying Aubrey often reported amusing but unlikely stories. That type of illogicality is left to literary commentators. Toland, who knew Aubrey well, testifies that he was 'most accurate in his account of matters of fact', a judgement supported by the weight of Malone's respect for his *Lives*. Aubrey no doubt held opinions shared by learned contemporaries that are regarded today as childish or superstitious, but that does not impugn Aubrey's truth, and Wood was the most peevish and ungrateful of men in his criticism of a helper to whom he was so deeply indebted. Aubrey was a founding member of the Royal Society, the friend of Wren and his associates, and in a recent study of the beginning of that society Aubrey's statement on that

topic is quoted without any mention of the doubtful
stories he recorded in other contexts. Aubrey's record
of the gossip he heard at Stratford does not prove, let
alone suggest, that his account of Beeston's observations
is in any way untruthful or inaccurate. The discussion
between Aubrey and Beeston of Jonson's remark on
Shakespeare's learning and Beeston's comment on it
are so well knit together that it is all or nothing; there
is no margin for a third view. Neither Farmer nor
Chambers dared to say Aubrey was lying; they tried
to beg the question by quoting the ungrateful Wood or
echoing his peevish sentiments. Aubrey's reliability
granted, the question of whether Beeston was well informed may then be asked.

That Beeston was likely to be well informed on the
question he discussed with Aubrey is suggested by his
being the son of an actor who must have known Shakespeare well, by his own long service in the theatre;
and added to this is the respect for his intelligence that
contemporary references to him indicate. Farmer and
E. K. Chambers, however, would put aside Beeston's
testimony, for it conflicts with their opinion of Shakespeare's beginnings as a dramatist. These scholars reject
the statement by Shakespeare's colleagues Heminge
and Condell that in publishing the First Folio edition
of Shakespeare's plays in 1623 they were giving the
public what Shakespeare himself had written. For some
of the pieces, which must date from Shakespeare's early
years in the theatre, suggest that their author had a
greater knowledge of Latin and keener interest in
Roman drama than these scholars are willing to credit
the youth from Stratford with. The author of *The
Comedy of Errors*, clearly an early work, has constructed
his ingenious plot by combining elements from two

plays by Plautus; this and the clever adaptation of the structure of Latin comedy to the local peculiarities of the London stage suggest in the dramatist an intelligent and professional interest in Plautine comedy. The earliest tragedy in the Folio is *Titus Andronicus*; here the author's interest in Seneca and Ovid is as obvious as is the debt to Plautus in *The Errors*. And in the early poems, *Venus and Adonis* and *The Rape of Lucrece*, poems, which only Baconians, and those of that way of treating the evidence, can deny to Shakespeare, there is found the same groundwork of Latin derivation, Ovid and Livy now providing the basic elements. In rejecting the ascription to Shakespeare of *The Comedy of Errors*, *Titus Andronicus*, and other of the early pieces, because of their Latin content, Farmer and E. K. Chambers are rejecting the authority of Shakespeare's first editors. To justify this attitude to the men who had been Shakespeare's colleagues for many years, actors in his plays, and the recognized managers of the company's affairs, Farmer and E. K. Chambers have naturally to reject Beeston's testimony. For if Shakespeare had been a schoolmaster in the country what more natural than his turning to account in his early essays as a dramatist the learning, however one cares to describe it, required in that age of a junior schoolmaster.

The master of the Grammar School at Stratford in Shakespeare's day, and earlier, was always a graduate of one of the English universities, for the provision made by Jolyf's endowment and subsequently by the Charter of Incorporation was sufficient to attract men of academic standing, some of whom came to Stratford on their way to promotion in church or state. No specific provision in the Charter was made for an

assistant in the school at Stratford; but we know from deeds establishing a schoolmaster elsewhere that the master was sometimes to have a scholar as his assistant. Every locality was not, however, as well provided for as Stratford. Fuller in the next generation laments the lack of good schoolmasters, for some young scholars take to it, he regrets, as a refuge, and even before they have taken any degree in the university commence schoolmasters in the country, while others use it only as a passage to better preferment and a more gainful calling, the rewards of teaching being often, as Fuller admits, miserable. Shakespeare without a degree could not have looked for promotion in the academic world; and no doubt even Fuller would have forgiven Shakespeare for deserting what that divine regarded as a profession most necessary in the commonwealth for an even more exacting and important calling.

It is natural, but not necessarily beyond question, to suppose that Shakespeare assisted the master at Stratford Grammar School. It was at Stratford that his first child Susanna was christened on 26 May 1583, and the christening of the twins Hamnet and Judith followed on 2 February 1585. Shakespeare must now have had to consider how best to support his family, for as an assistant in a school his remuneration would be small and his prospects in that profession negligible. Such considerations are by themselves sufficient to account for Shakespeare's departure to London. Bernard Shaw's explanation of his own reasons for leaving Ireland, and the factor's office there he had entered from school as a lad of sixteen, though made after the event, are not necessarily untrue to the promptings of his mind at the time itself: 'My business in life could not be transacted in Dublin out of an experience confined to Ireland.

I had to go to London the literary centre for the English Language.' For one with an instinct for the drama such as Shakespeare must have possessed there was no alternative. His business in life, which a man of genius is in some ways less free to choose than his less gifted fellows, is an adequate answer to questions about what took Shakespeare to London.

Chapter Two

LONDON

By the summer of 1594 Shakespeare was one of the
principal sharers in the company of actors that came to
be recognized as the leading theatrical group of their
time. With this company Shakespeare was to remain for
the rest of his professional life, and the successive
phases in his association as an actor and dramatist with
this company may be indicated by the theatres at which
in turn the company were to perform: the Theatre, the
Globe, the Blackfriars. The position Shakespeare held
in this newly formed Lord Chamberlain's company in
1594 was, however, determined by his work in his
earlier years in London, a period for which the information about his associations and his activities is less
direct and definite than that available for his years with
the Chamberlain's, later the King's, men.

i. EARLY YEARS

Shakespeare's early years in London, like those of
many distinguished men who have found their professional field there, have to be seen in the light that his
later achievements cast back on them. Yet references
to the period when Shakespeare was beginning to
make his mark in the theatre although few are in
no way ambiguous, and enable us to understand not
only his position in the theatrical world of 1594 but
his subsequent progress that in a few years was to
bring him recognition as the greatest dramatist of his
age.

The earliest guess about the date of Shakespeare's arrival in London is found in Aubrey's *Life*:

This William being inclined naturally to Poetry and acting came to London I guesse about 18 and was an actor at one of the Play-houses and did act exceedingly well: now Ben Jonson was never a good Actor, but an excellent instructor. He began early to make essayes at Dramatique Poetry, which at that time was very lowe, and his Playes tooke well.

For part of this statement support can be found from other sources; unfortunately Aubrey gives no indication at this point of his informant, and in any event Aubrey recognizes the latitude that must be allowed to his report by adding, 'I guesse'. Even did we suppose that Shakespeare left Stratford just before his twenty-first birthday, soon after the twins Judith and Hamnet were christened there in February 1585, that would allow him nearly ten years in which to make his reputation as a dramatist and to establish himself by 1594 at the head of his profession. The years between 1585 and 1594 in which Shakespeare could have been acting in London and making a regular contribution to the repertoire of a company there must, however, be reduced by almost two years, for on 23 June 1592 the Privy Council closed the theatres till 29 September (Michaelmas) as a consequence of a riot in Southwark. By August of that year the plague was spreading in London, and although there were short respites during which attempts were made to resume playing, the increasing severity of the infection in the early months of 1593 that culminated in the worst visitations of the Queen's reign kept the theatres all but closed till the summer of 1594, and drove the London companies to try their fortunes in the provinces. It was during these two

years that Shakespeare had leisure to write his poems *Venus and Adonis* and *The Rape of Lucrece*, sophisticated compositions that suggest the concentration of the study rather than the distractions of the open road.

Not long after the closing of the theatres in 1592 there appeared in a pamphlet entered in the Stationers' Register on 20 September 1592 the first undoubted mention in print of Shakespeare, from which it is clear that he was by that date not only an actor but an active and far from obscure dramatist. This pamphlet's title-page indicates at some length the contents as follows: 'Greene's Groats-Worth of witte bought with a million of Repentance. Describing the follie of youth, the falshood of make-shifte flatterers, the miserie of the negligent, and mischiefes of deceiving Courtezans' and to this is added the statement: 'Written before his death and published at his dyeing request.' Robert Greene (1558–1592), the pamphleteer and dramatist, had died in wretched circumstances on 3 September 1592; he had occupied the confinement to which the illness that proved fatal subjected him by retelling in the guise of fiction something of his own irregular life and of the circumstances in which he took to writing for the stage. Towards the end of his story he breaks off to put aside the character *Roberto*, who has so far been his mouthpiece, to speak in his own person and to offer the reader the admonition of a repentant sinner. This admonition he thinks should have a special appeal to 'my fellow Schollers about this Cittie' and he then inserts this open letter to them:

*To those Gentlemen his Quondam acquaintance
that spend their wits in making plaies, R.G.
wisheth a better exercise, and wisdome
to prevent his extremities.*

Like many sinners whose penitence seems to quicken their perception of their friends' faults and to prompt uninhibited reference to these failings, Greene begins by selecting three of his acquaintance, for special reproof and warning. Without mentioning names he makes the identification of those referred to plain to his contemporaries. Greene is obviously addressing Marlowe (1564–1593) when he writes: 'Wonder not, (for with thee wil I first begin) thou famous gracer of Tragedians, that *Greene*, who hath said with thee (like the foole in his heart) There is no God, shoulde now give glorie unto his greatness.' And Greene goes on to reprove Marlowe as a disciple of Machiavelli and as an atheist. Nashe is next introduced: 'With thee I joyne young *Iuvenall*, that byting Satyrist' who is reproved for his 'too much liberty of reproofe'. Then turning to the third acquaintance Greene says: 'Were it not an idolatrous oth, I would sweare by sweet S. George, thou art unworthy better hap, sith thou dependest on so meane a stay.' The 'meane stay' is the income to be derived from working for the actors, and Greene's acquaintance here is George Peele (1557–1596).

From his reference to Peele's 'meane stay' Greene passes at once to point out to his friends how the actors whom he has favoured with his plays have abandoned him in his distress, and how this will be the fate of his friends, more especially as one of the ungrateful tribe of players has set up as a dramatist and has had the effrontery to pose as a rival to Greene and his fellow scholars from the universities. That Shakespeare is the danger Greene now threatens his friends with is obvious in what follows:

Base minded men all three of you, if by my miserie you be not warnd: for unto none of you (like mee) sought

those burres to cleave: those Puppets (I meane) that spake from our mouths, those Anticks garnisht in our colours. Is it not strange, that I, to whom they all have beene beholding: is it not like that you, to whome they all have beene beholding, shall (were yee in that case as I am now) bee both at once of them forsaken? Yes trust them not: for there is an upstart Crow beautified with our feathers, that with his *Tygers hart wrapt in a Players hyde*, supposes he is as well able to bombast out a blanke verse as the best of you: and beeing an absolute *Iohannes fac totum*, is in his own conceit the onely Shake-scene in a countrey.

Yet Greene, although he affects to despise the style of this actor turned dramatist, obviously treats him as a dangerous competitor in the economic field; it is not this man's alleged self-satisfaction, though Greene would make this a fault, but the satisfaction that Shakespeare was giving his public that provokes Greene's jealous tirade.

The known reactions provoked by Greene's censures afford some measure of its effect on theatrical circles in 1592. As Greene was in his grave before their publication and beyond rebuke there was some suggestion that perhaps the pamphlet was the work of one of his circle. Greene and Nashe were known to have collaborated, and Nashe, who had already earned the reputation of a biting satirist, feeling that suspicion might easily put his name to the work, especially as a number of references to actors and dramatists in an earlier satirical essay by him were repeated and echoed by Greene, was prompt with his disclaimer. In his *Pierce Penniless* published some time in October 1592 Nashe wrote:

Other news I am advertised of, that a scald, trivial, lying pamphlet called Greene's Groats-worth of Wit is given

out to be of my doing. God never have care of my soul,
but utterly renounce me, if the least word or syllable in
it proceeded from my pen, or if I were in any way privy
to the writing, or printing of it.

Nashe was always ready to defend Greene's reputation
especially against the criticism of Gabriel Harvey;
Nashe cannot at this time have known, for his words
have the tone of truth, who wrote the pamphlet.

The responsibility for the publication could not,
however, be long concealed. The publisher's name was
on the title-page, but although the *Groats-worth* had
been entered to him in the Stationers' Register he no
doubt saw that he was handling explosive matter, and
as a measure of self-protection had added in the
Register the clause 'uppon the perill of Henrye
Chettle'. Chettle, however, made no attempt to evade
responsibility for his share in the publication. In
December 1592, Chettle in issuing a pamphlet of his
own composition, *Kind-Harts Dreame*, explained in an
introductory *Epistle* to the Gentlemen Readers his part
in the offending publication:

I had onely in the copy this share, it was il written as
sometime *Greenes* hand was none of the best, licensd it
must be, ere it could bee printed which could never be
if it might not be read. To be breife I writ it over, and
as neare as I could, followed the copy onely in that letter
I put something out, but in the whole booke not a worde
in, for I protest it was all *Greenes*, not mine nor Maister
Nashes, as some unjustly have affirmed.

Earlier in this *Epistle* Chettle had replied to two
dramatists who had taken exception to statements in the
Groats-worth. To leave no dubiety about his own
innocence Chettle explains that he himself did not

know them personally and could not therefore be the author of the references to them: 'With neither of them that take offence was I acquainted, and with one of them I care not if I never be.' The one whose acquaintance Chettle did not seek was clearly Marlowe; and he meets Marlowe's complaint by claiming that so far from deserving Marlowe's ill will he was entitled to credit from him for striking out one of Greene's insinuations:

For the first, whose learning I reverence, and, at the perusing of Greene's book, stroke out what then, in conscience I thought, he in some displeasure writ: or had it been true, yet to publish it was intolerable: him I would wish to use me no worse than I deserve.

To Shakespeare, however, Chettle offers a full and frank apology:

The other, whome at that time I did not so much spare, as since I wish I had, for that as I have moderated the heate of living writers, and might have usde my own discretion (especially in such a case) the Author beeing dead, that I did not, I am as sory as if the originall fault had beene my fault, because my selfe have seen his demeanor no less civill than he exelent in the qualitie he professes [that is acting]: Besides, divers of worship have reported his uprightnes of dealing, which argues his honesty, and his facetious grace in writting, that aprooves his Art.

Greene had charged Shakespeare as an actor with sharing in the dishonest treatment dramatists received from a greedy and callous crew of puppets and anticks: Chettle cites the testimony of men of standing to Shakespeare's honesty. Greene had treated Shake-

speare as a bombastic dramatist: Chettle finds that men of education admire his art.

The passage in the *Groats-worth of Wit* for which Chettle apologizes was recovered for scholarship by Thomas Tyrwhitt, who pointed out that the expression in Greene's attack, *Tygers hart wrapt in a Players hyde* was a parody of a line from Shakespeare's *3 Henry VI*, I. iv. 137,

O tiger's heart wrapp'd in a woman's hide!

This line is spoken by the Duke of York, taken prisoner by Queen Margaret and her forces at the battle of Wakefield. The Queen and others taunt the Duke as they prepare to kill him, and he replies in a tirade that contains the line Greene adapts to express his scorn of Shakespeare as a dramatist and his contempt for him as an actor. As Greene is quoting a passage to give point to his derision of Shakespeare's style he naturally quotes from a piece that was known to be by Shakespeare. We have here, therefore, a contemporary witness to the authorship of *3 Henry VI* that justified Tyrwhitt in dismissing the doubts of Pope, Theobald, and Warburton, about the place given to this play and its associated parts by Heminge and Condell among their colleague's works. Johnson had already pointed out the insubstantial nature of the conjectures by Theobald and others; to this Tyrwhitt added the positive evidence of Shakespeare's authorship provided by Greene's malicious comment.

Here the discussion might have ended, for the earlier editors had no satisfactory knowledge of the chronology of Shakespeare's work, and could not be expected to make allowance for the immaturity of certain pieces without some information about the date of their

E

composition. Yet it was the scholar who did so much
to determine the order of composition of the plays
who reopened the question of the authorship of the
Henry VI pieces. And, even more astonishing, it was
the same scholar, who had already questioned Rowe's
guesses about Shakespeare's lack of education, who
now gave his authority to the notion that Shakespeare
made a start as a dramatist by rewriting the plays of
some of the university men whom he found on his
arrival in London already established as dramatists.
In his dissertation on the Three Parts of *Henry VI*
Malone offered two principal reasons for asserting that
this trilogy was not originally by Shakespeare. The
'chief hinge of his argument' he found in the passage
from Greene that Tyrwhitt had just cited as proof of
Shakespeare's authorship. For Malone argued that the
phrase 'an upstart Crow beautified with our feathers'
was not merely another form of calling Shakespeare
one of 'those Puppets that spake from our mouths,
those Anticks garnisht in our colours' or of 'these
painted monsters' as Greene later calls the actors; it
meant, Malone insisted, that Shakespeare was a man
who in setting up as a dramatist had passed off as his
own compositions plots and dialogue he had stolen
from Greene and his friends. To substantiate this interpretation of Greene's words Malone then indicated the
very pieces that Shakespeare had taken over and that
Greene himself had indicated by his quotation, so
Malone believed, as stolen wares. The two pieces to
which Malone referred were issued in quarto format in
1594 and 1595 respectively; the earlier was described
on the title-page as *The First part of the Contention
betwixt the two famous Houses of Yorke and Lancaster*,
its sequel as *The true Tragedie of Richard Duke of Yorke*,

and the death of good King Henrie the Sixt. They give
in somewhat shortened and imperfect form versions of
2 and *3 Henry VI*, pieces not printed in their fuller form
till 1623, when Heminge and Condell included them
in the First Folio. Among many other resemblances
between the Quarto and Folio versions Malone noted
that the line adapted by Greene from York's tirade was
to be found in the *True Tragedie of Richard Duke of
Yorke.* His thesis, therefore, runs:

What does the writer [Greene] mean by calling him
[Shakespeare] 'a crow beautified with our feathers'? My
solution is, that Greene and Peele were the joint authors
of the two quarto plays . . . or that Greene was the
author of one and Peele of the other.

To Malone 'upstart Crow' means an upstart writer not
an upstart actor, and he supports this by the further
assertion, 'We have undoubted proofs that Shakespeare
was not above working on the materials of other men.
His Taming of the Shrew, his King John, and other
plays render any arguments on that point unnecessary.'
Greene therefore accuses Shakespeare with having
acted like the crow in the fable and dressed himself in
stolen colours, and to mark the theft Greene 'very
naturally quotes a line from one of the pieces which
Shakespeare had thus *re-written*'.

To show that Malone was mistaken in his interpretation of every material point concerning the authorship
of the *Henry VI* plays would be tedious, did the
evidence not indicate Shakespeare's theatrical connexions before his joining the Chamberlain's men in
1594, as well as enabling us to identify the plays that
had gained for him the reputation as a dramatist that
is not only mentioned by Chettle but provides the

explanation of his position in 1594 as a leading sharer
in the Chamberlain's company.

Malone, though he knew that stolen and mutilated
versions of some of Shakespeare's plays were published
by stationers during Shakespeare's years in London,
was not aware of the different forms such piracy might
take. For this reason he failed to see that *The Contention*
and *The True Tragedy*, although giving a much better
account of their originals than some later surreptitious
versions, had clearly all the marks of bad texts. They
provide no evidence whatever of Greene's or Peele's
authorship but only of the ability of some actors to put
together a version of plays they had acted in.

Malone's error about the nature of the stolen versions
of *2* and *3 Henry VI* puts out of court his guess that
these quartos were the work of Greene or Peele and the
foundation of Shakespeare's pieces, and leaves his
interpretation of the phrase 'an upstart Crow' a naked
and unsupported suggestion with nothing in the context to justify it though much to indicate its impro-
priety. We should therefore be free to return to
Tyrwhitt who took Greene's use of *his* before the
quotation from *3 Henry VI* as proof that Greene was
citing Shakespeare's own words as evidence of their
author's presumption and cruelty, were it not for an
objection by Professor Dover Wilson. Professor Dover
Wilson agrees that Malone was mistaken about the
origin of *The Contention* and *The True Tragedy*; nor
does he deny that Greene's use of *his* is parallel to that
in Mr Sergeant Buzfuz's indictment of Pickwick 'with
his heartless tomato sauce and warming pans'. The
evidence of Pickwick's systematic villainy the Serjeant
finds in the very instructions sent by Pickwick to Mrs
Bardell, his landlady. The use of 'his' may well indicate,

Professor Dover Wilson admits, that Greene is here quoting Shakespeare, but if so only, he implies, from a part added by Shakespeare to an original composition by Greene, Nashe, and Peele. For now Professor Dover Wilson relies on connoisseurship to apportion the scenes of *2* and *3 Henry VI*, as well as those of *1 Henry VI*, among the authors he feels must have contributed them. He has no evidence of the kind Malone fancied he had in the bad quartos. Against such impressionistic analysis, however refined on that practised by those whom Johnson condemned, the Doctor's objections still remain and in more cogent form. Only in the discussion of the plays themselves can the internal evidence be considered; meantime it may be observed that the assumption by which Professor Dover Wilson would justify his impressionistic disintegration of pieces attributed to Shakespeare by his first editors is, in its most material points, actually rejected by Professor Dover Wilson himself.

Professor Dover Wilson in recommending to us his procedure by observing that 'most scholars are agreed that Shakespeare spent at least part of his early years revising or rewriting the plays of other men' is forgetting what he himself has contributed to the rejection of this strange assumption. No doubt as long as Malone's dissertation on *Henry VI* was regarded as textually sound the assumption seemed plausible; for although Thomas Kenny in *The Life and Genius of Shakespeare* (1864) demonstrated the inadequacy of Malone's analysis of the texts, Malone's thesis was still accepted doctrine in 1924, as one can see from E. K. Chambers's Shakespeare Lecture of that year to the British Academy, a lecture called somewhat ironically *The Disintegration of Shakespeare*. For Chambers was

reproving others for going much further in dividing up
Shakespeare's plays among his contemporaries than he
himself was prepared to go; although at that time
Chambers had no doubt that we had in certain quarto
publications the very pieces Shakespeare revised or
rewrote in the form now found in the First Folio.
Since 1924, however, Professor Dover Wilson has
himself rejected the assumption, which Chambers
shared with Malone, that *The Contention*, *The True
Tragedy* and *The Taming of a Shrew* are original plays
which Shakespeare rewrote. There remain some other
pieces behind which the old assumption may still lurk,
but there is no proof, even of the kind once accepted
for the three named quartos, that these other pieces are
Shakespeare's originals. To refer us to what E. K.
Chambers and those who listened to him in 1924
thought on disintegration is not evidence; nor can we
return to Malone's position, for what he took for strong
points are lost for good. There is now no agreement
among scholars that Shakespeare had to begin by
rewriting the plays of better educated dramatists.

Professor Dover Wilson is therefore forced to find in
the phrase 'upstart Crow beautified with our feathers'
the sole external support to the extensive fabric of his
conjecture, and attempts to reinforce his interpretation
of it by citing other references by Greene to the fable,
especially to Greene's use of it in the form he adopted,
Professor Dover Wilson insists, from Horace's third
Epistle, that in which the Roman poet addresses Julius
Florus then serving in eastern parts on the staff of
Tiberius. Horace, as an old infantryman, seems to have
regarded the youthful staff officers as a group with
leisure for literary composition, for he enquires not
about their military tasks but about their latest poetical

ventures. The question in its playful and bantering tone just hints that Horace takes this part of their occupation as seriously as he takes their staff work. Is Titius, Horace asks, writing Pindaric odes or in the throes of tragic frenzies? And Celsus:

Pray what is Celsus doing; he who has been and must be often warned to search for resources of his own, and to refrain from laying hands on any writings which Apollo on the Palatine [the Imperial Library set up by Augustus in the Temple of Apollo] has admitted; lest if, perchance, the tribe of birds some day shall come to claim the plumage which is their own, he provoke laughter, like the wretched crow when stripped of her stolen colours.

Horace is laughing at a method of composition more extreme no doubt but somewhat similar to that attributed to Gray by Wordsworth: Gray 'wrote English Verses, as he and other Eton school-Boys wrote Latin . . . if I were to pluck out of Gray's tail all the feathers which, I know, belong to other birds he would be left very bare indeed'. There is, however, no suggestion in Horace or Wordsworth, who has obviously Horace in mind, that the subjects of their criticism are passing off as their own extensive compositions by other poets. Wordsworth does once elsewhere use the comparison where honesty is in question, when he talks of Macpherson owing 'his fine feathers' to the Bible, Shakespeare, Milton, and Pope. What was dishonest was Macpherson's pretence that he was translating from Ossian. Nor is Professor Dover Wilson's later reference to Greene's account of how Bathyllus claimed the distich which Virgil attached by night to the gates of the palace of Augustus, or how Varro rewrote Ennius,

although Greene here too introduces '*Ezops* Crowe', of any weight. For as Professor Dover Wilson himself points out, Greene uses the expression of actors, not because it is dishonest for an actor to declaim the words of the poet, but because the actor was taking the cash Greene felt the dramatist was entitled to. As a parallel Professor Dover Wilson quotes Byron's jibe at publishers. But Byron called them robbers not because they rewrote his works and published them as their own compositions, but because his Lordship regarded his share of the profits as inadequate. Actors were to Greene what publishers were to Byron, and Greene was no less outspoken about what he regarded as the actor's dishonesty; to Greene actors were robbers. As to Varro's modernizing of Ennius, that was as open as Dryden's rewriting of Chaucer, and in no way reflects on the honesty of the reviser.

Greene's most obvious use of the Crow fable to remind the actor of his inferior role in the theatre occurs in an interlude in Greene's sustained attack not on Shakespeare but on Marlowe, for in spite of Greene's pretence that he was calling Marlowe an atheist and something worse for friendship's sake, Greene had for some three years been invariably scurrilous in his references to Marlowe. In 1587 Marlowe's *Tamburlaine*, with Edward Alleyn in the title-role, had in the theatre world a triumph worthy of its hero's reputation in life. Both parts must have been on the stage by the end of that year, for in a letter of 16 November 1587 there is a description of an accident during the performance of *2 Tamburlaine*, v. i in which the Governor of Babylon is shot to death by Tamburlaine's men. Unhappily in shooting at the dummy figure an actor mishandled his piece and killed a woman and

child in the audience. Till 1587 and the publicity achieved by *Tamburlaine* Greene seems to have been indifferent to the financial possibilities provided by the theatre. His *Alphonsus King of Aragon* was, however, an early reaction to Marlowe's success; yet so obviously an imitation of *Tamburlaine* and so poor a one as to deserve the taunts that the Admiral's men allowed themselves at its lack of success. From this time, however, Greene regularly scoffs at Marlowe, and does not omit to remind Alleyn, who had made so successful an appearance as Tamburlaine, of his inferior status.

Greene's attack on Marlowe begins immediately after the failure of his *Alphonsus*. He introduces his next pamphlet *Perymedes the Blacksmith*, dated 1588, with a preface *To the Gentlemen Readers* in which he refers to the jeers of the Admiral's men at his *Alphonsus* and retorts with some observations on Marlowe's *Tamburlaine*:

I keepe my old course, to palter up some thing in Prose, using mine old poesie still, *Omne tulit punctum*, although lately two Gentlemen Poets made two mad men of Rome beate it out of their paper bucklers: and had it in derision, for that I could not make my verses jet it upon the stage in tragicall buskins, everie worde filling the mouth like the faburden of Bo-Bell, daring God out of heaven with that Atheist Tamburlan, or blaspheming with the mad preest of the sonne but let me rather openly pocket up the Asse at Diogenes hand: then wantonlye set out such impious instances of intollerable poetry: such mad and scoffing poets, as bred of Merlin's race, if there be any in England that set the end of scollarisme in an English blanck verse, I think either it is the humour of a novice that tickles them with selfe-love, or too much frequenting of the hot house (to use

the Germaine proverbe) hath swet out all the greatest
part of their wits . . . If I speak darkly Gentlemen, and
offend with this digression, I crave pardon, in that I but
answere in print, what they have offered on the stage.

In his earlier pamphlets Greene had proclaimed his
intention of honouring Horace's exhortation to combine amusement and instruction and used as a motto
on his title-page the line from the *Ars Poetica*: 'Omne
tulit punctum qui miscuit utile dulci.' Greene now
returns to the kind of composition he had for the
moment put aside to write for the stage; he tells us in
terms that are no longer fully intelligible of the satirical
comment his venture into the theatre provoked, but
however dark the nature of his complaint it is clear he
blames Marlowe and expresses strong disapproval of his
style and outlook.

The poor reception of *Alphonsus* did not, however,
discourage Greene from continuing in his *Orlando* and
his *Friar Bacon and Friar Bongay* to find suggestions
for his own pieces in Marlowe's plays; nor did this
continued interest in Marlowe's plays prevent his continuing to refer to Marlowe in disparaging terms. Even
in his *Menaphon* (1589), a pastoral romance in the mode
of Sidney's *Arcadia*, Greene manages to introduce a
sneer. Samela, the name the Princess Sephestia has
assumed after being cast ashore in Arcadia, is being
wooed by her husband Melicertus, from whom she has
been separated by shipwreck, without either identifying
the other; to Samela's objection that his affections are
placed elsewhere Melicertus replies:

Whosoever, Samela, descanted of that love, told you a
Canterbury tale; some propheticall full mouth that as
he were a cobbler's eldest sonne, would by the laste tell

where anothers shoe wrings but his sowterly aim was just
level thinking everie looke was love or everie faire word
a pawne for loyaltie.

As Marlowe was the son of a Canterbury shoemaker
there need be no question of Greene's aim, especially
as in the preface which Thomas Nashe contributed to
this work the attack on a rival group of dramatists and
players is open and inspired by Greene's affiliations and
enmities in this minor war of the theatre.

Greene maintained his reference to the 'cobbler' in
his *Franciscos Fortunes* (1590), but now he is not so
much concerned with Marlowe as with the actors who
are enjoying not merely the applause that should be
reserved for the dramatist but the profit that is, Greene
feels, by right the author's. Under cover of what pur-
ports to be a discourse on the theatre in Rome Greene
introduces his attack on Alleyn. According to Greene
'men of great honour and grave account' were once
willing to perform in comedies before the Senate and
Consuls, the important feature in this arrangement
being the rich rewards that were given the authors, not
the actors, of these comedies. Unhappily mean men
took to acting; their performance could not be faulted
but they were rich and insolent, among them none
more famous than Roscius. In his pride and pretensions, however, he was reminded of his place by
Cicero:

Why Roscius, art thou proud with *Esops* Crow, being
pranct with the glorie of others feathers? of thy selfe thou
canst say nothing, and if the Cobler hath taught thee to
say *Ave Caesar*, disdain not thy tutor, because thou prat-
est in a Kings chamber: what sentence thou utterest on
the stage, flowes from the censure of our wittes, and what

sentence or conceipt of the invention the people applaud for excellent, that comes from the secrets of our knowledge.

The 'Cobler' is Marlowe. Greene found a cobbler in his source and made it another excuse for a jibe at the cobbler's son. Roscius is Alleyn, famous as Tamburlaine and Faustus.

Greene uses the same terms in describing Alleyn as he does in his attack on Shakespeare: Alleyn is a proud crow 'being pranct with the glorie of others feathers'; Shakespeare is 'an upstart Crow beautified with our feathers'. There is, however, a difference: Alleyn of himself can say nothing; but Shakespeare is an upstart for though an actor he thinks himself a dramatist as good as or better than Greene and his friends. The context in which Greene applies the terms to Shakespeare requires us, if we are to make sense of the passage, to take 'upstart Crow beautified with our feathers' as meaning an upstart actor.

The reference to actors as crows wearing the feathers of the dramatists Greene may have had suggested to him by Nashe who, on coming down from Cambridge, associated himself for a time with Greene and contributed the Preface *To the Gentlemen Students of Both Universities* to Greene's *Menaphon*. Nashe is here covering up Greene's failure to rival Marlowe's pieces for the stage by a kind of counter-attack on the more successful dramatists. He begins by referring to 'their idiote artmasters, that intrude themselves to our eares as the alcumists of eloquence, who (mounted on the stage of arrogance) think to outbrave better pens with the swelling bumbast of a bragging blanke verse.' Later we hear of dramatists whose scholarship seems deficient to Nashe:

a sort of shifting companions, that runne through every
arte and thrive by none, to leave the trade of *Noverint*,
whereto they were borne, and busie themselves with the
indevors of Art, that could scarce latinize their necke-
verse if they should have neede; yet English *Seneca* read
by candle light yeeldes manie good sentences, as *Bloud
is a begger*, and so foorth; and, if you intreate him faire
in a frostie morning, he will affoord you whole *Hamlets*,
I should say handfulls of tragical speaches. But O griefe!
tempus edax rerum, what's that will last alwaies? The sea
exhaled by droppes will in continuance be drie, and
Seneca let bloud line by line and page by page at length
must needes die to our stage: which makes his famish
followers to imitate the Kidde in Æsop, who enamored
with the Foxes new fangles, forsooke all hopes of life to
leape into a new occupation, and these men, renouncing
all possibilities of credit or estimation, to intermeddle
with Italian translations: wherein how poorelie they have
plodded . . . let all indifferent Gentlemen that have
travailed in that tongue discerne by their twopenie
pamphlets.

Nashe is careful to express himself in forms that hint
rather than assert. Some years later he was to declare
that he never attacked Marlowe, but there can be little
doubt that 'the idiote art-masters' and their 'bragging
blanke verse' would suggest Marlowe to many readers,
especially as Greene was at this time referring to Marlowe, as he does in *Menaphon* itself, in contemptuous
terms, and Nashe was contrasting Greene's *Menaphon*
with plays more showy but less truly eloquent in style.
The reference to Kyd, the son of a scrivener, is also
clear. The mention of *Hamlet* has, however, given rise
to much speculation. The assumption that Shakespeare
rewrote the plays of other dramatists has given the
ground for the further assumption that this early

Hamlet was by Kyd and rewritten by Shakespeare many years later when at the height of his creative powers in the form we now know as his. The assumption itself rests on false assumptions, and the subsequent information about this early *Hamlet* indicates that it was by Shakespeare.

Nashe, in addition to his impertinent references to well-known dramatists, is contemptuous in his treatment of actors. It is here that he describes the actors as dressed in the feathers of the dramatists: 'Sundrie other sweete Gentlemen I know, that have vaunted their pens in private devices, and trickt up a companie of taffata fooles with their feathers'; and Nashe adds the further detail, which Greene also incorporated in his *Groatsworth of Wit*, about the actors playing such pieces as *Delfrigus* and the *King of the Fairies* till the scholars provided them with real dramas. In his mention of Alleyn, however, whom he refers to as Roscius, Nashe recognizes his deserved reputation and regards him as alone providing 'the rabble of counterfets', that is the other actors of the company, with their appeal to the public.

Nashe's *Preface* is a brisk fusillade in defence of Greene, now against rival dramatists, now against actors. It is here that the actors are treated as 'counterfets' dressed in the feathers of the dramatists, an image adopted by Greene with the added suggestion that the actors by underpaying the dramatist were guilty of a form of theft. For this Chettle apologized by acknowledging Shakespeare's reputation for honesty. To add with Professor Dover Wilson: 'Whatever his (Shakespeare's) grand friends said about his honesty in general neither he nor they had been able actually to deny the particular charge Greene brought against him' is to

beg the whole question of the cause of Green's complaint. To go on to say that we shall never know the reason for Greene's reference to the line 'tigers heart wrapt in a womans hide' is to draw on oneself the question, what did Greene mean when he ended his letter by saying of the actors 'a whole booke cannot containe their wrongs'? Had Greene in mind a catalogue of wrongs we shall never know?

The root of Greene's complaint against the actors as against Shakespeare was financial in kind, and Shakespeare was to Greene twice an offender by ignoring the line of demarcation that Greene felt should separate actor and dramatist. Without copyright protection as that is now understood the dramatist was selling on a buyer's market, parting with his productions for a modest payment down; in comparison with Edward Alleyn or the sharers in Shakespeare's company the dramatists were poor men. Although Greene could tell Alleyn 'of thy selfe thou canst say nothing', Alleyn could purchase in 1605 the manor of Dulwich for £5,000, and spend another £5,000 on his project there, while the cobbler's eldest son that provided him with his famous parts was a comparatively poor man who came to grief among a group of men living by their wits. The uneven distribution of takings between the actor and the dramatist was not, however, a feature peculiar to the Elizabethan age, or evidence of Shakespeare's greed. In what is often regarded as the most civilized world of Louis XIV the average earnings of Racine in the thirteen years (1654–1667) he served the theatre were, according to Mr J. Lough's calculation, a little over a thousand livres a year, while a full sharer in Molière's company in the period 1659–1673 averaged 3,500 livres a year. We may regret that Racine on

making a respectable marriage abandoned the stage for more courtly and lucrative employment, but La Bruyère's sketch of the actor in his carriage and the dramatist on foot: 'Le comedien, couché dans sa carrosse, jette de la boue au visage de Corneille, qui est à pied' may help to our understanding of Racine's choice. Corneille himself indicated that what he needed was money even more than fame. The bitterness that the type of situation indicated by La Bruyère might engender in the mind of Greene, galled no doubt by his own reckless conduct, is only too easily understood. In the very act of confessing his follies Greene attributes his misery to others, his attack on the actors verging on persecution mania. Had Greene had any real injury to attribute to Shakespeare he would not have hesitated to say what it was. The man who could call Marlowe an atheist and something more that Chettle couldn't bring himself to transcribe, and all this for old acquaintance sake, was not too nice to tell the worst about the man he regarded as an enemy. To wonder what offence other than his success as an actor and dramatist we are to impute, on Greene's words, to Shakespeare is to misunderstand not merely Greene's grammar but his unhappy state of mind.

The misunderstanding of Greene's words that set Malone and later scholars searching for the wrong Greene had suffered at Shakespeare's hands also suggested to them that Shakespeare had just started his career as dramatist in 1591, otherwise Chettle could not have been unacquainted with him. But Chettle was also unacquainted with Marlowe, who had been a notable figure in the world of the London theatre since 1587. Further Shakespeare was already regarded by 'divers of worship' as an excellent dramatist. How they

could do so unless they were familiar with his plays need hardly be asked. Fortunately the very pieces that Malone, at the prompting of Farmer, offered as evidence of Shakespeare's early efforts as a reviser of other men's pieces enable us to reconstruct in part Shakespeare's early associations and to see the context in which some of his first plays were written.

In his dissertation on the *Henry VI* plays Malone had attributed the quartos *The Contention* and *The True Tragedy* to Greene and Peele. At the further prompting of Farmer, his evil genius in this affair, Malone changed his mind and decided they were the work of Marlowe. It is true the quartos contain many passages and lines identical with or similar to lines and passages in Marlowe's *Edward II*. The passages, however, were not inserted by Marlowe but by the actors who put together these quartos from memory; and they inserted the passages from Marlowe because, having played in *2* and *3 Henry VI* as well as in *Edward II*, their memories failed to keep clear and distinct the differences between many situations in Shakespeare's pieces and Marlowe's history that might very easily be confused. That the same company of actors played in these pieces is clear from the title-pages of *The True Tragedy* and *Edward II* where they are described as having been acted by Pembroke's company. *The Contention* clearly belonged to the same company, and the reason why some of Pembroke's men put together from memory versions of *2* and *3 Henry VI* is indicated in a letter which Henslowe wrote to Alleyn while the latter was on tour with Lord Strange's men during the plague of 1593. Alleyn had written enquiring about Pembroke's men who were also touring the provinces and was told in Henslowe's reply of 28 September 1593: 'As for my

lord of Pembrokes which you desire to know where they
be, they are all at home and have been this 5 or 6 weeks,
for they cannot save their charges with travel as I hear
and were fain to pawn their apparel for their charge.'
As the players' costumes were among their most important possessions, the company was clearly in difficulties when they disposed of them. That they disposed of
their play-books too is evident for several reasons,
amongst others the fact that some leading members of
the company put together from odd parts and memory
versions of *2* and *3 Henry VI*. How Marlowe's
Edward II came to be in their repertory, and became
in part confused with Shakespeare's plays, we learn
from another letter of this period.

Marlowe's *Tamburlaine* was performed by the Admiral's men, and they too seem to have owned *Faustus*,
as well as *The Jew of Malta*, and *The Massacre at Paris*,
although the latter pair were in the repertory of Lord
Strange's men at the Rose, probably because Alleyn, an
Admiral's man, was able to make them available, Alleyn
being at this time with Strange's men while the majority
of the Admiral's men were touring abroad. *Edward II*
as a Pembroke piece stands by itself outside this
group, and the reason why Marlowe wrote this piece and
this alone for that company is found in the letter which
the dramatist Thomas Kyd wrote to Sir John Pucker-
ing, the Lord Keeper, some time after 12 May 1593.

On that day Kyd was arrested by those authorized by
the Privy Council to arrest and bring to confession, by
torture if necessary, those who were suspected of helping to stir up ill-feeling and action against foreign
craftsmen in London. The searchers found nothing to
implicate Kyd in this matter, but in turning over his
papers came on a copy of a document written by a

Unitarian while under examination for heresy by Cranmer in 1549. The author of this treatise had recanted; it now seemed to the authorities vile and heretical, being a denial of the divinity of Christ, and Kyd was examined about his interest in these views under torture it would seem. In his distress Kyd wrote to the Lord Keeper explaining that the document in question had belonged to Marlowe; they had been associated for a brief period in the service of the same nobleman, worked together in the same room, and the document had been in error transferred to Kyd's papers when they separated. Kyd further explains that he had been some six years in his Lordship's service; Marlowe had been engaged not as a member of his Lordship's household, but only to write for his company of players. On learning, however, of Marlowe's irreligious views his Lordship at once dispensed with his services. Kyd does not name his patron; it cannot, however, be the Lord Admiral for whose company Marlowe first wrote and to whose company, as represented by Alleyn, his later pieces belonged; for although Strange's men acted *The Massacre at Paris* and *The Jew of Malta* at the Rose, these pieces remained with Alleyn and the returned Admiral's men at the Rose after Strange's men had become incorporated in the Lord Chamberlain's new company. With the Admiral and Lord Strange eliminated, there remains only Lord Pembroke, and this is confirmed by Kyd's letter which explains how Marlowe's connexion with his company was cut short, so that a single contribution by Marlowe to the repertoire of Pembroke's men would be what we might expect as evidence of this brief association. As *Edward II* was published as a Pembroke play, the only piece by Marlowe so described, and as it is so closely associated

with *2* and *3 Henry VI* through their bad quartos *The Contention* and *The True Tragedy*, the unauthorized reconstructions of their lost play-books by Pembroke's men, only the most clear and unequivocal evidence to the contrary can rule out the conclusion that Kyd's patron was Pembroke. When, therefore, Kyd tells the Lord Keeper that two years had passed since he and Marlowe had shared the same room, Marlowe's *Edward II* can be dated 1591, some time in May or the early part of the year.

It may be noted in passing that Kyd's arrest was followed by an order from the Privy Council dated 18 May requiring Marlowe to appear before it. Marlowe was at that time residing with Thomas Walsingham, cousin to Sir Francis Walsingham, the organizer of Elizabeth's secret service. Marlowe presented himself on 20 May and was told to report daily till otherwise instructed. His death on 30 May at Eleanor Bull's tavern at Deptford, when supping with three men engaged in secret service work, anticipated any action the Privy Council may have felt called for by reports of his atheistical opinions.

Now that *The Contention* and *The True Tragedy* can be dismissed as unauthorized versions put together after the failure of Pembroke's company in 1593, and the suggestion that the recollections from *Edward II* that these pieces contain are evidence of Marlowe's authorship is seen to be baseless, it is possible to compare *2* and *3 Henry VI* directly with *Edward II*. This comparison reveals a number of parallels between them; but as Professor Dover Wilson in his Introduction to *2 Henry VI* has summed up the matter:

Once the parallels are studied in relation to the sources of *Henry VI*, Marlowe is revealed as unquestionably the

borrower, since, in three cases, the passages in *Edward II* are neither guaranteed by history nor required by the dramatic context, while those in *Henry VI* are obviously taken from the chronicles.

2 and *3 Henry VI* as we have them in the First Folio were, therefore, in existence when Marlowe was writing *Edward II* for Pembroke's men in 1591. As there is no evidence that Greene, or Nashe, or Peele, had ever any connexion with Pembroke's company, that is but one more objection, were further argument required, against the suggestion that any of these writers had a part in those pieces.

It is now possible to reconstruct the evidence of Shakespeare's connexion with Pembroke's company, the errors of Malone and those who have been mis-directed by him put aside. Marlowe, when he came to write for Pembroke's men, found Shakespeare one of the company and his *2* and *3 Henry VI* in their reper-toire; that these pieces were by Shakespeare is attested by Heminge and Condell, Shakespeare's editors, and this is confirmed by Greene's offering as an example of Shakespeare's bombast a line from *3 Henry VI*. Mar-lowe finding these plays popular set himself to write something on the same lines. The notion that Marlowe was the originator of the English history play, and that Shakespeare was, in Mr Bakeless' words, beginning slowly and clumsily to follow in the way Marlowe had marked out for him, is an assumption that rests on the assumption that Shakespeare could not yet write for himself and completely misrepresents the relationship between *Edward II* and *2* and *3 Henry VI*. That Marlowe had an influence on Shakespeare is not denied; Shakespeare was too perceptive a dramatist not to see how much better some of Marlowe's motifs could be

treated; *Edward II* itself no doubt was in Shakespeare's
mind as he wrote his *Richard II*. In *Edward II*, however, Marlowe was learning from Shakespeare how to
put together a plot, a tribute to Marlowe's discernment,
for it is clear not only from *2* and *3 Henry VI*, but from
the other plays by Shakespeare in Pembroke's repertoire, that already Shakespeare easily excelled anyone
writing at that time for the stage in this most important
feature of stage-craft.

Fortunately two sources of evidence enable us to
assign to this period some at least of the plays Shakespeare had written before joining the Chamberlain's
men. Not only are the bad quartos of *2* and *3 Henry VI*
evidence that these pieces were Pembroke plays, the
bad quarto of *The Taming of the Shrew* is also described
on the title-page as acted by Pembroke's servants. The
good quarto of *Titus Andronicus*, published early in
1594, has on its title-page 'As it was Plaide by the
Right Honourable the Earl of Darbie, Earle of Pem-
brooke, and Earle of Sussex their Servants'. We can
follow the passage of this piece from Pembroke's men to
Shakespeare's new company, the Chamberlain's men.
On the break-up of Pembroke's men about August
1593, while some of Shakespeare's pieces in that company's repertory appeared in unauthorized and mutilated versions, *Titus Andronicus* alone was printed from
a good and sound copy. A copy had fallen into Henslowe's hands and was acted by the company, servants of
the Earl of Sussex, playing at his theatre the Rose
during January 1594. Henslowe put against it his mark
'ne' which indicates either a new piece or one having its
first performance at his theatre; as *Titus Andronicus*
had been a Pembroke play Henslowe or the company
must have acquired it as a result of the failure of

Pembroke's men. It next appears in Henslowe's diary
in his record of the short season at Newington Butts,
when the Lord Admiral's and the newly formed Lord
Chamberlain's company had during ten days in June
1594 a joint season there. By that time it is clearly part
of the repertory of the Chamberlain's men, and it never
again figures in Henslowe's diary. Shakespeare must
have bought back or asserted his right to the piece, for
had it remained in Henslowe's possession it would have
surely been revived at the Rose, since the takings at the
three earlier performances there by Sussex's men were
considerable.

In addition to the evidence provided by those Pembroke plays that found their way into print in good or
mutilated texts, there is the record in Henslowe's diary
of the season at Newington Butts shared by the
Admiral's and Chamberlain's men. Of the four pieces
presented by the Chamberlain's men three were by
Shakespeare: *Titus Andronicus*, *Hamlet*, and *The Taming of the Shrew*. *Titus* and *The Shrew* had been Pembroke pieces; that *Hamlet* was also by Shakespeare is
suggested by the context in which it is here mentioned,
and this is confirmed by features in the play itself and
by its later history. Shakespeare had now transferred
himself and his plays to the Chamberlain's men, a
company obviously ready to make the most of the work
of a dramatist who had already gained for himself a
standing, as Chettle indicates, among gentlemen who
were interested in the theatre.

The Chamberlain's men, however, were naturally
desirous of attracting to their performances not merely
those whom the custom of the age recognized as gentlemen but all who were ready to pay their penny or two-
pence to the gatherers at the entrances. In Shakespeare

they saw a dramatist with a wide appeal, if we are
to judge by the readiness publishers showed in their
printing of even imperfect copies of his plays, and the
evidence of what may be called his box-office appeal.
The record of Henslowe's share of the takings during the
brief season at Newington Butts can be put aside, since
the playhouse there was out of the way and its occupation by the Admiral's and Chamberlain's men a very
temporary arrangement. But *Titus Andronicus* when
performed earlier at the Rose proved a marked financial
success, and if *Harey the VI*, first performed at the
Rose on 3 May 1592, was one of Shakespeare's pieces,
the sustained support of his work by the theatre-goers,
as reflected in Henslowe's share of the receipts, was
outstanding. As Shakespeare was attached to Pembroke's men at this time, and as *2* and *3 Henry VI* were
in their repertory, the *Henry VI* at the Rose, if Shakespeare's, must be *1 Henry VI* and have passed to
Strange's men who performed it at Henslowe's Rose
from a company to which Shakespeare belonged before
he joined Pembroke's. Just as *Titus Andronicus* after
the failure of Pembroke's men is found at the Rose, so
the first part of *Henry VI* may have been written at an
earlier period of Shakespeare's career for a company
that he had acted with before he joined Pembroke's.
That this earlier company was the Queen's men has
been suggested by A. W. Pollard. If that were so
1 Henry VI may have passed from them to Strange's
men, for the latter are known to have taken over some
pieces from the Queen's company. There is another
entry in Henslowe's diary that suggests a connexion
between Shakespeare and the Queen's men. During the
few days at Easter 1593, when the Queen's men shared
the Rose with Sussex's men, Henslowe records on

6 April a performance of *Kinge Leare*. It is generally accepted that this is another piece that Shakespeare rewrote in his later years, that *King Leir*, published in 1605, represents this early version, that *King Leir* is an original composition by some unknown dramatist whose piece Shakespeare rewrote. This conclusion, now that the notion that Shakespeare was in the habit of revising old plays by other men is seen to be unsupported by any concrete evidence, must be reconsidered, for Shakespeare's *Lear* may be like his *Hamlet* his revision of one of his own earliest pieces. While Shakespeare's first associations in the theatre world must remain for the present a matter for conjecture and further investigation, his connexion with Pembroke's men in the years immediately preceding the plague of 1592–4 are so clearly indicated as to put his association with Marlowe and Kyd beyond reasonable question. To this early period may be assigned the three parts of *Henry VI*, *Titus Andronicus*, *The Taming of the Shrew*, and an early version of *Hamlet*; these assignments can all be supported by external evidence, and they provide a body of work that enables one to see how *The Comedy of Errors* and some other of his plays have features that may point to their production in this period. Only such a body of work enables us to understand Chettle's reference in 1592 to Shakespeare's reputation as a dramatist, and to the leading part he took in the company he had joined when regular playing was resumed in 1594.

Between Shakespeare's association with Pembroke's men and his appearance with the Chamberlain's men lie the two years when the London theatres were closed except for the briefest of respites. Some at least of this time Shakespeare occupied with the writing of *Venus*

and Adonis, entered in the Stationers' Register on 18 April 1593, and *The Rape of Lucrece* a year later on 9 May 1594. Unlike the editions of his plays that were printed during his lifetime with too many errors to allow us to suppose the dramatist read the proofs, the two narrative poems were carefully produced, a courtesy in keeping with their presentation to the Earl of Southampton in dedicatory epistles over Shakespeare's own name. Proof-reading, at a time when the printer had to work with a limited stock of type and so had to print a work of any size in stages, required the regular attendance of the author if he wished to supervise the work. If Shakespeare ever gave such attention to a publication it was to these two poems. Although regular writing for a company would not be required in such a state of theatrical emergency, there might be some special occasion at some noble house that called for a new production. Allowing for such an exceptional composition, we cannot suppose the companies were requiring new pieces for their visit to the provinces or, in their difficulties, willing to lay out more money than that demanded by their immediate needs.

ii. THE THEATRE

With the passing of the worst phase of the plague, acting in London was resumed in the summer of 1594, not, however, without important changes in the organization of the companies. The company Shakespeare now joined was a new formation under the patronage of the Lord High Chamberlain, Henry Carey the first Lord Hunsdon. Lord Hunsdon was the son of Mary Boleyn, Anne Boleyn's sister, so the Queen's cousin, and for his own sake trusted as well as liked by the Queen. His new company drew its personnel from

three distinct sources. The main body of the new company had acted at the Rose under Henslowe's management from the middle of February 1592 to the closing of the theatres on 23 June of that year. Their patron at that time was Lord Strange who, soon after becoming Earl of Derby on 25 September 1593, died on 16 April 1594. While at the Rose they were strengthened by Edward Alleyn, a member of the Admiral's company. Although many of that company were on tour on the continent Alleyn had remained in England, no doubt because he was about to marry Joan Woodward, Henslowe's step-daughter, the ceremony taking place on 22 October 1592. When the closing of the London theatres forced Strange's men to tour the provinces, they travelled under a warrant from the Privy Council dated 6 May 1593 that names the principal members of the company: 'Edward Allen, servant to the right honourable the Lord High Admiral: William Kemp, Thomas Pope, John Hemminges, Augustine Phillipes and George Brian, being all one company, servants to our very good Lord the Lord Strainge.' With the return of the Admiral's men Alleyn rejoined them, leaving the members of Strange's company to form part of the new Chamberlain's men. In place of Alleyn they were fortunate to secure Richard Burbage, who was to succeed Alleyn as the leading tragic actor of his time. The third source from which the new company drew their strength was Shakespeare.

As Strange's men had been at Henslowe's Rose when the theatres were closed, the new formation made its first appearance in London, again under his management, during a short season at Newington Butts from 3 to 27 June 1594. They shared this theatre with the reorganized Admiral's men, the companies performing

on different days, each in its own pieces. The Chamberlain's men put on four plays, three of them by Shakespeare: *Titus Andronicus*, *Hamlet*, and *The Taming of the Shrew*. None of these plays was in their repertory during their season at the Rose; of the twenty-three plays they performed there only one, *Henry VI*, has a name that suggests it was by Shakespeare. That it was indeed by Shakespeare is probable if we may regard it as a version of *1 Henry VI*, written before Shakespeare joined Pembroke's company and subsequently acquired by Strange's men. Strange's men had also become possessed of a copy of *Titus Andronicus*, no doubt like Henslowe or Sussex's men, after the failure of Pembroke's men, for Derby's men are mentioned with those of Pembroke and Sussex on the title-page of the quarto of 1594, published early that year as the entry in the Stationers' Register of 6 February 1594 suggests. The joint season at Newington Butts over, the Admiral's men occupied the Rose, while the Chamberlain's men made the Theatre their headquarters, although in the winter months they may have performed at the Cross Keys, in Gracechurch Street, an inn-yard in the City adapted for playing.

With Richard Burbage one of their number it was natural for the Chamberlain's men to use the Theatre owned by James Burbage, Richard's father. James Burbage, originally a carpenter, had turned to acting, and he was one of those mentioned in the Letters Patent issued under the Great Seal of England on 10 May 1574 authorizing the Earl of Leicester's men to act in London and elsewhere in spite of any regulation to the contrary, provided their plays had been seen and allowed by the Master of the Revels. Playing was not, however, to take place during plague or 'in the time of

common prayer'. This unique privilege was granted to defeat the determination of the City Fathers to make professional acting in London impossible. The City retaliated by imposing restricting regulations. The building of the Theatre in 1576 was James Burbage's reply to this continued hostility.

Burbage's building stood in the north-east, some distance outside Bishopsgate. Two circumstances governed his choice of site. This was the Liberty of Holywell, once the possession of Benedictine nuns. At the dissolution of the religious houses their ground became the property of the Crown, but, though subsequently given away or sold, the privilege enjoyed by the monastery or nunnery of being exempt from local jurisdiction still adhered to the site. This was also true of the Liberty within the City, Blackfriars, as well as the Liberties of the Clink and Paris Garden on the south bank of the river. Burbage's theatre was therefore outside the direct control of the City Council. There was the further attraction that Holywell was beside Finsbury Fields, a favourite recreational resort of Londoners.

Burbage's example was soon followed. Next year, 1577, the Curtain was constructed south of the Theatre separated from it by Holywell Lane. And towards the end of 1587 the Rose was built in the Liberty of the Clink. Further exploitation of the Liberties in the interests of the theatre were to follow, Burbage again proving an innovator.

James Burbage was driven to his next venture as the lease of the ground on which he built his theatre was due to expire in April 1597; for he had taken only a twenty-one year lease, and although he had bargained that the lease should be renewable, it was clear that the owner of the ground, Giles Alleyn, was prepared to

quibble over the terms in a way that gave little hope of
agreement. To meet this difficulty Burbage bought in
February 1596 for £600 the old dining-hall once used
by the monks of Blackfriars. The Blackfriars was a
Liberty in one of the most important districts of the
City, the hall was large enough to allow, at the cost of
another £300, the erection of a stage, gallery accommodation, and other furnishings; as a theatre it would
be an all-weather house, securely roofed and with artificial lighting.

The advantages of such a theatre are no doubt obvious, but may have been suggested to Burbage by the
performances given in roofed buildings by the Children
of the Royal Chapels and by those of St Paul's. Hitherto
the public theatres were all of the same general design
as the Theatre: an unroofed yard into which the stage
projected from the tiring-room, the whole enclosed by
a timber and plaster wall that carried three internal
galleries, the topmost protected by a thatched roof. On
the other hand the choristers from Windsor and the
Royal Chapel performed in a hall in the Blackfriars from
1577 to 1584, and the boys of St Paul's continued their
acting to 1590 in the singing-school beside their cathedral. Ten years later the boys were to resume their performances on a more professional scale. It was for this
early phase of the boys' theatrical activities that John
Lyly (1555–1606), the author of *Euphues*, wrote his
plays, among others his *Endymion*, *Campaspe*, and
Midas, courtly entertainments which the Queen herself
had played before her. In these pieces Shakespeare
found suggestions for his own production as Burbage
perhaps did in the halls where they were played.

Unfortunately for Burbage's scheme, the aristocratic
inhabitants of the Blackfriars, which was a somewhat

select area, surrounded by its own wall, its gates shut
at night, objected to having a common playhouse in the
precinct, and their petition to the Privy Council moved
that body to forbid James Burbage to use his newly
acquired building as a theatre. Two months before the
lease of the Theatre expired James Burbage died in
February 1597, leaving his difficulties to his sons:
Cuthbert now had the Theatre and the problem of its
future to see to, while his younger brother Richard was
left the new Blackfriars theatre in which acting was
forbidden.

In the solution of the problem posed the Burbages
by these difficulties Shakespeare and some of the senior
members of the company were to take an important
part. Meantime Dr Hotson has produced evidence that
the company's first notion in the emergency was to
transfer their playing to the recently erected theatre on
the Bankside called the Swan. This theatre was built
by Francis Langley, a wealthy goldsmith, though a
member of the Drapers' Company, on the Liberty of
Paris Garden, which he had purchased no doubt with
the hope of profiting by the obvious popularity of play-
going. The building was a large and handsome erection
completed probably in 1595. Two pieces of evidence
support Dr Hotson's conclusion. In 1595 Shakespeare
had been living in the Parish of St Helen's, Bishopsgate,
close to the Theatre. His residence must have been of
some size as it was assessed, for purposes of calculating
the occupant's share of any subsidy voted by Parliament
to the King, at £5, a larger sum, as Quincy Adams
noted, than that borne by the dwellings of either Cuthbert or Richard Burbage. The instalment due on 1 February 1596 was paid by Shakespeare in St Helen's, the
second on the same assessment due on 1 February 1597

had to be recovered from the Bishop of Winchester's officials, as Shakespeare was now residing in the Liberty of the Clink and so within the Bishop's jurisdiction. Shakespeare's removal is followed by his association with Francis Langley in a bitter dispute with William Gardiner, a Surrey Justice of the Peace, whom Langley described, very justly as Dr Hotson shows, as 'a false perjured knave'. That Shakespeare's connexion with Langley came about because the Chamberlain's men were acting at the Swan is confirmed by a reference to the early *Hamlet* in Dekker's *Satiromastix*: 'My names Hamlet revenge: thou hast been at Paris Garden, hast not?' Paris Garden being the site of the Swan.

If Dr Hotson is right, and his argument seems well founded, the Chamberlain's men were for a time at the Swan; they cannot, however, have continued at the Swan long, for the revived Pembroke's company began playing there on 21 February 1597. The contract Pembroke's men made with Langley gave them the use of the Swan for a year; unhappily the performance of a piece there in July called *The Isle of Dogs*, in which both Nashe and Jonson had a hand, gave such offence that the Privy Council ordered the arrest of the authors and actors. Playing in London was forbidden, and there was an order to dismantle the theatres that was fortunately not put into execution. The Swan, however, remained closed during the remainder of the reign; and although the Chamberlain's men had to travel in the provinces till the Queen's anger had blown over, they were allowed to be one of the two companies, the other being the Admiral's men, that might resume playing in London.

In giving place to Pembroke's men at the Swan, the Chamberlain's men may have used the Curtain, as they

certainly did after they were permitted to act again in
London in the autumn of 1597. By this time the lease
of the Theatre had expired. Cuthbert Burbage had
allowed the building to remain, as Giles Alleyn seemed
willing to come to terms; this proved to be a ruse on
Alleyn's part to secure the building, for Cuthbert Burbage had been entitled to dismantle the Theatre while
the lease was still in force, and doubtless also by oral
agreement if the subsequent negotiations came to
nothing. Alleyn, however, offered impossible terms and
claimed the building still on his ground.

Giles Alleyn no doubt felt he had had the better of
the deal; he had miscalculated the resource of his
tenants. Having declared the fabric of the Theatre forfeit Giles Alleyn, towards the close of 1598, withdrew
to the country to enjoy the Christmas season there, to
find on his return that the Theatre had vanished. How
this happened Alleyn explained to the Courts from
whom he sought redress for this trespass:

The said Cuthbert Burbage, having intelligence of your
subject's purpose herein [to take over the fabric], and
unlawfully combining and confederating himself with
the said Richard Burbage and one Peter Street, William
Smith, and diverse other persons to the number of
twelve, to your subject unknown, did about the eight
and twentieth day of December, in the one and fortieth
year of your highness reign . . . riotously assemble themselves together, and then and there armed themselves
with diverse and many unlawful and offensive weapons,
as, namely, swords, daggers, bills, axes, and such like;
and so armed did then repair unto the said Theatre,
and then and there armed as aforesaid, in very riotous,
outrageous, and forcible manner, and contrary to the
laws of your highness realm, attempted to pull down
the said Theatre. Whereupon, diverse of your subjects

G

servants and farmers, then going about in peaceable manner to procure them to desist from that their unlawful enterprise, they, the said riotous persons aforesaid, notwithstanding procured then therein with great violence, not only then and there forcibly and riotously resisting your subject's servants and farmers, but also then and there pulling, breaking, and throwing down the said Theatre in very outrageous, violent, and riotous sort.

Peter Street was a master carpenter who had no doubt helped to erect the Globe. William Smith was a financial supporter of the enterprise. The widow of James Burbage, to encourage her sons, 'was there, and did see the doing thereof, and liked well of it'. The timber framework was then taken across the river for incorporation in the new theatre that the Burbages were going to erect in the Liberty of the Clink.

As the Burbages had invested very considerable sums in the Blackfriars theatre that could not at present be used for playing, they were no doubt glad to take as partners in the new venture five of the leading sharers in the Chamberlain's company: Shakespeare, Heminge, Phillips, Pope, and Will Kempe. The Burbages were to keep half the shares for themselves; the actors each to have a fifth of the other half. This arrangement not only helped the Burbages to raise the capital required, but ensured that the Globe, as the theatre was to be called, would be the house used by the Company to which the sharers belonged. As the Courts did not sustain Giles Alleyn's claim against the Burbages for some £800 damages, the removal from the Theatre cost little more than what would have had to be expended normally on such an operation; and the change of situation and opening of a new and more handsome playhouse, even if forced on the company, proved a profitable investment.

During the years between the summer of 1594, when the Theatre became the house of the Chamberlain's men, and the company's move in 1599 to a new building on the Bankside, Shakespeare shared the financial success that his own work had been a major factor in bringing to his company. The tide of his affairs seemed set for fortune, when his son Hamnet died in his twelfth year and was buried at Stratford on 11 August 1596. It is possible that Shakespeare when residing in Bishopsgate had his family with him, otherwise the extent of the assessment on his dwelling there is difficult to explain; he may even have taken them to the Bankside when he moved there. The loss of his son, however, seems to have made Shakespeare decide to have a house of his own in Stratford which his wife and daughters could occupy, and on 4 May 1597 he bought New Place for £60 from William Underhill. By ill chance Underhill was poisoned some two months later by his half-witted eldest son, who was executed in March 1599; as soon as Underhill's second son, to whom his brother's forfeited property had been regranted, came of age in 1602, Shakespeare's lawyer took the precaution of having Shakespeare's title to New Place confirmed.

New Place stood at the corner of Chapel Street and Chapel Lane opposite the guild chapel, and the property purchased by Shakespeare included two barns and two gardens. New Place is sometimes confused with The Great House, now the Shakespeare Hotel, which Sir Hugh Clopton, the Lord Mayor of London, had built, no doubt, as H. E. Forrest in his *Old Houses of Stratford-upon-Avon* maintains, for business purposes.

In 1596 John Shakespeare, perhaps at his son's prompting, obtained from the College of Heralds the grant of the coat-of-arms he had a right to as a former

Bailiff of Stratford. At an earlier date he had obtained a 'pattern' of a proposed coat, but had at that time taken the matter no further. The arms now granted are as described in the previous chapter; to the detail there given may be added the statement in the draft that John Shakespeare's ancestors had been 'advanced and rewarded' by Henry VII 'for their valiant and faithful services'; this would be true of Mary Arden's ancestors, but so far none of John Shakespeare's ancestors have been found to whom this description may be applied. The only objection to this grant was made by the York Herald in 1602, Ralph Brooke who was at odds with his fellows in the College; his complaint, a purely technical one, that Shakespeare's arms were not sufficiently differentiated from those of Manley was answered conclusively by William Dethick, Garter King, and William Camden, Clarenceux King of Arms. In 1599 John Shakespeare made application for the right to quarter his arms with those of Mary Arden his wife. The further draft made by the Heralds seems to acknowledge Shakespeare's right to the arms of one of the branches of the Arden family, but the dramatist does not seem to have taken the claim further after his father's death.

The assessment on Shakespeare's residence in London as well as his purchase of New Place indicate the easy financial circumstances in which he was living; and this is confirmed by the only letter to Shakespeare that has come down to us. It was written on 25 October 1598 from the Bell in Carter Lane by Richard Quiney and bears the superscription *To my Loveinge good ffrend and countreymann Mr. Wm. Shackespere deliver theese.* Quiney had been on Stratford business in London, and asks Shakespeare to lend him £30 to pay his debts there.

Shakespeare may have called on Quiney at the Bell before the letter was dispatched, for the letter remained in Quiney's possession and was among his papers at the time of his death. As he died during his second term as Bailiff his papers that included this and other letters were retained in the borough archives. Whether Shakespeare received the letter or not it is certain he saw Quiney that day, for on the same day Quiney wrote to Stratford indicating that Shakespeare had seen him and arranged for Quiney's immediate needs as well as talking over with him other financial matters.

Already in 1594 Shakespeare on joining the Chamberlain's men was recognized by the company as a dramatist whose plays they were ready to produce, for on their first recorded appearance in London after the plague of 1592-4 they played in four pieces at Newington Butts, three of them by Shakespeare: *Titus Andronicus*, *Taming of the Shrew*, and the early *Hamlet*. His standing is also indicated by the wording in the Treasurer's account, when he was paying the new company for their performances before the Queen during the Christmas season: 'To William Kempe, William Shakespeare, and Richard Burbage, servants to the Lord Chamberlain . . . in all xxli.' This £20 was made up of £13. 6s. 8d. for performances on 26 and 27 December 1594, the remaining £6.13s. 4d. being 'by way of Her Majesty's reward'. Kempe, Shakespeare, and Burbage, were accepting payment on behalf of their company; Kempe and Burbage were in their respective parts the leading comic and tragic actor of the troupe; that Shakespeare was associated with them because of his standing as a dramatist is not a conjecture prompted by our knowledge of his later reputation, but a conclusion justified by the company's choice of his pieces on their

appearance at Newington Butts, as well as by their readiness to act his plays on special occasions. The titles and authorship of 'the two several comedies or interludes' played before the Queen on 26 and 27 December are unfortunately not recorded. The following evening, however, 28 December, the company performed at Gray's Inn, as part of what was to have been the most important entertainment of that society's Christmas celebrations; for that occasion the company chose Shakespeare's *Comedy of Errors*. The piece performed on this occasion is known only because the failure of the organizers of the entertainment to limit the invitations they sent out to the capacity of the hall offended their guests from the Inner Temple who withdrew in displeasure. A mock court of enquiry held next night found that *The Comedy of Errors* was a fitting ending to 'The Night of Errors'. A later invitation to the members of the Inner Temple made all well again.

The expectations of the company that Shakespeare's plays would prove attractive to their public, indicated by their readiness in these early days of their association to produce them, were not disappointed. By 1598 Shakespeare was proclaimed in a work published that year as the leading dramatist of the day. Its author, Francis Meres, was a graduate of Cambridge and from 1602 till his death in 1647 rector of Wing in Rutland. During his years in London it is clear he associated with those both interested and informed about the theatre, his own interest prompting these connexions. For although critical of what he regarded as misguided conduct or of writings encouraging loose behaviour, Meres had no Puritanical aversion from the stage and while admiring Sidney and Spenser could also enjoy Nashe's satire. His *Palladis Tamia: Wits Treasury* was

entered in the Stationers' Register on 7 September 1598, and there exists a copy containing a dedication dated from London 19 October 1598. Meres describes his work as 'A comparative discourse of our English Poets with the Greeke, Latine, and Italian Poets'. The comparisons he institutes are often of the most obvious kind; those suggested for Shakespeare merely reflect contemporary opinion; the mention, however, Meres makes of certain of the plays provides most valuable aid in determining the chronology of Shakespeare's work.

The most important references to Shakespeare in Meres follow:

As the soule of *Euphorbus* was thought to live in *Pythagoras*: so the sweete wittie soule of *Ovid* lives in mellifluous and hony-tongued *Shakespeare*, witnes his *Venus* and *Adonis*, his *Lucrece*, his sugred Sonnets among his private friends.

As *Plautus* and *Seneca* are accounted the best for Comedy and Tragedy among the Latines: so *Shakespeare* among the English is the most excellent in both kinds for the stage; for Comedy, witnes his *Gentlemen of Verona*, his *Errors*, his *Love labors lost*, his *Love labours wonne*, his *Midsummers night dreame*, and his *Merchant of Venice*: for Tragedy his *Richard the 2*. *Richard the 3*. *Henry the 4*. *King John*, *Titus Andronicus* and his *Romeo* and *Juliet*.

As *Epius Stolo* said, that the Muses would speake with *Plautus* tongue, if they would speak Latin: so I say that the Muses would speak with *Shakespeares* fine filed phrase, if they would speak English.

Meres makes no claim to be giving a complete and up-to-date list of Shakespeare's work; he is supporting by examples, as his word 'witness' shows, his assertions about Shakespeare's excellence as a poet and dramatist.

Here as elsewhere Meres adopts a symmetrical arrangement, balancing six comedies against six tragedies.
That Meres makes no mention of the three parts of
Henry VI, or of *The Taming of the Shrew*, or of the
early *Hamlet*, is no evidence against Shakespeare's
authorship of these plays. Nor does he mention *The
Merry Wives of Windsor*, almost certainly performed,
as Dr Hotson has shown, in 1597. Close on the plays
mentioned must come *Much Ado*, *As You Like It*, and
Henry V, all referred to in the Stationers' Register on
4 August 1600; yet it is probable that they were composed and played before *Julius Caesar*, which was seen
at the Globe in the autumn of 1599. If one may hazard
a guess as to the play written for the opening of the
Globe, one might suggest *As You Like It* or *Henry V*.

By the opening of the Globe Shakespeare had written
at least twenty-one of the thirty-six plays attributed to
him by Heminge and Condell in the First Folio edition
of his works. As the list provided by Meres gives a
suitable reckoning point from which to make a brief
survey of the chronology of Shakespeare's plays, the
division of the pieces among the periods so far mentioned may be outlined tentatively as follows. Beginning
with the last period, that which extended from the
occupation of the Theatre by the Chamberlain's men
in 1594 to the opening of the Globe in 1599, the following plays were written in these five years:

Histories: *Richard II*, *1* and *2 Henry IV*, *Henry V*.
Comedies: *Merchant of Venice*, *Midsummer Night's
Dream*, *Merry Wives of Windsor*, *Much
Ado about Nothing*, *As You Like It*.
Tragedy: *Romeo and Juliet*.

From the closing of the theatres on 23 June 1592 to

the summer of 1594, when the leading companies reformed in London, belong *Venus and Adonis*, *Rape of Lucrece*, and *Love's Labour's Lost*.

There remain for placing:

Comedies: *Comedy of Errors*, *Taming of the Shrew*, *Two Gentlemen of Verona*.

Histories: *1*, *2*, and *3 Henry VI*, *Richard III*.

Tragedies: *Titus Andronicus*, *Hamlet* (the early version).

As some of these plays can be attributed to Shakespeare's attachment to Pembroke's company such 'dated' pieces provide a guide to style and treatment by which the others may be grouped. As Shakespeare wrote at least ten plays in the first five years of his association with the Chamberlain's men, to assign nine plays to the years before 1592, when Shakespeare may have been acting and writing for eight or so years, is in keeping not only with the external evidence, imperfect as that is, but with the rhythm of production as it were that we may, from later data, ascribe to these years. For no doubt some of his earlier pieces may like his *Hamlet* have come down to us only in a revised form. And this possibility must be considered in connexion with *King John*, mentioned by Meres, but not assigned here so far to any of the periods already described. Just as the lost plays of Molière's thirteen years in the provinces are to be found, however changed in form, in his later work, and not to be written off as stolen by an aged dame as he hastened back to Paris, so traces of Shakespeare's earliest work may be found in such pieces as *The Troublesome Raigne of King John* and *King Leir*, though these pieces have generally been treated not as borrowings from Shakespeare but as his source

plays, because of the erroneous notions of Shakespeare's
beginnings as a dramatist fostered by Farmer and
Malone. Once Farmer's picture of the untaught Shakespeare is seen to be the creation of his own fancy, and
Malone's treatment of *Henry VI* the unfortunate sequel
to Farmer's dogmatism, the question of Shakespeare's
earliest work for the stage may be considered without
our distorting the evidence to fit so strange a pre-
possession as the conviction that Shakespeare was so
illiterate that he had to steal from so notorious a
pilferer of other men's work as Greene.

iii. THE GLOBE

The formal lease for thirty-one years of the site chosen
for the Globe was signed on 21 February 1599 by the
owner of the ground Nicholas Brend. In a schedule of
the property left by his father Thomas Brend dated
16 May 1599, the theatre is described as 'newly erected'
and 'in the possession of Shakespeare and others'. As
the contract for the Fortune theatre, a document preserved with Alleyn's papers at Dulwich College, the
specifications in which were closely modelled on those
of the Globe, allowed twenty-six weeks for its construction, the Globe may have been completed by May;
much of the framework was taken in part ready-made
from the Theatre, and we hear of no hindrances to
progress such as delayed the building of the Fortune.

Shakespeare alone of the company is named in the
schedule setting out the possessions of Thomas Brend,
no doubt because he was regarded as the most important of the new owners; his financial share, however,
in the transaction was as mentioned earlier the same as
that of the other four actors who shared equally between
them the half interest in the house that remained after

Cuthbert and Richard Burbage had taken the other half. Shakespeare is now what was called a 'householder' in addition to being a sharer in the company. The first charges on the company's takings would be the rent to the householders and the salaries of the hired men; what remained was divided among the sharers.

With the leading sharers in the Chamberlain's men also householders in the Globe the success of the new theatre was assured; there would be no danger of its being left untenanted like Langley's Swan. Within a year of the opening of the Globe their neighbours at the Rose found the competition from the new arrivals so severe that the owners, Henslowe and Alleyn, decided to build a theatre in another district. They leased a site to the north-west of the City outside Cripplegate, and commissioned Peter Street, the master carpenter responsible for erecting the Globe, to build the new theatre more or less on the lines of the Globe but with a square exterior. It was opened in December 1600 and named the Fortune.

It is unfortunate that chance has not preserved for us the play with which the Chamberlain's men opened their famous years at the Globe. Various suggestions have been made. In *As You Like It* the words of Jaques,

All the world's a stage
And all the men and women merely players

offer a version of the motto, *Totus mundus agit histrionem*, on the sign displayed at the entrance to the theatre, the sign itself, as the reference to it in *Hamlet* II. ii. 358 indicates, showing Hercules carrying the world on his shoulders. An alternative suggestion for the opening play is *Henry V*. Some, however, think its references to the 'unworthy scaffold' point to the

ageing Curtain rather than the splendid Globe. But the 'wooden O' of the Prologue to *Henry V*, even were it the Globe, would fall just as short as the older Curtain, or any other arena, of providing 'A kingdom for a stage'. To call the old house names seems less in keeping with Shakespeare's manner than the slightly deprecatory yet tactful reference to the features of their new and handsome home. Certainly by September the new theatre was in full production, for on 21 September 1599 the Swiss traveller Thomas Platter was ferried over to the Globe to see *Julius Caesar*, the first in the great cycle of tragedies that was to return at the end to Roman subjects with *Antony and Cleopatra* and *Coriolanus* and to include *Hamlet*, *Othello*, *King Lear*, and *Macbeth*.

It is this tragic sequence that has given rise to the notion that Shakespeare was now overcome by some sense of disillusion with life generally, or with a particular dark lady, or with the political situation as the Queen's long reign drew to its inevitable end. Yet this does not seem reflected in *Twelfth Night* which was written about the same time as *Hamlet* and may even follow that tragedy.

It is true the uncertainties of the closing years of the Queen's reign were given a gloomier colouring by the folly of Essex. A scholar and a soldier, who had distinguished himself at Zutphen, and especially at the capture of Cadiz in 1596, Essex unfortunately lacked the discretion and self-restraint demanded of the successful general. His mishandling of the Islands Voyage in 1597 and his quarrel with Raleigh, whose direction had made the Cadiz venture a success, and would if heeded have made the later operations fruitful, instead of warning Essex of his need of wise counsel made him

the victim of flattering adventurers. He foolishly thrust
himself into the command of the force Elizabeth felt
compelled to send to Ireland to suppress the activities
of Tyrone. Setting out on 27 March 1599, with what
seemed all London cheering him on his way, Essex
returned on 28 September 1599 with a few intimate
followers, secretly and contrary to the Queen's express
orders, having nothing to report but failure. Deprived
of the monopolies that provided the money for his
extravagant way of living, he tried without success on
Sunday, 8 February 1601 to raise London against the
government. Condemned on 19 February for treason,
he was beheaded on 25 February 1601.

Shakespeare cannot have been unaffected by this
most unhappy episode, for Southampton to whom he
had dedicated *Venus and Adonis* and *Lucrece* was sen-
tenced to death with Essex. Southampton had modelled
himself on Essex, serving with him on the Cadiz expe-
dition of 1596 and on the Islands Voyage. In 1598 he
had married Elizabeth Vernon, a maid of honour and
cousin to Essex, in circumstances that so displeased
the Queen that both were for a time imprisoned. In dis-
favour at Court Southampton followed Essex to Ireland and took part in the attempt to raise London. The
Queen spared his life but he remained in prison till her
death. Yet to attempt to find this and other events of the
time displayed in Shakespeare's tragedies as in a mirror, would be as uncritical as to suppose that *Macbeth*
somehow reveals Shakespeare's gloom at the arrival of
a sovereign from a country so barbarous that its kings
accepted at their peril their subjects' hospitality.

The fears that Elizabeth's death might be followed
by a disputed succession, with foreign malice reinforc-
ing domestic strife, were not unnatural. The peaceful

arrival of James from Scotland is described by Bacon as
the awakening from a fearful dream: 'But so it was,
that not only the consent but the applause and joy was
infinite, and not to be expressed, throughout the realm
of England, upon this succession.' The relief felt by
Bacon was not merely the reaction of a nervous politician, the feeling was general. Yet Shakespeare who had
written *Julius Caesar* and *Hamlet* before the fall of
Essex continued with *King Lear* and *Macbeth* after the
accession of a king who was specially gracious to the
actors. Doubtless in a later part of James's reign were
sown the seeds of political dissension that were to spring
up as armed men in the Great Rebellion; but Shakespeare had retired before the statesmen brought up
under the discerning eye of Elizabeth had given place
to the favourites James in his indulgence raised to
power. The troubles that brought with them the closing
of the theatres in 1642 may no doubt be traced in part
to the Scottish king's lack of financial grip in his new
and more opulent realm; meantime, however, the actors enjoyed a patronage more lavish than that bestowed
on them by his careful predecessor.

The Queen died on the morning of 24 March 1603;
James reached Whitehall on 7 May 1603, and on 19 May
1603 by letters patent made Shakespeare and his fel-
lows the King's men; those named being: Lawrence
Fletcher, William Shakespeare, Richard Burbage,
Augustyne Phillippes, John Heminges, Henrie Condell,
William Sly, Robert Armyn, Richard Cowly. Lawrence
Fletcher, though an Englishman, had come south with
James from Scotland where he had as an actor enjoyed
the King's protection and patronage. Soon after the
leading players were made Grooms of the Royal Chamber, and it was in that capacity, and not as actors,

that they attended on the Constable of Castile, Juan Fernandez de Velasco, Duke de Frias, who arrived in August 1604, with some hundred noblemen and an even larger body of attendants, to negotiate a treaty of peace between Philip III of Spain and King James. The King's men for this occasion numbered twelve, and they would be recognized among the Constable's entourage as, to borrow the words of Ernest Law, 'a group of twelve gentlemen in red doublets and hose, with cloaks of the same, embroidered in gold with the King's cypher crowned'. The Constable and his suite occupied Somerset House. On Sunday, 19 August, the solemn ratification of the treaty at Whitehall was followed by a state banquet and a ball at which the Earl of Southampton, who had been released on James's accession, had the honour of acting as the Queen's partner in two of the dances. Next morning the Constable had a slight attack of lumbago and had to delay his departure till 25 August. For their services from 9 to 27 August the King's men were paid £21. 12s. There would be in addition some token to each of the Constable's regard. A record of the event may be seen in the picture in the National Portrait Gallery, in which the Spanish and English Commissioners face each other across a richly covered table, on which rests, beside a single pewter inkpot and pen, the treaty itself in front of Secretary Cecil, later Earl of Salisbury.

At this date Shakespeare was lodging in Silver Street, in the north-west of the City. Although he had moved to the Bankside some years before the building of the Globe he did not continue there long after its opening and by 1602, his family now being at New Place, he had moved to the house of Christopher Mountjoy, a Huguenot who had settled in London after the

Massacre of St Bartholomew. Mountjoy had an extensive business as a tire-maker; Falstaff in *The Merry Wives of Windsor* (III. iii. 61) when he assures Mistress Ford that were she a lady of rank and fashion her beauty would become 'the ship-tire, the tire-valiant, or any tire of Venetian admittance', is picturing her in some of the more elaborate forms of contemporary head-dress. Mountjoy lived in one of the more select districts and must have had a well-to-do clientele who required their hair to be dressed and adorned by his art. Mountjoy had an apprentice Stephen Belott, also of French extraction, who married his master's daughter Mary Mountjoy in November 1604. Two years later Madame Mountjoy died, and there followed a dispute between Belott and his father-in-law, who now lacked the steadying influence of his wife, about the financial arrangements made at the time of Mary's marriage. The matter came before the Courts and on 11 May 1612 Shakespeare gave evidence about his stay with the household and his part in the events preceding the marriage. He had known the parties to the case, he told the Court at Westminster, for some ten years; Belott he described as 'a very good and industrious servant'; he had himself at the request of Mary's mother moved and persuaded the young man to marry Mary; he could not, however, remember the details of the financial arrangements. In the deposition to which Shakespeare put his signature he is described as 'of Stratford-upon-Avon . . . gentleman'.

By 1612 Shakespeare had retired to Stratford-on-Avon and was living in New Place, which he had acquired in 1597. To this important purchase he had added, during the years he was working at the Globe, 107 acres of arable land near Stratford; this he bought

in May 1602 from William Combe and his nephew John Combe for £320, and in September of the same year he bought a cottage and ground in Chapel Lane near New Place. In July 1605 followed an even more important transaction: he acquired the lease of certain tithes for £440. These tithes had originally belonged to the College of Priests; leased by the College in 1544 to a private individual for 92 years they were quickly sub-divided among several purchasers, and from one of these intermediate parties Shakespeare acquired his very considerable holding. The return on this investment was in 1611 valued at £60, less certain payments to prior interests, and in 1625 when the annual value was £90 the Corporation was able to acquire them from Shakespeare's heirs for £400, since the lease was due to expire in 1625 and these particular tithes by the Charter of 1553 would pass to the Corporation, the College having been dissolved by the Chantries Act.

During these early years at the Globe there were important changes in the Shakespeare family. Shakespeare's father died in September 1601, a few weeks after helping his friend Richard Quiney, Bailiff for the second time, to draw up a document dealing with the infringements of the Borough's charter by the over-bearing lord of the manor Sir Edward Greville. Next year Quiney himself was injured in attempting to suppress a brawl started by Greville's men and died in May 1602. On 5 June 1607 Shakespeare's elder daughter Susanna married John Hall a physician, a graduate of Cambridge, who had after study on the Continent settled in Stratford, and was beginning to make in the Midlands the reputation he gained as a distinguished practitioner. Hall's Croft, now preserved by the Birth-place Trustees, tradition indicates as their home. In

the year of Susanna's marriage Shakespeare's youngest brother was buried on 31 December 1607 with a 'fore-noon knell of the great bell' in the church of St Saviour's, Southwark; the Register describes him as a 'Player'. Next year, on 8 February, Elizabeth Hall was born, who was to prove the Hall's only child; late in 1608 came the death of Shakespeare's mother, who was buried on 9 September. Of Shakespeare's two surviving brothers Gilbert was buried on 3 February 1612 and Richard on 4 February 1613, both at Stratford.

iv. THE BLACKFRIARS

Some twelve years after James Burbage was forbidden to use the hall he had acquired in the Blackfriars as a theatre his sons had an opportunity to carry out their father's plan. Rather than let the hall lie empty Richard Burbage had leased it on 2 September 1600 for twenty-one years to a group, represented by Henry Evans, who planned to revive the performances formerly given in the Blackfriars by the Children of the Royal Chapels. The inhabitants of the precinct did not object to these 'private' performances, which, however, were now on a more commercial scale than formerly and supported by dramatists well known in the theatre world. The new theatre proved for a time a rival to the Globe, and the reference in *Hamlet* II, ii. 36 to the children that 'so berattle the common stage that many . . . dare scarce come thither (to the common theatres)' indicates not merely the popularity of the Children but the satiric vein cultivated by their dramatists. With the Children of St Paul's also performing again there was started an exchange of abuse between Marston and Dekker at Paul's and Jonson at the Blackfriars, whose *Cynthia's Revels* and *Poetaster* in 1600 and 1601 respec-

tively so provoked the Chamberlain's men that they produced Dekker's *Satiromastix, or The Untrussing of the Humorous Poet*. Although peace was made between the dramatists the satirical licence fostered at the Blackfriars did not spare royal personages, and this liberty was followed by their suppression. Evans was therefore ready to surrender his lease to Burbage.

On 9 August 1608 Richard Burbage formed a group of seven 'householders' to manage the Blackfriars. They included himself and his brother, Heminge, Shakespeare, Condell, Sly, and Thomas Evans representing Henry Evans. They would share the rent of £40 payable to Richard Burbage and divide the rent the Company would pay the householders. This proved a most successful venture; their standing as King's men now made their occupation of the theatre acceptable to the inhabitants of the precinct; and by using this well-roofed house during the winter months and playing at the Globe only in summer the Company's takings were greatly increased.

With the King's men at the height of their popularity Shakespeare made arrangements to take up residence at Stratford. In a note dated 9 September 1609 Thomas Green the town clerk of Stratford, who was lodging with Shakespeare's wife and daughters at New Place, indicated that he could stay another year there. Meantime he had purchased a house for himself. The dates here tally with the production of *The Tempest*, that cannot be earlier than the last months of 1610, in which Shakespeare is taking a farewell of the stage.

In the years that followed Shakespeare, though normally in residence at Stratford, was frequently in London. On 11 May 1612 he was at Westminster to give his evidence in the Mountjoy case. Important events at

Court must have called for his presence in London again towards the end of that year.

On 16 October 1612 Frederick, the youthful Elector Palatine, and later for a brief period King of Bohemia, arrived at Whitehall to visit King James and ask the hand of his daughter Elizabeth in marriage. Elizabeth was just sixteen, the Prince a few days her junior. By ill chance her brother Henry, Prince of Wales, on whom so many had set their hopes, was struck down by a fever after bathing in the Thames and died, calling on his sister; he was buried in the Abbey on 7 December 1612. Matters of State had, however, to go on, and on 27 December Elizabeth was betrothed to the Prince. From then till their marriage on 14 February, St Valentine's Day, 1613, and thereafter to their departure from London on 10 April 1613, the King's men were performing regularly at Court, their payment for twenty performances with the King's reward coming to £153. 6s. 8d. During this period fell the King's Accession Day, 24 March 1613, which was celebrated by a tournament at which the tilters bore shields with appropriate emblems and mottoes. For this occasion Francis Manners, who had just become sixth Earl of Rutland, had his device and motto chosen by Shakespeare and painted by Burbage, whose skill as an artist is mentioned by contemporaries. For their services each received 44 shillings in gold.

While in London at the marriage celebrations Shakespeare bought from Henry Walker a house in Blackfriars known as the Gate-House for £140, putting down £80 in cash and mortgaging the dwelling to Walker for the remaining £60, to be paid by 29 September 1613. Heminge acted as one of the trustees for Shakespeare. As Dr Hotson has shown, William

Johnson, who also acted for Shakespeare, and signed the Conveyance, dated 10 March 1613, and the Mortgage, 11 March 1613, was host of the Mermaid, doubtless where Shakespeare was lodging during his prolonged stay in town.

On 29 June 1613 Shakespeare's *Henry VIII* was being produced at the Globe with special magnificence as a tribute to the master who had returned once more to the scene. The firing of one of the stage cannon during the first performance set the thatch above the galleries on fire and the theatre was burnt to the ground. The event was thought worthy of recording in the continuation of Stowe's *Annales*:

Upon S. Peters day last, the play-house or Theater, called the Globe, upon the Banck-side near London, by negligent discharging of a peal of ordinance, close to the south-side thereof, the thatch took fire, and the wind sodainly disperst the flame round about, and in a very short space the whole building was quite consumed, and no man hurt; the house being filled with people to behold the play, viz. of Henry the Eighth. And the next spring it was new builded in far fairer manner than before.

Happily there is no mention here or in any of the other accounts of this mishap of any loss of play-books, as there is in that of the burning of the Fortune on 9 December 1621:

On Sonday night here was a great fire at the Fortune in Golden-Lane, the fayrest play-house in this towne. It was quite burnt down in two howres, and all their apparell and play-bookes lost, wherby those poor companions are quite undone.

After securing an extension of their lease the Burbages and their associates rebuilt the Globe, among

their improvements being the replacement of thatch by tiles. *Henry VIII*, however, was Shakespeare's last contribution to their repertoire. He was in London again on 17 November 1614, for Thomas Greene, already in London on Stratford business, made a note of their meeting that day: 'At my Cosen Shakspeare commying yesterday to towne I went to see him how he did.' As Dr Hall was with him Shakespeare may not have been in the best of health; he had no doubt made the journey at that inclement season because of the Company's probable commitments at Court. His conversation as recorded by Greene, however, dealt with the intention of William and Thomas Combe to enclose certain common land near Stratford. This the borough strongly resisted. Although Greene noted that Shakespeare 'and Mr Hall say they think there will be nothyng done at all', it required much expense and effort to defeat the scheme.

Whatever the state of his health in 1614 Shakespeare on some date before 10 February 1616, perhaps in January of that year, had his will drawn up by Francis Collins who was to succeed Greene as town clerk. The marriage, however, of Shakespeare's daughter Judith to Thomas Quiney, the son of Richard Quiney who had died in 1602, made some alterations necessary. The young couple had been married by the Vicar during a prohibited season and the Bishop threatened them with excommunication. Perhaps some of the safeguards now attached to her father's bequests to Judith may have been prompted by the somewhat casual conduct of the bridegroom, who was to prove unfortunately a very different man from his reliable father.

Shakespeare's will, now preserved in Somerset House, was recovered for modern times only in 1747.

Unfortunately the inventory that would have been lodged at the same time is, as are those for so many wills of that date, missing. The will is on three sheets, the first replacing that of the first draft; pages 2 and 3, which remain from the first draft, are brought into accord with the new provisions on page 1 by interlinings. The whole is now dated 25 March 1616.

Shakespeare's intention was to provide a substantial inheritance that his daughter Susanna could hand on to her eldest surviving son; failing that, the inheritance was to go to his grand-daughter Elizabeth and then to her eldest surviving son; failing that, to the male heir of his daughter Judith. Meantime Shakespeare leaves Judith £300, half, however, with certain conditions attached. To his sister Joan, whose husband William Hart died some days before Shakespeare himself, he gave the use of the Western house in Henley Street and £20, and £5 each to her three sons; to the poor of Stratford £10; to certain Stratford friends, including Hamlet Sadler, who had been his son's godfather, 28s. 6d. each for memorial rings, and a similar bequest for rings to the surviving members of the old Chamberlain's company, Richard Burbage, John Heminge, and Henry Condell. To the overseers of his will Thomas Russell Esquire and Francis Collins gent. £5 and £13. 6s. 8d. respectively.

The item in the will that has given rise to most speculation is the single reference to his wife, to whom he leaves 'my second best bed with the furniture'. As the best bed would be in the guest room in New Place the second best was the bed he shared with his wife. As she was to live with her daughter Susanna, who was devoted to her, if the words on her mother's gravestone have any meaning, Shakespeare's wife was safely

provided for and the bequest a gesture more intimate than any formula of farewell.

The identification of Thomas Russell, one of the
overseers of the will, by Dr Hotson has revealed
Shakespeare's acquaintance with an important group
among his contemporaries. Thomas Russell was born
in 1570, the younger son of Sir Thomas Russell of
Strensham House in the village of Strensham, some
miles down the river from Stratford. A student at
Oxford, later at sea with the distinguished sailor Sir
George Gifford, Russell was also a friend of men of
learning and courtly parts but preferred for himself the
life of a country gentleman. His manor at Alderminster, some four miles from Stratford, gave him connexions in that borough. To Alderminster he brought
in 1600 his second wife, the widow of Thomas Digges,
the soldier and mathematician. Her younger son
Leonard Digges, an Oxford don, contributed verses to
the First Folio, and there is good reason to believe
Shakespeare knew the elder son, later Sir Dudley
Digges and Master of the Rolls.

On 23 April Shakespeare was dead. As a tithe-
holder he was buried within the chancel rail of the
church on 25 April. The lines on the flagstone over his
coffin beginning

> Good friend for Jesus sake forbeare
> To dig the dust enclosed heare;

and the curse that follows on meddlers have so far discouraged busy-bodies and sextons from disturbing his
bones. Some time before 1623 his family placed on the
wall of the chancel the monument that shows the poet
in the act of composition and that records in Latin and
English verse his unrivalled genius.

In 1623 his wife was buried beside him; his son-in-law
Dr Hall died in 1635 and his grave is next Shakespeare's
on the other side; Susanna who died in 1649 was buried
next her husband, and next her again lies Thomas Nash,
the first husband of Elizabeth Hall. She later married
John Barnard, himself a widower with a family. On
Susanna's death they occupied New Place for a time but
later moved to Abington Manor in Northamptonshire.
At the Restoration Barnard, a strong royalist, was made
a baronet. Lady Barnard died in 1670 and her husband
in 1674, both at Abington. As Lady Barnard died
childless Shakespeare's estate would have passed to
Judith and her sons. Judith, however, had died in 1662,
aged 78, and her three sons had long predeceased her.
Lady Barnard was therefore the last of Shakespeare's
direct descendants. But through Thomas Hart, the
second son of Shakespeare's sister Joan, there are today
not a few descendants of John Shakespeare and Mary
Arden living in England and America.

Chapter Three

THE COMEDIES

SITTING in the theatre enjoying a play the audience instinctively adjusts its mind to the degree of illusion demanded by the nature of the representation; and good actors as they play their parts help to establish the mode in which their words and actions are to be interpreted. This give and take between actor and audience, though apparently spontaneous and automatic, is a form of interpretation and judgement, yet requires the further discipline of the understanding to yield the precipitate that may be recognized as criticism. This interaction of instinct and understanding that alone can give coherence and authority to what seems to begin as impression and feeling must still, however, work within the limits imposed by the kind of representation that prompts the initial response. This is the point of Horace's precept, *ut pictura poesis*, and admits of no exception. To see some pictures to advantage one must stand some distance from them, while others require to be viewed at shorter range. Rembrandt's remark to some impertinent fellow that pictures were not for smelling is a corollary to Horace's proposition, and should serve as an admonition to those who would look at a play as if they were scrutinizing a historical or legal document. The standpoint in drama should be what we would attribute to the ideal spectator at an ideal performance. To say that in the study we discover faults that are invisible in the theatre is to pride oneself on the form of impercipience rebuked by Rembrandt.

To this type of mental myopia a play such as *Lear* is as confused a spectacle as is a canvas in Titian's later manner to the individual who stands with his nose against it.

The range of adjustment Shakespeare expected from his audiences is indicated generally by the three-fold division of his work into Comedies, Histories, and Tragedies. The attempt to be more precise by inventing such categories as tragical-comical-historical-pastoral, Shakespeare treats as a ludicrously pedantic approach to a matter of such infinite variety. The accommodation required varies from play to play and the terms Comedy, History, and Tragedy, are sufficient to remind us that criticism must adjust its standpoint in conformity with the design of the dramatist.

As Shakespeare produced comedies in every period of his work for the theatre, and as each phase of this career is marked by fresh developments, we must expect even the comedies to call for a considerable latitude of response: *The Comedy of Errors*, which must be among the earliest of Shakespeare's essays in this mode, is obviously very different from the last, *The Tempest*. Between them lies a wonderfully varied series of pieces that reveal the dramatist's constant effort to develop the range of his art and to deepen its significance.

There are three of Shakespeare's comedies that may be taken as belonging to the years before 1592: *The Comedy of Errors*, *The Taming of the Shrew* and *Two Gentlemen of Verona*. The first recorded performance of *The Comedy of Errors* took place on 28 December 1594 in the hall at Gray's Inn. There is no reason to suppose that it was written specially for this occasion. In the jesting about the kitchen wench's looks at III. ii. 127 we have a reference to France 'In her fore-

head: armed and reverted making war against her heir'. The pun on 'hair' and 'heir' refers to the war between the Catholic League and Henry of Navarre who became heir to the throne on the death of the Duke of Anjou in June 1584. When the King, Henry III, died on 12 August 1589, Henry of Navarre was legally King, and was so regarded in England. There is nothing in the play to rule out a date before 1589 and much to support it. *The Taming of the Shrew* was one of the plays performed by the newly formed Chamberlain's men at Newington Butts in June 1594. A stolen and imperfect version printed just before this in May 1594 describes it as having been performed by Pembroke's company; the original play Shakespeare had brought with him to his new company. For the date of *The Two Gentlemen of Verona* there is no satisfactory external evidence. The style and treatment, however, suggest that it too belongs to this early period.

These three plays reveal something of the scope and professional accomplishment of the dramatist even in his earlier years. It is unfortunate that the Inventory of his possessions lodged with his will has been lost, for it might have given us, as the corresponding document for Molière's estate does, the contents of his library. Molière's library was largely composed of play-books; these were part of his stock-in-trade as a writer for the theatre, and his own productions reveal how he turned this reading to account. His reply to some pedant who charged him with plagiarism, *Je prends mon bien où je le trouve*, has the ironic implications so characteristic of this master of his art. For Shakespeare, although we have no Inventory, a study of his sources proves how he took the same professional interest as Molière in works for the stage and in forms that could be adapted

to its requirements. The three early pieces to be briefly discussed show Shakespeare's use not only of Latin comedy but of the forms in which Latin comedy had been adapted by humanists for the Italian stage. Shakespeare's grammar school training first as a pupil and then as a junior schoolmaster could not but make him acquainted with the Latin dramatists, Plautus and Seneca especially. His interest in the Italian development of classical comedy was an obvious extension of his early schooling for one with his professional bias.

The Comedy of Errors is a complete transformation for the English stage of the *Menaechmi* of Plautus, in which the Latin dramatist exploits the confusions and misunderstandings in which twin brothers become ludicrously involved. Just, however, as the Roman comic dramatists might combine in one piece features from more than one Greek comedy, so Shakespeare incorporated in his play an important episode from a second play by Plautus. In the *Amphitruo* Jupiter and Mercury impersonate Amphitryon, the Theban general, and his man Sosia. The deceivers are entertained by Alcmena, the general's wife, while her true husband and his servant, on their arrival, find the doors shut against them. Shakespeare had therefore to provide his twin masters with twin servants.

To object that Shakespeare by doubling the twins, without the supernatural sanction claimed by Plautus for his impersonations, has outraged probability is to miss the logic of the type of comedy being presented. A classical scholar has criticized the plot of the *Menaechmi* as 'thin and improbable, merely affording a background for ludicrous situations and for a highly diverting game of cross-purposes'. As this diversion was the end for which the plot was devised the criticism is

clearly another breach of Horace's law 'ut pictura
poesis'. Shakespeare has developed the mechanism of
the Latin comedy to the limit of exploitation. To describe it, as *The Times* of 4 August 1960 did, as an old
clockwork farce, and to report that the audience re-
sponded enthusiastically to every quip, is as much as
to say that though everyone enjoyed the pudding it
was mouldy. The unexpected vein of charm and magic
The Times correspondent found in the piece he attributed to the producer.

Shakespeare's play is not merely a *tour de force* of
theatrical manipulation, it transposes the asperities of
the Plautine treatment into a more gracious key. The
Menaechmi are, it must be admitted, crudish fellows.
At the end when the brothers have discovered each
other, the married twin decides to return to Syracuse
with his brother and meanwhile sell up his possessions
in Epidamnus—his wife too, as his brother's servant
suggests, if he can find a buyer. In place of this Shakespeare finishes with a family reunion and a gossips'
feast.

The *Menaechmi* is one of the few plays by Plautus
that have no love interest. This Shakespeare supplies
by giving the wife of the married twin a sister who is
greatly distressed by the advances of one she takes to
be her sister's husband but happily proves to be her
sister's husband's brother. And the harmony is deep-
ened by another technical resource. Instead of the
Latin Prologue the play opens at dawn with a Syracusan
merchant, condemned to death, explaining to the Duke
of Ephesus how his search for his lost family has
brought him to this fate. Respited till evening on the
chance that someone may ransom his life, the unhappy
man is again on his way to execution when there is a

brawl outside a Priory which the Abbess in person quells, to find she is the merchant's lost wife and the twin masters her sons. All are now reunited with the blessing of the Duke himself.

The Unity of Time, with the progress from morning to evening carefully marked, is strictly observed, and that of Place, with the three houses as in the Roman theatre, carefully preserved. Almost every feature of Latin comedy that can be transplanted successfully is found in this piece. Those who regard it as too scholarly a production for the young Shakespeare may be asked to indicate the scholar who brought to his studies the craft and brio of this comedy.

The Taming of the Shrew in style and treatment belongs to the same genre as *The Errors*. Though not derived directly from Latin comedy *The Shrew* combines a folk-motif with a sub-plot derived from an Italian comedy on Latin themes. Ariosto's comedies for the court at Ferrara were inspired by his enthusiasm for Roman comedy, and his *I Suppositi* (1509), which adapts features from the *Captivi* of Plautus and the *Eunuchus* of Terence, was known to Shakespeare, perhaps in the original but certainly in George Gascoigne's version in English called *Supposes* (1566), in which, as Gascoigne says in his Argument, 'you shall see a master supposed for a servant, the servant for the master' and similar mistakings.

In Ariosto, and in Gascoigne, a young man, as in the *Eunuchus*, gains admission to the household of the girl he loves in the guise of a servant; to cover his deception he makes his servant impersonate him, as in the *Captivi*. When an elderly suitor seems likely to interrupt the secret association of the lovers, the masquerading servant comes forward to offer a better settlement than

the old but wealthy rival. To support this handsome offer the servant produces a bogus father to confirm his promises. The young man's real father, distressed at lack of news from his son, now appears. His fear and anger on discovering the servant posing as his son, and the sense of outrage and wrath of the girl's father on discovering the nature of the intrigue, provide an excellent foil to the happiness of all parties when confession clears up the confusion and marriage is pronounced desirable not merely by the lovers but by their parents.

Shakespeare adopts and adds to the 'supposes' of his original. Lucentio changes places with his servant Tranio, and is introduced as a suitable instructor for Bianca; Tranio meanwhile posing as Lucentio presents himself as a rival to the aged Gremio for Bianca's hand. Pressed by Bianca's father to make good his promises Tranio produces a supposed father. Shakespeare adds a fourth 'suppose' in the disguise Hortensio, another of Bianca's suitors, assumes as a music master. Roughly handled by Bianca's elder sister Katherine the Shrew, who breaks his lute over his head, Hortensio discovers Bianca's preference for Lucentio and takes himself off to marry a rich and willing widow. In the final scene Hortensio and his widow join Petruchio and Katherine, Lucentio and Bianca, at the banquet and celebration in which the three brides are submitted to the test of wifely obedience that vindicates Petruchio's faith in his Kate.

The skill with which Shakespeare has combined the affair of Petruchio and Katherine the Shrew with the intrigue for Bianca her sister has been very justly praised by Johnson. Although no other dramatist of the period to which this piece belongs is known who was

capable of so dexterous a piece of stage carpentry, some commentators still persist in supposing that Shakespeare found his plot ready made. This they deduce from the existence of a piece named *The Taming of a Shrew* entered in the Stationers' Register on 2 May 1594 and printed as having been performed by Pembroke's men.

The relation between *the Shrew* and *a Shrew* was determined by Farmer solely on the ground that Shakespeare was too illiterate to be regarded as other than the imitator of what Farmer regarded as an old play, although he himself had on his own confession never seen a copy of *a Shrew*. This view was unchallenged till Samuel Hickson (*Notes and Queries*, 30. iii. 1850) proved that the 1594 version was a pirated version of *the Shrew*. As E. K. Chambers, on what might be thought later evidence, rejects Hickson's conclusion, a brief note on his opinion is necessary.

Three features indicate the dependence of *a Shrew* on *the Shrew*. Admitting that passages in *the Shrew* have often more point than parallel passages in *a Shrew*, Chambers argued that just as Shakespeare picks phrases and passages from Holinshed and other chronicles he may have taken phrases from *a Shrew*. What Chambers omits to observe is that no one can say of these passages in the chronicles what Hickson demonstrates of several passages in *a Shrew* that 'their purpose and sometimes even their meaning is intelligible only in the form in which we find it in Shakespeare'. Of the handling of the parallel episodes in *a Shrew*, which provide even more damning evidence of the pilferer's procedure, all that Chambers can say is that Shakespeare's collaborator, another gratuitous assumption, must have consulted Ariosto or Gascoigne.

I

As it is obvious that the author of *the Shrew* must have consulted Ariosto or Gascoigne, how this proves that *a Shrew* is the original of *the Shrew* is beyond the scope of logical argument. To assume it must be so is characteristic of the illogical procedure known as begging the question. To these irrelevant objections to Hickson's contention Chambers adds a third and even more misleading assertion. The pirate of *a Shrew* padded out his sadly distorted thievings from Shakespeare with ludicrous insertions from Marlowe's *Tamburlaine* and *Faustus*. We are not to take this, were we to believe Chambers, merely as the resort of a magpie compiler who furnishes his piece with the bright but unrelated things that catch his fancy, for Chambers observes that some other bad quartos are put together on a different principle. As he had been taught by Crompton Rhodes and others that pirated texts are of various kinds and that the type to which *a Shrew* belongs is not unknown, Chambers was not attempting to argue but merely expressing his incapacity to believe that he had for long been mistaken on this issue.

The pirate transfers the scene from Shakespeare's Padua to Athens, for having some, perhaps hearsay, knowledge of Marlowe's *Hero and Leander* being concerned with Sestos, he makes the son of the Duke of Cestus one of his lovers, and has to find a university as near the Hellespont as maybe.

As with *The Errors*, Shakespeare sets his *Shrew* in a frame, provided on this occasion by the Arabian-Nightlike experience of Sly the tinker. Unfortunately the final scene, in which Sly departs to try, with what success we can all guess, the taming recipe on his wife, is missing from the Folio and has to be understood in the light given by the imperfect report in the stolen version.

What is clear, however, is that in the Prologue and Epilogue dealing with Sly the dramatist is providing a comic contrast to what some might regard as the artificial and unacceptable moral of the play; just as Chaucer gives the Clerk of Oxford, after telling his tale of patient Griselda, a Ballade to warn husbands that Griselda is dead long ago and that they would be foolish to expect the patience of which Griselda is so surpassing a pattern to have survived her.

That Shakespeare was himself perfectly familiar that he was still working in part in the Latin comic tradition is suggested by his borrowing the names, Tranio and Grumio, of the town and country slaves in the *Mostellaria* of Plautus for the corresponding roles in his own comedy.

The third comedy that can be assigned on internal evidence to the same formative period as *The Errors* and *The Shrew* is, as they are, in the Latin-Italian tradition; Shakespeare here, however, first employs a device that the Italian *commedia erudita* had added to the resources of Latin comedy. Italian scholarly comedy took over from Roman comedy the rule that excluded respectable unmarried girls of good family from being represented on the stage. This Plautus sometimes evaded by having his heroine free-born but in the possession for the time being of some procurer or slave-dealer. In the *Curculio* the heroine Planesium, who takes a prominent speaking part in the action, is in this plight, though Plautus takes care to inform us of her chaste condition. The discovery of such a girl's parentage makes her marriage to her lover agreeable to their elders. In his *Persa* Plautus has given a prominent part to the charming girl who is disguised by her father as a Persian; as her father is a parasite no breach of decorum

could be imputed to the author. The advantage of
having the female parts unrestricted by such conven-
tions was clear to Renaissance dramatists; to secure this
freedom, while observing the letter of the law, the
Italian dramatists devised plots that allowed them to
present their heroines in male disguise. Without offending classical susceptibilities the respectable girl masquerading as a boy could now play a leading and often
decisive part in the action. English audiences lacked this
scholarly sense of propriety that ruled in Rome and
Renaissance Italy; to them what was sauce for the
gander was sauce for the goose; their dramatists, perhaps helped by the female roles being played by boys,
were free to give the sexes an equal footing on their
stage. This was a great gain in comic resource; the
English dramatists, however, had not the machinery for
creating complications that the exposing of children
and the activities of slave-dealers gave the Roman
dramatists. Shakespeare therefore welcomed the scope
the Italian device of disguising the girl gave him and
employed it repeatedly.

Shakespeare's first heroine to play a boy's part is
Julia in *The Two Gentlemen of Verona*. This comedy
though not directly derived from an Italian original
inherited this important feature from a comedy first
produced at Sienna in 1531. In that city a literary
society calling themselves the Academy of the Intronati, the Thunderstruck by Love, produced for the
carnival season a comedy, *Gl'Ingannati* (The Cheated),
that was to set an international fashion in plotting and
to interest many translators and adapters. Shakespeare
used it later in his *Twelfth Night*, where he took from
Gl'Ingannati the twins of different sex, the girl masquerading as a boy, acting as page to the man she loves

and employed as his messenger to the lady on whom for the moment his fancy had settled. This last motif, the girl as page, was taken over by Shakespeare in *The Two Gentlemen* in the form the Portuguese poet Jorge de Montemayor had given it in his Spanish prose romance *Diana Enamorada*. Book II of this romance, in whatever form it was known to Shakespeare, provided the train of events that leads to Julia's disguise and her acting as page to Proteus.

In the *Diana* three nymphs enjoying the charm of the pastoral life are suddenly attacked by three armed savages; fortunately a strange shepherdess carrying a bow and arrows, as well as a sharp-pointed staff, saves the helpless girls by shooting down two of their attackers and braining with her staff the third miscreant. This fair warrior confides to the nymphs that she is the love-lorn Felismena wandering in search of Don Felix. Shakespeare takes the following episodes from the story she tells: her reproof of her maid for bringing a letter from Felix; his dispatch to court by his father; her following him there in male disguise; her lodging at an inn and hearing Felix serenading Celia; her employment as a page by Felix and as a messenger to plead with Celia for her master. Here Shakespeare abandons Montemayor. There Felismena tells how Celia fell in love with her disguised as the page and died of despair, and how Felix in his turn fled the court. This episode ends like Shakespeare's play in a wood, but the circumstances are very different. Felismena comes on a fray in which a single knight is being set upon by three opponents. He slays one, but is saved from further danger by Felismena who with unerring aim kills one with an arrow through his head; the other she shoots through his heart. The knight

who is thus saved is Felix, and all ends happily in marriage.

Bartholomew Yonge published his translation of the *Diana* in 1598. There is no evidence that Shakespeare saw this in manuscript, although it was completed some sixteen years earlier. Shakespeare, however, may have known *The History of Felix and Filiomena*, as this was a play recorded in the Revels Accounts as performed at court the Sunday following New Year's Day 1585. The anonymous author may have drawn on the Felix Felismena episode in the *Diana*. Even, however, if this were so and Shakespeare knew the piece, his own *Two Gentlemen* combines this material with other motifs, and all is ordered by the dramatic idea that now informs every part. The strands in *The Shrew* are finally drawn together in the concluding wager; so in the final scene of *The Two Gentlemen*, Shakespeare presents the conflict from which the play arises in its extremest form, when Valentine having rescued his Silvia from Proteus offers to yield her in the name of perfect amity to this erring but repentant friend. Though this is the culmination of the struggle between love and friendship that is foreshadowed in the very title of the piece, it has been criticized as entirely out of keeping with the work as a whole, and even regarded as a botcher's effort to provide a conclusion—for Shakespeare's ending must have been, it has been felt, much more romantic and perhaps rejected only because found theatrically ineffective.

It would be hard to find a conjecture that flies so patently in the face of fact—of what we find in the play and what we know of Shakespeare's command of his stage. This is to misrepresent both Shakespeare's technique and his idea. *The Two Gentlemen* illustrates as does *The Shrew*, which also offends those who insist

on looking at it as Horace might say in the wrong light, the almost ruthless way Shakespeare works out his idea. But the idea of *The Two Gentlemen*, if reflected in Valentine's gesture, would, it might be said, make Quiller-Couch's jest about there being *no* gentlemen in Verona a true criticism of the piece. Yet in what has been described as the earliest work in English on moral philosophy, *The Governor*, that grave moralist Sir Thomas Elyot included *The wonderful history of Titus and Gisippus, and whereby is fully declared the figure of perfect amitie*, the perfect amitie being made manifest by the manner in which Gisippus renounces to Titus his 'title and interest' in the lady he is about to marry. To effect this gesture he goes through the ceremony of marriage only to allow his friend to take his place secretly in the marriage bed and become in fact the bride's husband. Gisippus acts thus in spite of the reproach and hatred his conduct may provoke; in the end his friends approve his sacrifice. Such notions may no longer have a place in our philosophy, but Shakespeare was entitled to make what use he could of this once familiar motif, especially as he gave it a context that neutralizes what may be censurable in its effects.

Elyot's story takes no account of the bride's feelings about her bridegroom's disposal of her; in *The Two Gentlemen*, however, there are two ladies about whose wishes we have very precise knowledge, and at the crisis Julia produces the ring that arrests any further flights of male fancy. Shakespeare thus contrives to have it both ways: the two gentlemen have their proper partners and yet in perfect amity. No doubt Shakespeare is somewhat brusque with us at the finish and has to wrong Eglamour as a character, the actor who played the part being needed in another guise at the close.

We naturally allow a latitude to the narrator of an amusing story that is denied the teller of tragic news.

The play exhibits in many places the fusion of poetry and drama, each enhancing the other, that is the glory of the later masterpieces. As has been pointed out, the scene between Julia and her maid which announces Julia's plan to follow Proteus in disguise, though charming in itself, is greatly enriched by the reflected lights from the immediately preceding scene in which Proteus confesses to himself his broken faith. And it is difficult to find even in Shakespeare a more lovely and at the same time more cunningly constructed scene than that in which Julia listens to Proteus serenading Silvia. The perfection of the song is a kind of enchantment that might seem to need no more commendation than the host's delight in the music, but it opens as a spell for us the hearts of the listeners gathered in the darkening air, discovering the guile of Proteus, the simplicity of Thurio, the intelligence and scorn of Silvia, and the heartache of Julia. The scene is as much plot as poetry. The sleepy host is stirred by the wakeful Julia with the question, 'Where lies Sir Proteus?' and we know that fate is now closing in on the unsuspecting deceiver.

The heroines of Shakespeare's comedies have been admired by Ruskin and others as showing a purpose and resource that rescue their somewhat slower-witted lovers from their doubts and difficulties. Even at their most masterful, however, Shakespeare's heroines observe a decorum that is unknown to Laelia, the clever contriver in *Gl'Ingannati*, who is quite uninhibited and ruthless in the pursuit of her purpose. Montemayor's Diana, though the complete Amazon in her encounters with armed bandits, is a pattern of scrupulous behaviour in her wooing. Shakespeare's next comedy *Love's*

Labour's Lost maintains the tradition of feminine discretion and resolute purpose in a whole group of ladies in their adventures at a royal court.

Love's Labour's Lost, though at one time because of its abundance of rhymed verse regarded as the earliest of Shakespeare's comedies, deals in so allusive and familiar a way with topics debated in courtly and literary coteries about 1594 or so, that it cannot be the work of a new-comer to these circles. Many of its features suggest that it was originally written for private performance before the circle round Essex; Southampton, to whom Shakespeare dedicated his narrative poems first in 1593 and then most cordially in 1594, was a devoted partisan of Essex and could very easily be the intermediary that prompted the commission.

The King of Navarre and three of his gentlemen agree to devote themselves to study. From this academy, as it were, women were to be rigidly excluded. Hard on this comes the announcement that a Princess of France with three of her ladies has just arrived to discuss important state affairs; and the scene is set for the antagonistic forces.

Although the King of Navarre is called Ferdinand, no doubt to rule out any assertion that Shakespeare was introducing Henry of Navarre, King of France since 1589, Shakespeare gives to his gentlemen names that could not but recall Henry IV's struggle with the Catholic League for his inheritance. Berowne and Longueville are obviously called after Henry's supporters the Maréchal Biron and the Duc de Longueville; Dumain recalls the Duc de Mayenne defeated at Ivry by Henry but later an ally. As Essex had himself in 1591 commanded a force to help Henry IV to besiege Rouen, the treatment of Navarre and his entourage

would doubtless convey more, however indirectly, to the Essex circle than it can to those not so initiated.

The visit to Navarre of a Princess of France also recalls the meeting at Nerac in 1578 between Henry and Marguerite de Valois his wife, though separated from him, to settle matters about her dowry that involved Aquitaine. Marguerite was accompanied by her mother Catherine de Medici and, to ease the negotiations, a group of fascinating ladies-in-waiting known as *l'escadron volant*. At v. ii. 14 the lines beginning 'He made her melancholy, sad, and heavy' may refer to the death of Hélène de Tournon two years before this meeting, an event recorded in the Queen's *Mémoires*.

The apparent dilemma between learning and love could not but remind the Essex circle of an earlier debate on these issues. Essex had married Sir Philip Sidney's widow Frances Walsingham, and Penelope Devereux, the Stella of Sidney's sonnets, was Essex' sister. While Sidney was writing his sequence to Stella, he was exhorted by Giordano Bruno, then a visitor to England, to give up comparing a lady's eyes to stars and turn his thoughts to tasks more in keeping with the heroic aspirations of the mind such as astronomy; for Bruno was a disciple of Copernicus and a pioneer in scientific speculation, an enthusiasm that made the Inquisition consign him to the flames in 1600. Navarre's academy, one gathers from Berowne's tirade about the relative importance of what may be learnt from the eyes of women and the study of stars, seems to have had astronomy somewhere on the curriculum.

This debate is sustained in the sub-plot by the minor characters; Holofernes and Sir Nathaniel, whose learning is sorely tried by the wit of Moth and the observations of Costard, reflect the controversy between

John Florio and Gabriel Harvey on one side and Nashe and John Eliot on the other. Shakespeare quotes from Florio's *First Fruits* and *Second Fruits*, manuals to teach Italian, as well as from Eliot's *Ortho-epia Gallica or Eliot's Fruits for the French*, which, under cover of teaching French, provides a satiric commentary on foreign teachers of languages and pedants generally. Of the Nashe–Harvey controversy, which Whitgift the Archbishop of Canterbury ended by having their publications burnt, Eliot's views are summarized in the remark: 'The Book-worme was never but a pick-goose; it is the Multiplying spirit, not of the Alchimist, but of the villainist, that knocketh the naile one the head, and spurreth cutt farther in a day, than the quickest Artist in a weeke.' Here 'Artist' means scholar, the advocate of learning, while the villainist is the man of the world and experience, who may find, Nashe argues, in prison more real instruction than a pedant in a college.

The love and learning, artist–villainist, controversy Shakespeare rounds off by introducing some considerations ignored by the contending parties. The gay round is halted by the entrance of the messenger in black who brings the Princess word of her father's death. The Princess and her ladies decline to entertain the proposals of marriage now pressed upon them, at least for a year. The King if still of the same mind after a year's meditation in a hermitage may ask again, while Berowne to prove his faith must spend the year in a hospital, not the hygienic, aseptic, institution of today, where anaesthetics help to ease the ordeals of the inmates, but a centre of infection and unrelieved pain where only the determination and the duty to hope rather than hope itself could live. The ladies have put

the questions at issue into a more realistic perspective than their gallants.

The charming debate between the Owl and the Cuckoo which now provides the final note is an addition for later performances perhaps to mask the austerity with which the original argument had ended.

The face of the dark lady of the Sonnets seems to appear occasionally, and especially at the very end of Act III, in *Love's Labour's Lost*. In 1598 Meres refers to the Sonnets as in circulation among private friends, and in 1599 William Jaggard included Sonnets 138 and 144 in a collection he named *The Passionate Pilgrim*. As these two sonnets refer to the Fair Youth and the Dark Lady, the episode in which they took part, if it has any historical warrant, must be dated before 1598. Further if Southampton was the Fair Youth, we may treat the episode as earlier than his association about 1595 with Elizabeth Vernon, one of the Queen's maids of honour. His sudden marriage with the lady in 1598 brought on him the Queen's displeasure and a term of confinement in the Fleet. If Southampton were the Fair Youth, references to the Dark Lady in a piece presented to the Essex circle, in which Southampton moved, would no doubt have been appreciated by those in his confidence.

The Sonnets, as a whole, were not printed till 1609. Thomas Thorpe, who entered them in the Stationers' Register on 20 May 1609, dedicated them to a Mr W. H. as their 'onlie begetter'. Who Mr W. H. was, and what precisely 'onlie begetter' means in this context, are only two among the many questions provoked by this publication that still await a definite answer.

That Mr W. H. was Mr William Harvey, who in 1598 married the twice-widowed mother of Southamp-

ton, has been suggested; for, on the death of Lady Southampton in 1607, he might have been prevailed upon to allow the world the privilege of seeing a document that Lady Southampton could not bring herself to give the public. Further, as Sir William Harvey had married Cordelia Annesley in 1609, Thorpe's hope that the 'onlie begetter' enjoy 'that eternitie promised by our ever-living poet' could then be interpreted as a wish that this marriage be blest with children, for Shakespeare had in the Sonnets urged marriage on the Fair Youth that he might enjoy a similar immortality. Strangely enough Cordelia Annesley had, as Professor Sisson has pointed out, defended her father in his old age from the attempt by her two older sisters to take over his estate—an almost Lear-like situation.

The great attraction of the Pembroke view is that this would allow the dark lady to be identified as Mary Fitton. But Pembroke was only sixteen in 1598, and Mary Fitton could not have been described by that date as a married woman.

The Merchant of Venice and *A Midsummer-Night's Dream* are probably among the earliest comedies Shakespeare wrote for the newly formed Chamberlain's men. In them Shakespeare's craftsmanship, though as assured as in his earlier comedies, is less obtrusive, so strongly have other elements in the complex developed.

The blessing of the house by Oberon with Titania and their train that provides the Epilogue to *A Midsummer-Night's Dream* suggests that the play itself was in fact as in form an Epithalamion. The fairy band that sing and dance is also a feature of *The Merry Wives of Windsor*, which, as Dr Hotson has shown beyond reasonable doubt, was written for a special performance before the Queen. Why a singing and dancing

troupe of children was at the poet's service in *The Merry Wives* is explained by the importance of the occasion for the Lord Chamberlain, who was in a position to provide choir-boys to help out with a performance that had about it something of a celebration. The importance given to the fairies in *A Midsummer-Night's Dream*, while strictly functional and in keeping with the theme of the piece, does raise the practical question of their recruitment, which would be answered if we knew that Shakespeare wrote the play for the marriage of the Lord Chamberlain's grand-daughter Elizabeth Carey to Thomas Berkeley on 19 February 1596. We have unfortunately no record of the celebrations, but the Queen who had a deep attachment to her cousin the first Lord Hunsdon would certainly have honoured the occasion by her presence; and the poet's homage to Her Majesty as 'the fair vestal throned by the west' would have graced such an occasion as fittingly as it provides the key to what may be called the mechanism of the plot, which turns on the very diverse effects that follow the application of Dian's bud or Cupid's flower to the eyes of the sleepers in the moonlight.

There are in the Comedies many causes that lead to those misunderstandings by characters and between characters that amuse the omniscient spectator, who may truly say of himself what Berowne in *Love's Labour's Lost* mistakenly felt of his superior position,

> Like a demi-god here sit I in the sky,
> And wretched fools' secrets heedfully o'er-eye.

In all the Comedies except *The Dream* the reasons for these mistakings become known in the end to the victims themselves and peace and happiness replace the confusion; but in *The Dream*, although Titania may

yet learn from Oberon how she became enamoured of an ass, and although all the lovers are happily united, the mortals will never know what increased and then resolved the cross-purposes and confusions in the wood near Athens. The account the lovers try to give of their doings seems to Theseus as inconsequent as the discourse of poets and lunatics, and he is prevented from answering the mild dissent to his opinion expressed by Hippolyta by the arrival of his guests. To the spectators who know better than Theseus and who have seen how 'Cupid is a knavish lad', there is a gaiety as well as a satisfaction about the outcome, most appropriate were the spectators themselves the guests at some marriage festivity.

Theseus seems above the strife and exempt from the accidents to which lesser mortals are subject; yet it is from the Fairy King and Queen whom his wedding has drawn to Athens that we have a glimpse of an earlier time. Titania provoked by Oberon can call Hippolyta 'the bouncing Amazon, Your buskin'd mistress and your warrior love' and draw from Oberon in his turn some remarks on Theseus' earlier adventures. Shakespeare had been reading in Plutarch's *Lives*, perhaps in the new edition of 1595 published by Field, his friend the printer from Stratford, and adjusted the portrait of the hero he found in Chaucer, there as in Shakespeare the ironic commentator on the effects of love, to his humorous transformation of *The Knight's Tale*, a tribute that the elder master would have enjoyed more perhaps than Shakespeare's later treatment of his *Troilus*.

This fantasia on love themes is completed by the very tragical mirth of the lamentable comedy of Pyramus and Thisbe which provides a remarkable pedal

point, for the construction of the piece resembles less a fantasia in the way the themes are run in counterpoint than a complicated fugue, before the final close. No composition, if one may again borrow, however extravagantly, for a moment the terms of a sister art, can show a more admirable Episode than the wooing of Bottom by Titania.

The skill with which Shakespeare combines his subject, the marriage of Theseus and Hippolyta, with contrasting counter-subjects is a developed form of the technique found in *The Errors* and the other early comedies. Now to this is added his growing powers of characterization that make Bottom the weaver the first of Shakespeare's masterpieces in this kind. And there is still to be added the poetry, that invests the scene with the moonlight which lies like an enchantment over it, or that restores the morning air alive with the sounds of day. It was this strain in the magic of the play that so captivated Milton and Keats.

Bernard Shaw has called *The Merchant of Venice* a safe play; an ambitious actor-manager can hardly destroy its balance, and even if he plays Shylock, the villain of the piece, that will not obscure its charm. Yet the play might seem put together from a set of motifs of so ancient an origin that all potency would have deserted them: the bond that sets the flesh and life of one against the money of another; the choice of caskets; the will that prescribes such a choice, the exchange of rings, the wicked Jew.

Shakespeare's immediate source was in an Italian collection of stories *Il Pecorone* (The Dunce) published in 1558 and attributed to Ser Giovanni Fiorentino. The first story of the fourth day tells how Giannetto, living with his godfather Ansaldo, a wealthy merchant

of Venice, was persuaded to ask permission to visit Alexandria. Ansaldo provided a splendid ship and merchandise merely to gratify Giannetto's wish, not in hope of gain. Putting in at the port of Belmonte, the young man encounters the beautiful and capricious widow who invites wealthy visitors to share her bed, on the condition that they will forfeit their possessions if they fail to enjoy her. Her victims are given a drugged wine that leaves the lady free to take possession of the goods of her sleeping guest. Twice Giannetto visits her and twice he loses everything. Yet Ansaldo furnishes him for a third venture, having, however, to borrow ten thousand ducats from a Jew, which he must repay by the feast of St John or forfeit a pound of his flesh. The third time Giannetto warned by the lady's maid not to drink embraced the lady as his wife and became her husband. Enjoying his new state Giannetto forgets his godfather's plight, till a procession on St John's Day reminded him of the bargain with the Jew. Provided with a hundred thousand ducats by his wife, Giannetto hastens to Venice only to find that the Jew insists on having Ansaldo's flesh. Meantime, however, the lady from Belmonte has come secretly to Venice, and disguised as a lawyer she challenges the Jew, who has refused her offers of money, to take the flesh without spilling blood. He sees he is defeated, but his offer to take the money is now rejected, and he tears up the bond in his fury. Giannetto offers the lawyer the hundred thousand ducats; this, however, is declined and he has to give his ring instead. Once more at Belmonte all is explained, and to complete the general happiness Ansaldo marries the damsel who had warned Giannetto against the doctored wine.

As the test to which the visitors had to submit in

the Italian tale was unsuitable for the stage Shakespeare replaced it with the three caskets from a story in the *Gesta Romanorum* as translated by Richard Robinson. There a lost girl, by birth a king's daughter, has to choose between three caskets to win the Emperor's son. Shakespeare now makes the prize the lady of Belmont, and her suitors those who must try to choose the winning casket. This lottery we learn was devised by Portia's virtuous father in a moment of holy inspiration; and we are to understand, if we believe what Nerissa tells her mistress, that the winning casket 'will, no doubt, never be chosen by any rightly but one who you shall rightly love'. When we hear later in this scene of a scholar and a soldier called Bassanio who is approved of by the ladies, we can settle down to enjoy the way he will no doubt surmount the obstacles to his own and the heroine's happiness.

'Every book', William de Morgan the ceramist and novelist claimed, 'has a right to an assumption intrinsically improbable to make things go.' How far this claim is admissible may be questioned, but hardly to be denied by those who are willing to enjoy a comedy. To reject the verdict of the caskets and denounce Bassanio as a vulgar fortune-hunter is by hypothesis, one may fairly say after we have heard of Portia's holy and inspired father, absurd.

Having established the authority of the test, Shakespeare now develops its dramatic potentialities in a manner without parallel in the sources. In the central scene of the play as Bassanio stands before the caskets, we know from the earlier failures of Morocco and Arragon where Portia's picture is enclosed, so that we follow Bassanio's choice with the apprehension such knowledge brings with it. And we also know, as Bassanio

and the company do not, that Antonio's ships have not come home although the three months allowed for repayment of the loan are soon to expire, and that Shylock vexed by the elopement of his daughter has, were it needed, an added incentive to revenge. It is not merely the lovers' happiness that is in jeopardy, for Portia makes no concealment of her fears; and the release of the tension that follows Bassanio's resolution not to be intimidated by the threat on the leaden casket *Who chooseth me must give and hazard all he hath*, and that makes the happy lovers' exchange of greetings a specially welcome resolution to the anxious expectancy of the ordeal—this rejoicing immediately gives place with the arrival of the news about Antonio to fears that seem to mock Bassanio's fortune and the happiness it promised. From sunshine we pass into shadow again.

The trial scene compared with the corresponding part in the Italian story shows the same skill in maintaining an ebb and flow of apprehension, although in this phase of the action, instead of our contemplation of happiness being shadowed by our knowledge of approaching danger, we see the apparently desperate plight of Antonio and the misery of his friends touched with the hope that our knowledge of Portia's presence gives.

Quite apart from Shakespeare's skill in setting off one aspect of the action against a contrasting part, one has only to compare his treatment of Shylock with the Jew in *Il Pecorone* to see Shakespeare's power of conferring on a static image of a figure the movement and energy of life. Undoubtedly Marlowe's Jew of Malta and his daughter Abigail were in Shakespeare's memory as he fashioned Shylock, who is, however, a human being beside Marlowe's monster.

There was still the episode of the borrowed ring to

round off the story, and this simple motif, in the original a pleasant jest to confirm the bond between the lovers, suggests to Shakespeare the moonlight and stars which Lorenzo and Jessica contemplate from Belmont, and the music of the spheres, as a fitting prelude for the homecoming and fun of the reunion, and the news that Antonio's ships are safe in port.

In his *Epistle* to *The Comicall Gallant* (1702), a comedy based on *The Merry Wives of Windsor*, John Dennis refers to Shakespeare's play as written at the Queen's command in fourteen days. Rowe in 1709 elaborates the tradition a little: 'The Queen was so well pleas'd with that admirable character of *Falstaff*, in the two parts of *Henry* the Fourth, that she commanded him to continue it for one Play more, and to shew him in love.' Traditions that are not heard of till 1702 require confirmation; and this has been provided by Dr Hotson who has given the most cogent reasons for regarding the play as written for performance before the Queen at the Garter Feast held at Westminster on St George's Day, 23 April 1597.

There had been no election to the Order of the Garter since 1593, and that of 1597 was not merely of unusual importance in itself, it had a special interest for Shakespeare's company, as their patron George Carey Lord Hunsdon was one of the five new Knights of the Order. His father Henry Carey, first Lord Hunsdon, was the Lord Chamberlain who became patron in 1594 of the company of which Shakespeare had just become a member. On his death the office of Chamberlain was taken over by William Brooke, seventh Lord Cobham. On Cobham's death in March 1597 he was succeeded as Chamberlain by George Carey, second Lord Hunsdon, who had on his father's death taken under his

patronage his father's company. He was like his father greatly loved by the Queen, who treated him as a junior and favourite cousin to whom she subscribed herself, as in the letter quoted by Dr Hotson, 'Your most affectionate loving Sovereign'.

Although five Knights were elected only four made the journey on 23 May to the Installation ceremony next day at Windsor, for Frederick, Duke of Württemberg had been elected *in absentia*. In 1592 Frederick, then Count of Mömpelgart, had visited the Queen and requested to be given the Garter. On his return to Germany he kept pestering the Queen, who at last had him elected without having, however, to be bored by his company, or indeed going to the very considerable expense of giving him the insignia of the order, an extravagance she left to her successor from Scotland. On 23 April, therefore, Shakespeare was free to remind the company, to whom the circumstances would not be unknown, of the absent candidate in the remark Dr Caius makes to the Host of the Garter Inn: 'it is tell-a-me, dat you make grand preparation for a Duke *de Iamanie*: by my trot: der is no Duke that the Court is know to come.' In the finale in which Falstaff is trapped in Windsor Park by the Fairies led by that Welsh fairy Sir Hugh Evans, and Fenton carries off Anne Page in spite of the diverse schemes for her marriage put on foot by her father and mother, we have the reference by the Fairies to the Installation at Windsor that will follow the Garter Feast in London. Crier Hobgoblin gives the order,

> Cricket, to Windsor chimneys shalt thou leap.
> Where fires thou find'st unrak'd and hearths unswept,
> There pinch the maids as blue as bilberry.
> Our radiant queen hates sluts and sluttery.

And there follows the reference to the chapel and the motto of the Garter, *Honi soit qui mal y pense*, which the Fairy band as they danced no doubt displayed

In emerald tufts, flowers, purple, blue, and white.

In the opening scene we have the punning reference to the luces in Shallow's coat that nearly a hundred years later prompted the speculation that gave Sir Thomas Lucy a deer-park he never possessed from which Shakespeare might steal the mythical buck that transported him to London and future fame.

The comedies that follow, *Much Ado about Nothing*, *As You Like It*, and *Twelfth Night or What You Will*, have generally been regarded as the culmination of this phase of Shakespeare's art, and that in spite of Bernard Shaw's objection that their very titles betray Shakespeare's lack of the seriousness which a disciple of Ibsen expects even in comedy. What Shakespeare's audience enjoyed were amusing and pleasant love affairs, the matter of comedy since the time of Menander; they were willing to forget for the moment the toils and troubles of life in the contemplation of the happiness it may also bestow on mortals who are not too wise in their own conceit. The instinct in his audience that Shakespeare sounded so surely finds expression in the demand that the later and no doubt more sophisticated lover of comedy Stendhal makes on the dramatist: *il faut que des gens passionnés se trompent, sous mes yeux, d'une manière plaisante, sur le chemin qu'iles mène au bonheur.* Johnson's assertion that love 'has little operation in the dramas of a poet who caught his ideas from the living world and exhibited only what he saw before him' is no doubt his way of expressing his disapproval of much contemporary dramatic business, and

indirectly his feeling for the reality which lovers'
meetings in Shakespeare, however literary or artificial
their antecedents, leave upon us. What may be called
the mechanism of the plots of the three comedies of this
mature phase of Shakespeare's development is no less
artificial than that of their predecessors, and is sometimes treated even more casually; but the plot now
seems little more than an excuse for allowing us to
enjoy without delay Rosalind or Viola or the many characters like Touchstone, or Sir Toby, or Dogberry and
Verges, who seem to crowd in on the scene from nowhere as soon as Shakespeare sits down to improvise, as
it were, on some theme that has caught his fancy.

Shakespeare found suggestions for the Claudio–Hero
theme in a tale from Bandello, where the action is laid in
Messina and the characters include King Pedro and
Messer Lionato, father of the heroine. The subject of
Claudio's wooing and rejection of Hero is not a very
promising one, and indeed is never in itself satisfactory.
Shakespeare is careful to keep his audience fully informed of the wrong that is being so mistakenly done to
the lady; for Dogberry and Verges have already secured
the evidence that will convict Don John of his infamy
and convince Claudio and the Prince of their error,
and all before the wedding scene that ends so unhappily; Leonato, however, is hastening to the church and
cannot spare the leisure that is necessary, if he is to
follow the meanderings of the minds of the Constable
and the Headborough in their report on the conspiracy.

It is what may be called the counter-subject that gave
the play its popularity with the Elizabethans, and that
still provides its attraction. It treats of what Goethe described in the version of the theme he introduced as an
episode in his *Kindred by Choice* as 'a violent, so to

speak innate liking concealed under the form of resist-ance', where his heroine's apparently unfriendly ges-tures are an innocent means of directing attention to herself. And Shakespeare does not hesitate to use the difficulties of the Claudio–Hero situation to give an added point to the Benedick–Beatrice relationship that places Benedick under the necessity of submitting to her passionate injunction to kill Claudio.

Bernard Shaw will have it that Shakespeare has covered poverty of thought and coarseness of innuendo by the grace and dignity of the diction he has given his teasing lovers. But poets and dramatists are no more able than other men to gather grapes of thorns or figs of thistles, or to give grace and dignity and charm to what is coarse or indecent. 'No matter how poor, coarse, cheap and obvious the thought may be, the mood is charming, and the music of the words expresses the mood.' One would think that to please such a critic Beatrice and Benedick should have consulted some manual of deportment on how to be less vulgar and thoughtless and less obviously happy with one another.

The presence of the names Kempe and Cowley, in place of Dogberry and Verges in the manuscript the company sent to the printer in 1600, shows that Shakespeare wrote the piece before Kempe left the company in 1599.

Compared with *Much Ado* and its intricate web of intrigue and pretences *As You Like It* offers a compara-tively simple situation. All turns on the masquerade to which Rosalind and Celia resort in their distress. Rosa-lind, confined in the court of her usurping uncle, finds escape in the forest of Arden and freedom to indulge the holiday humour to which her encounter with Orlando has given release. Rosalind is the 'practiser', the magi-

cian as she explains to Orlando who will make all even, yet she herself is under a spell that gives to her teasing of the devoted but ignorant Orlando the undercurrent of keen and ardent feeling, without which her brilliant descant on the hopes and fears of marriage would lack its charm and power. The warring elements that give such life and reality to the comedy of the wooing of Ganymede are resolved for us in the coda-like dialogue that concludes the scene where Celia voices one strain as she complains: 'You have simply misused our sex in your love-prate. We must have your doublet and hose plucked over your head, and show the world what the bird hath done to her own nest'; and Rosalind in her defence confesses to the other, 'O coz, coz, coz, my pretty little coz, that thou didst know how many fathoms deep I am in love!' This central situation is set off as in Thomas Lodge's *Rosalynde: Euphues Golden Legacie*, which gave Shakespeare the outline of his plot, with the very different encounter of Celia and Oliver as well as that of Phebe and Silvius. To this Shakespeare added Touchstone and Audrey, and to stress the gaiety of the love-making in the forest he added a sardonic commentator in the melancholy Jaques.

Shakespeare does not even pretend to round off his action in the plausible manner adopted by Lodge. With everyone in the forest married or settled it is time to return to duty, so the usurping Frederick after meeting an old religious man abandons the Dukedom to its rightful possessor and withdraws to the retreat in which Jaques proposes to seek him out. To complain that such an ending is too casual is not to take the play too seriously but to miss where in his source Shakespeare found his interest and indeed his inspiration.

That Shakespeare had been reading Marlowe's *Hero*

and Leander, published in 1598 some five years after Marlowe's death, is suggested by several passages, but principally and beyond question by Phebe's reference at III. v. 80,

> Dead Shepherd, now I find thy saw of might,
> 'Who ever loved that loved not at first sight'

A tribute to a former colleague unique in Shakespeare, and yet strangely in place in what seems at first sight so very incongruous a setting.

On 2 February 1602 *Twelfth Night* was performed at the Middle Temple as one of that society John Manningham noted in his diary: 'At our feast wee had a play called "Twelve Night, or What You Will", much like the *Commedy of Errores*, or *Menechmi* in Plautus, but most like and neere to that in Italian called *Inganni*.' Shakespeare could have looked over two plays called *Gl'Inganni* (The Cheats), the first by Nicolo Secchi dated 1562, and that of 1592 by Curzio Gonzaga where the disguised heroine takes the name Cesare, which may have suggested Viola's presenting herself as Cesario. Both the Italian versions derive from the piece performed in 1531 at carnival time in Siena by the society of the Intronati (Thunderstruck by Love) called *Gl'Ingannati* (The Cheated). From this play descend all those versions dramatic or narrative in which the confusions and misunderstandings come from the presence of twins, not brothers as in the *Menaechmi*, but brother and sister; for the girl disguised as a boy, according to the Italian convention that allows an unmarried girl of respectable family only when disguised to take an active part in the plot, is confused with her brother when he unexpectedly appears on the scene. In *Gl'Ingannati*, the heroine Lelia, for-

gotten by her former lover Flamminio, enters his service disguised as a page called Fabio and acts as his messenger to Isabella with whom he is now enamoured. Isabella falls in love with the page, who does not scruple to encourage Isabella to transform her indifference to Flamminio into active hostility. Meantime Fabrizio, Lelia's brother, arrives in Modena, is mistaken by his father for the disguised Lelia and locked up with Isabella. The marriage of Isabella and Fabrizio being announced, Flamminio now becomes aware of the devotion of Lelia and makes her his wife.

Shakespeare had already in *Two Gentlemen of Verona* used this motif of the girl disguised as a page acting as messenger for the man she loves to the lady that now occupies his fancy. There Shakespeare had in mind Montemayor's adaptation of the situation in *Gl'Ingannati*. Now Shakespeare returns to the original Italian arrangement in which a brother makes good the part that disguise has as it were thrust upon his twin sister. Shakespeare took the title of his piece from the Prologue to *Gl'Ingannati*: 'The story is new, never seen nor read, and only dipped for and taken out of their own industrious noddles as your prize-tickets are dipped for and taken out on Twelfth Night (la Notte di Beffana).' That Shakespeare had looked at some of the later stage versions derived from *Gl'Ingannati* seems probable; of the prose versions, that by Barnaby Riche, the story of Apolonius and Silla, in *Riche his Farewell to the Militarie Profession* (1581) cannot have been unknown to Shakespeare, for, as Professor Muir has shown, Shakespeare used in *Twelfth Night*, and nowhere else in his works, four unusual words that stand in Riche's volume; and it may well be that Shakespeare took from another story in the volume suggestions for the scene

in which Malvolio is treated as a lunatic. In *Apolonius and Silla* there is a shipwreck that leads to Silla's adopting her brother's name and male disguise.

Dr Hotson has suggested that Shakespeare wrote *Twelfth Night* for a performance before the Queen on Twelfth Night 1601, when she had as a guest the youthful Orsino, Duke of Bracciano. Unfortunately in the accounts of this entertainment on which Dr Hotson draws there is no indication of the precise piece performed on that occasion. Shakespeare would find *Orsino inamorato* as a character in *Il Viluppo*, and the Duke's visit may well have reminded him of the name in the Italian piece as suitable for his love-lorn Duke. To have given any excuse at a command performance for drawing public comment on the Queen's guest would have been tactless; the reference to the Duke of Württemberg in *The Merry Wives* is to an importunate bore whose absence was obviously happily contrived by the Queen, and provides no precedent for the Orsino suggestion.

Of all Shakespeare's comedies *Twelfth Night* perhaps combines most happily dignity and charm with the more amusing aspects of human nature. Olivia's household, a wonderful picture of a wealthy Elizabethan establishment, conducted, as it seemed to the newly arrived Sebastian, 'with such a smooth, discreet, and stable bearing' might appear to an outsider suitable material for the grave brush of a Velasquez: the lady herself in mourning for her brother, the precise and serious steward to maintain the order and decency required by the position of his mistress, the shrewd waiting-woman, the uncle whose relationship with Olivia gives him a privileged position in so apparently sober and staid a precinct. The world was to be shut out from

the veiled walks of this cloister. By the time Sebastian finds himself within its influence the appearance may in part remain but the reality makes him wonder whether it is he or the lady who is mad. We are not astonished he should ask himself such a question, but having had the privilege of following the happenings in this sequestered spot we understand the method in the madness that perplexes Sebastian.

The smooth functioning of the household has been disturbed by tensions that develop within its bounds. Maria means to have Sir Toby and become a lady, for, as the knowing Feste tells her, 'if Sir Toby would leave drinking, thou wert as witty a piece of Eve's flesh as any in Illyria'. And Malvolio is persuaded by Maria that his dream of marrying Olivia is more than an idle fancy; while Olivia herself as she resolutely shuts out such distractions as Orsino's suit becomes in her turn the victim of a more passionate delusion. Meantime Sir Andrew, regarding himself as another of Olivia's suitors, is merely providing Sir Toby with a handsome subsidy for encouraging him in his fatuity. From these determinations or delusions Shakespeare develops the most wonderful sequence of scenes, and matters have become entangled apparently beyond all unravelling when Sebastian stumbles unawares into the midst of this confusion, which only his presence can resolve into harmony and happiness.

If the lines by Leonard Digges can be trusted, the Elizabethan audiences found in Malvolio the focus of their interest,

> The Cockpit Galleries, Boxes, all are full
> To hear *Malvoglio* that crosse garter'd gull.

and Charles I whose taste in art or letters cannot be

described as vulgar scored out in his copy of Shakespeare, a second Folio now in the library at Windsor,
the heading 'Twelfth Night' and substituted 'Malvolio'.
The day-dreams of an Alnascar, the fifth and most idle
of the Barber's brothers, may entertain us, and his
hopes of marrying and bullying the Vizier's daughter
end appropriately in the loss of the basket of glass on
which he had been building his castles in the air; the
imaginings of Malvolio are no less vain and insubstantial and are no doubt, because he is a responsible and
serious-minded being, all the more ludicrous and ridiculous. 'He might', as Lamb observed, 'have worn his
gold chain with honour in one of our old round-head
families.' Yet, as Lamb felt, there is 'a deep sense of
the pitiable infirmity of man's nature that can lay him
open to such frenzies' and in Malvolio Shakespeare
anticipates the darker portrait of a not very dissimilar
temperament in the Angelo of *Measure for Measure*.
However, what is all but tragic in Vienna is in Illyria
pitiable, no doubt, but also fair game for the comic
spirit.

The fun and frolic of the piece makes an immediate
yet lasting appeal, but without the poetry that discovers
for us the depth of sensibility in Viola, and in Olivia
even in her delusion, *Twelfth Night* could not be regarded as perhaps the most enchanting of the comedies.

The comedies that follow, *Measure for Measure* and
All's Well that Ends Well, offer a more realistic treatment of some social problem than their predecessors, and
it was this feature that allowed Bernard Shaw to regard
them as superior to *As You Like It* and *Twelfth Night*
and indeed as foreshadowing, however faintly, what
Shaw regarded as the more intellectual and adult treatment of such problems by Ibsen or indeed by himself.

Measure for Measure was performed at Court on 26 December 1604. Shakespeare found the story from which he constructed his plot in Giraldi Cinthio's *Hecatommithi* (1565), a collection of tales which he had already drawn on for *Othello*. Cinthio later dramatized in his *Epitia*, with important variations, the story of how Juriste, left by the Emperor to govern Innsbruck, condemns the youthful Vico to death for rape, pretends to Epitia, who is Vico's sister, that she can ransom her brother by yielding herself to his will, and breaks his promise by having Vico executed. The Emperor petitioned by Epitia orders the deputy to marry her and then suffer death. Epitia now begs for her husband's life so earnestly that the Emperor pardons Juriste. In the dramatic version the governor of the prison has a murderer executed in place of Vico; when Juriste is exposed, his sister Angela (whose name may have suggested Shakespeare's Angelo) pleads with Epitia, who is unmoved till she learns that Vico is indeed still alive and safe. *Epitia*, though not printed till 1583 some ten years after Cinthio's death, seems to have been known to Shakespeare. He did certainly know the two five-act *Discourses* adapted from Cinthio's story that George Whetstone published in 1578 with the title *Promos and Cassandra*. As in Cinthio, Cassandra pleads for her brother Andrugio, and Whetstone anticipates Cinthio's device in *Epitia* by substituting a dead man's head for Andrugio's. Andrugio appears from hiding and secures the pardon of Promos. In 1582 Whetstone made a prose version of the story for his *Heptameron of Civill Discourses* as 'reported by Madam Isabella', the name that Shakespeare adopts for his heroine.

From Whetstone's play Shakespeare took the suggestion for his background of low life, and from Cinthio

the problem of reconciling justice and mercy. This was a problem that had exercised the pen of England's new sovereign, and immediately after Elizabeth's death reprints of treatises by James, particularly his *Basilikon Doron*, were quickly put on sale by London publishers. The King's opinions were naturally prescribed reading for those in any standing at Court, and Shakespeare did not neglect in this play, as in *Macbeth*, to show his knowledge of his new sovereign's philosophy. In *Macbeth* this in no way disturbs the imaginative integrity of the dramatist's conception; in *Measure for Measure*, however, the part of the Duke, in which Shakespeare incorporated features that were obviously drawn from James, including his dislike of crowds, is a somewhat artificial role. From the first it is clear the Duke is conducting an experiment, for after explaining to Friar Thomas his reasons for disguising himself as a Friar he concludes, referring to Angelo his newly appointed deputy,

> Hence shall we see
> If power change purpose, what our seemers be.

We see, as Tolstoy has said in another connexion, the author's intention and we are put off. To treat the play as an exposition of Shakespeare's considered thoughts on justice and mercy is to suppose Shakespeare as muddle-headed and inconsistent as James himself often proved. The comments of Lucio on the Duke's philosophy and conduct seem to come from a part of Shakespeare's mind that hardly acquiesced in the formal design of this exposition of 'the properties of government', according to the new and reigning fashion.

The power of the play lies in the encounters between Angelo and Isabella. It was impossible for Shakespeare

at the height of his powers not to make something memorable from the contrast and contest between the very different types of austerity represented by the deputy and his petitioner. Shakespeare, however, escapes from the tragic consequences of their uncompromising wills by a series of subterfuges, including the substitution of Mariana for Isabella as the deputy's bed companion, that transpose the action into a key more in keeping with comedy. We are no doubt relieved that all ends happily, but as neither of the contestants has been allowed to realize the natural consequence of their attitude the issue between Angelo and Isabella becomes obscured by the manipulations required to avoid it.

The confusions of judgement over the moral issues of this play that so trouble commentators have been attributed to some crisis in the dramatist's own experience. It is more likely that they arise from Shakespeare's attempt to accommodate something of his new patron's moralizings to an action where the issues involved are more numerous and complex than those treated in the King's philosophy.

The place of *All's Well that Ends Well* among the comedies is uncertain. It is, however, convenient, and possibly correct, to regard it as a comedy that Shakespeare felt was required by his company at a time when his own interests were absorbed in another type of work.

The story that provides Shakespeare with his plot comes from Boccaccio's *Decameron* and is there related on the third day, when the theme prescribed for that session requires the narrators to tell of those who by their exertions and determination obtain what they greatly admire or regain what they have lost. William Paynter retold the story in his *Palace of Pleasure*, a

collection of tales first published in 1566. How closely Shakespeare follows his source may be seen from the synopsis prefixed to Paynter's version:

Giletta a Phisition's daughter of Narbon, healed the French King of a Fistula, for reward whereof she demanded Beltramo Counte of Rossiglione to husband. The Counte being maried against his will, for despite fled to Florence, and loved another. Giletta his wife, by pollicie found meanes to lye with her husbande, in place of his lover, and was begotten with childe of two sonnes: which knowen to her husband, he received her againe and afterwards he lived in great honour and felicitie.

The story in Shakespeare's source belongs to the well-known type of folk-tale in which a wife is required to vindicate her claim to her husband's affection by performing some apparently impossible task. Here the interest is concentrated on the skill with which the challenge is met. The regained husband is merely the token of success. In Boccaccio the interest can be focused on the skill and determination of the quest. In drama, however, the moral position of the husband cannot be concealed. Dr Johnson described Bertram as

A man noble without generosity and young without truth; who marries Helen as a coward, and leaves her as a profligate; when she is dead by his unkindness sneaks home to a second marriage, is accused by a woman he has wronged, defends himself by falsehood and is dismissed to happiness.

The idea that Helena should deign to pursue a man who scorns her love is equally unwelcome to other critics. Shakespeare has made some effort to make Bertram worthy of affection; he is a soldier and he discovers his lack of discernment in his association with Parolles.

Nothing, however, that Shakespeare can do can make after-reflection on the piece, however cleverly it is contrived as a stage production, anything but confused and unsatisfactory, unless we accept the convention on which Shakespeare relies. And this particular convention is no longer congenial to the spirit of comedy.

The three comedies that Shakespeare wrote after his company took over the Blackfriars theatre offer such a contrast to the tragedies, and indeed to the comedies of what has been called the tragic period, that commentators have tended to feel that the explanation of the change of tone and interest must lie in some happening in the dramatist's private life. E. K. Chambers imagines Shakespeare the victim of his own endeavour to find in his tragedies a means of unburdening his mind of its disillusion and despair. Only a nervous breakdown, according to this commentator, brings the sequence of tragedies to an end, and the comedies that follow are the work of a kind of convalescence, the comforting reflections of his last and less vigorous years. Taking up this notion of the dramatist overcome by his own communings with his unhappy thoughts, Lytton Strachey would regard the final comedies as an escape from reality into a world of fantasy and poetry, were it not that Shakespeare is still haunted by bad dreams that in the shape of Cloten, or Caliban, or the other unpleasant intruders, disturb this realm of make-believe. Strachey, however, could not but admit that while he scoffed at what he regarded as the sentimental attitude of Dowden and E. K. Chambers to the Romances, as these comedies came to be called, he accepted their interpretation of the tragedies and built on it his paradoxical treatment of the last plays. Strachey's own

interpretation merely develops in a contrary fashion the same uncritical and naïve assumption about the tragedies that gave rise to the opinions he satirizes.

Cymbeline seemed to Dr Johnson a hopeless confusion of the names and manners of different times. Certainly Shakespeare has put together features from many different sources. Into the reign of Cymbeline, a mythical descendant like Lear of the mythical Brutus, who according to Geoffrey of Monmouth, writing in the reign of Stephen, civilized Britain, Shakespeare introduces an intrigue from Boccaccio.

In Boccaccio Shakespeare found the story of the Genoese merchant who entered into a wager about his wife's chastity, and thinking he had lost gave orders for his wife's death. She escapes in male disguise and having unmasked the villain who belied her is reunited with her husband. The villain, as in Shakespeare, had been smuggled into her bedroom in a chest; he takes away during the night a girdle and other articles to show the husband, as well as noting the mole on his wife's breast. Shakespeare also read the story in the English version *Frederyke of Jennen*, but this version does not contain the fate that overtakes the villain in Boccaccio, which Shakespeare introduces jocularly in *The Winter's Tale* where Autolycus at IV. iv. 772 frightens the clown by telling him of the punishment awaiting a shepherd's son: 'He has a son—who shall be flay'd alive, then 'nointed over with honey, set on the head of a wasp's nest . . .' and finally 'with flies blown to death.'

To mythical history and bourgeois intrigue Shakespeare adds the folk-motif of the sleep that resembles death, and an adaptation of Holinshed's account of how a Scots husbandman Hay and his two sons turned

defeat into victory at the battle against the Danes at Loncart in A.D. 976.

That the dramatist who wrote *Julius Caesar* and *Antony and Cleopatra* must have known that Frenchmen, Dutchmen, and Spaniards did not meet in the Rome of Augustus and wager ten thousand ducats on their respective mistresses has given rise to the suggestion that the play is a composite production by various hands; the complicated intrigues, however, are resolved in the final scene in a manner that indicates precise and skilful planning, as Granville Barker who favoured a divided authorship had to admit. The parts, however diverse, are closely interwoven in a manner that rules out casual additions or conflicting designs. As Professor Bertrand Evans demonstrates in his analysis of how the audience are enabled by Shakespeare to follow every movement of his characters in the maze of events in which they find themselves wandering and often lost, *Cymbeline* is Shakespeare's greatest achievement in this particular technique.

The design of the play has something in common with those sometimes found in early Renaissance tapestries, like that of silk and silver in Imogen's bedchamber showing 'Proud Cleopatra when she met her Roman', where the splendour of the work does not depend on historical accuracy in costume or setting. There is a richness in the colouring and texture especially in the dramatist's treatment of his heroine that captivated Tennyson, who felt the charm of the art that so sets off the fear and niceness of the courageous and generous Imogen.

Ben Jonson regarded *The Winter's Tale* and *The Tempest* with a dissatisfaction very similar to that Dr Johnson expressed in his criticism of *Cymbeline*; for in

the Induction to *Bartholomew Fair* Jonson disclaims the liberties that Shakespeare seems to take with probability: 'If there be never a servant-monster in the fair, who can help it, he says, nor a nest of antiques? He is loth to make nature afraid in his plays, like these that beget tales, tempests, and such like drolleries.' It is doubtless true that Shakespeare makes little concession to probability in coming to the point where his own interest lies. In *Pandosto, The Triumph of Time* (1588), Shakespeare's principal source, Greene had attempted to give the jealousy of Pandosto, King of Bohemia (for Shakespeare reverses the roles of Bohemia and Sicilia), some sort of colour. In Shakespeare it merely attacks Leontes, King of Sicilia, like some fever or disease. And in the need to cut off the exposed Perdita from all contact with the land of her birth and knowledge of her parentage, Shakespeare does not hesitate to enlist the complicity of his audience in his disposal of Antigonus, by treating his fatal encounter with the bear as a comic episode. This allows Shakespeare to bring us to the sheep-shearing, a pastoral scene that is entirely Shakespeare's creation, for though such a scene is mentioned in *Pandosto*, its realization is entirely Shakespeare's, and one of his most splendid creations. On the surface all is gay with music and dancing, and even Autolycus, who is there to profit by the simplicity of such as Mopsa and Dorcas and their rural swain, brings to the feast a tuneful voice as well as a dexterous hand at picking and cutting purses. Yet this country frolic is only a brilliantly devised background that takes its dramatic significance from the presence of Florizel and Perdita. And their love duet in its turn is heard against the muffled disapproval of the disguised Polixenes that bursts out into what seems an absolute contradiction and denial of the

love theme, that is not, however, to be silenced though
resumed in a darker but no less firmly established key.
To Camillo's warning that

> Prosperity's the very bond of love,
> Whose fresh complexion and whose heart together
> Affliction alters,

Perdita's reply

>   One of these is true:
> I think affliction may subdue the cheek,
> But not take in the mind,

is as Camillo recognizes worthy of a true princess,
although only the audience knows that she is indeed the
daughter of a king.

The return to Sicilia is suggested by Camillo, but it
is Autolycus who turns it to his own and to the Prince
his master's good. To make Perdita's homecoming complete Hermione had to be restored to her daughter and
husband, and Shakespeare with a little mystification
that takes our attention from the precise nature of the
trick or deception he is practising on us, produces to
our astonished but satisfied eyes the long-lost Queen.

In September 1610 news reached England from Virginia of the unexpected arrival in Jamestown of a ship's
company given up for lost who had a remarkable tale
to tell of their survival.

In June 1609 a fleet of nine vessels sailed from
Plymouth to take much-needed reinforcements to the
recently established colony in Virginia. The *Sea-Venture*, carrying the Admiral as well as Sir Thomas Gates,
the new Governor of the colony, had in a storm that
scattered the fleet to be driven ashore on the Bermudas
to avoid foundering. Fortunately there was no loss of

life; and in two pinnaces, which they constructed during their stay on the island, the company reached Jamestown on 23 May 1610.

Soon after the news reached England in 1610, Silvester Jourdan who had been in the *Sea-Venture* published *A Discovery of the Barmudas, Otherwise called the Ile of Devils*, while the Council of Virginia printed *A true Declaration of the estate of the Colony of Virginia, with a confutacon of such scandalous reportes as have tended to disgrace so worthy an enterprise*. A letter from William Strachey, secretary to the Governor, giving a candid account of conditions in the colony was not, however, printed till 1625, after the Council had been dissolved. In *Purchas his Pilgrimes* it stands as *A true Repertory of the wracke and redemption of Sir Thomas Gates, Knight*. Shakespeare drew on all three accounts for detail; that he had access to Strachey's confidential document was made possible, Dr Hotson has very reasonably conjectured, by his acquaintance with Thomas Russell of Alderminster whose stepson Sir Dudley Digges was an important member of the Council of Virginia.

Shakespeare took from Richard Eden's *The Historie of Travayle* (1577) the name Setebos; this he found in the account of Magellan's circumnavigation of the world applied to a Patagonian 'devil'. While no obvious source has been discovered for the plot, the presence in a play *Die Schone Sidea* by Jacob Ayrer of Nuremberg, who died in 1605, of a disinherited princely magician with a daughter who marries his enemy's son, a ministering spirit, a log-carrying episode, a sword fixed by enchantment in its scabbard, suggests that there may have been some story on which both dramatists drew independently. English actors did visit Germany, and

Shakespeare might have heard indirectly of Ayrer's plot. Unfortunately the explanation of the similarities must remain a matter for conjecture.

Gonzalo's picture of the ideal commonwealth, based on a report of an ideal state in the New World that Montaigne included in his essay *Of the Canniballes*, provides an ironic introduction to affairs on the island. Alonso's party contains two important members who have no scruples about advancing their status by cold-blooded murder; and in Caliban the island itself provides another conspirator whose scheme to murder Prospero seems good to Trinculo and Stephano, although they lack Caliban's concentration and purpose. It is these stratagems that made Lytton Strachey feel he was in a more dangerous world than the merry England disguised as Athens that Bottom and his fellows inhabited. Certainly happenings in Virginia were very different from the order and content Montaigne and Gonzalo speak of.

The suggestion that in *The Tempest* the dramatist is himself taking leave of the stage, and that Prospero's renunciation of his magic is Shakespeare's farewell to his art, is hardly to be rejected. Yet Prospero had he despaired of society could hardly have felt so hopefully about the dreams of the younger generation; and Prospero's rejoicing in their affections is the characteristic note of these last comedies, including *Pericles* which, though not included in the First Folio, bears clear marks of Shakespeare's hand. Unlike the disillusioned Tolstoy who felt afraid of such tender feelings and had never found, so he declared, a single spark of truth in that kind of love, Shakespeare makes it the theme of the Romances. All his comedies it may be said are on this theme; but if the Romances do indeed

present us with a more threatening world than the earlier comedies, if there are more unpleasant and dangerous characters in *The Tempest* than in *As You Like It*, so much the stronger must be the faith that looks beyond the ignorant present and is not afraid to hope.

Chapter Four

THE HISTORIES

'In order that a drama may be properly historical, it is necessary that it should be the history of the people to whom it is addressed.' Shakespeare's editors, Heminge and Condell, or whoever was responsible for the grouping of the contents of the First Folio, anticipated Coleridge's judgement by putting the plays dealing with the history of England from King John to Henry VIII in a group by themselves, between the Comedies and the Tragedies, and describing them as Histories.

The terms History and Tragedy are used in Quarto publications without much distinction. The Stationers' Register describes *Richard II* as a Tragedy, while *Lear* is called a History; and the second quarto of *Hamlet* combines the terms on its title-page, which introduces it as a 'Tragicall Historie'. It might be said that the doings of Lear or Cymbeline were, although the invention of Geoffrey of Monmouth, still generally regarded in Shakespeare's day as historical and that Macbeth was indeed a historical character; further, Coriolanus even if he is not as well vouched for by history as Julius Caesar and Antony and Cleopatra, stood equally with the others in Plutarch's *Lives* and in Shakespeare's imagination. The Roman plays, however, do not deal with the history of England nor does *Macbeth*; and although Cymbeline may have seemed to many a historical figure, his story like that of Macbeth and the Romans lacks the one feature essential in a 'History' play.

This essential feature is isolated in *Some Words about 'War and Peace'* in which Tolstoy discusses the difference between the historian's and the artist's treatment of events: 'The historian has to deal with the results of an event, the artist with the fact of the event.' This distinction has been explained clearly by Professor Wade-Gery in his discussion of the *Iliad*: 'Homer was not a historian but an artist. He has no concern with the results of the Trojan War: he does not treat it as the title of the Greeks to Asia, he did not think of it as having in any way created the world he lived in.' And Professor Wade-Gery having explained this important distinction goes on to illustrate it by reference to Shakespeare:

In *Richard II*, and in *Richard III*, Shakespeare is something of a historian: these plays deal with the start and finish of a war which had directly created the world in which the poet lived. The *Iliad* does not: rather (as I have suggested) it resembles *Macbeth*. In *Macbeth*, Shakespeare has no concern with the results of the event —no serious concern: James's descent from Banquo is not a serious issue—his central concern is with the fact of the event, with the tragic experience of the characters.

From *King John* to *Henry VIII* Shakespeare is dealing with events that his audience could well understand as creating the world in which they were living. King John had lived nearly four hundred years earlier, but the struggle with the Papacy was a living issue, and the dynastic struggle that followed the deposition of Richard II was a terrible prelude to the rule of the Tudors. Neither Shakespeare nor his audience could look on the acts of Richard II or those of Richard III in the disinterested way that it was possible for an

Elizabethan or Jacobean to view the affairs of ancient Rome.

It might be said by way of objection to this distinction that the performance of *Coriolanus* in Paris just before the last European war was received so riotously that it clearly presented a living issue to the French, one not to be contemplated disinterestedly. This was, however, a political issue not a national issue that divided the audience, although this division no doubt affected the national will; and the political question in Shakespeare's play is only a background for the great sacrifice that saved Rome. Had the play been understood in the spirit in which it was written, who shall say how much folly and suffering might have been spared not only France but the world. This episode provides no parallel to the attitude of Shakespeare's audience: no one supposes that when at the end of *King John* the audience heard the lines

> Come the three corners of the world in arms
> And we shall shock them

many rose to their feet in protest at such bellicose or patriotic sentiments and set about attacking their neighbours or wrecking the theatre. Doubtless later critics in a more sophisticated generation, Hazlitt the life-long admirer of Napoleon, with Yeats and Shaw from Ireland, may disapprove of what has come to be called Shakespeare's jingoism. And it is certainly true as a distinguished American critic has said that 'No patriotic Frenchman of Elizabethan times and no internationalist of our own could watch the performance of such a play as *King Henry the Sixth* without having his sense of justice grossly wounded'. There is no doubt, as Shakespeare would have admitted himself, that he

takes advantage at times of the strong national feeling in his audience; but *1 Henry VI* is a very early piece written when Shakespeare was determined to get his audience with him, and if *Henry V* is later and yet not beyond criticism on the same score Shakespeare has himself provided mitigating circumstances.

The hero of the History plays, it has been said, is England, and it follows that the acts of a Richard or a Henry cannot be dissociated from their consequences to the nation. Shakespeare is not so concerned about the effect on Rome of the murder of Caesar as he is about what follows in England from the murder of Richard II. Brutus can be praised as the noblest Roman of them all, while Bolingbroke cannot forget the dangers to the country's peace his example may provoke. In *Julius Caesar* the tragic fate of Brutus is the main theme; in *Richard II* the King by his wanton neglect of the duty that England expects from all her sons, and not least from those in high estate, forfeits something of the sympathy the truly tragic figure evokes, and that although the tragic protagonist may be a more actively wicked man than Richard. A king of England is accountable to an English audience on a score a Roman soldier or an early king of Scotland is not; the result of this reckoning inevitably colours the reaction of the dramatist and his audience to his fate however unhappy that may prove, for they cannot be, at least could not be in Shakespeare's day, disinterested spectators of their country's fortune.

The editors of the First Folio, or those acting with their approval, arranged the Histories in the order suggested by their historical content, beginning with *King John* and ending with *Henry VIII*. We know from other sources that *Henry VIII* was the last play written

by Shakespeare; this, however, is a coincidence from which no general conclusion can be drawn about the order in which the Histories were composed.

The production of *King John* is assigned by E. K. Chambers to the winter of 1596–7, the years when Shakespeare was producing very different Histories in the two parts of *Henry IV*. There is, however, neither external nor internal evidence for the date suggested by Chambers, which seems to be merely the echo of an old notion that the lament of Constance for her son Arthur in the play gives expression to Shakespeare's feelings at the death of his son Hamnet in August 1596.

The suggestion that the piece dates from 1596 carries with it the corollary that Shakespeare was here rewriting more or less scene by scene an anonymous production that was printed in 1591 with the title *The Troublesome Raigne of King John*. This was described on the title-page as having been acted by 'the Queenes Majesties Players'.

The publication of *The Troublesome Raigne* was prompted by the publication of the two parts of *Tamburlaine* in 1590. In some verses addressed 'To The Gentlemen Readers' the author asks those who have applauded the infidel Tamburlaine 'to welcome (with like curtesie) A warlike Christian and your Countreyman'. And he continues,

> For Christs true faith indur'd he many a storme,
> And set himselfe against the Man of Rome.

asking his readers to think what follows 'was preparde for your disport'. As *Tamburlaine* was published in two parts, *The Troublesome Raigne* is also published in two parts, 'quite unnecessarily' as Professor Bullough observes 'for it was obviously written as one piece', the

division having no real theatrical or dramatic justification. The two parts of *Tamburlaine* are related much as the two parts of Shakespeare's *Henry IV*, and each part would be produced independently; the division of *The Troublesome Raigne* is merely the result of a mechanical form of imitation, for the parts could not be produced independently.

Not only does the author of *The Troublesome Raigne* adopt the two-part form of *Tamburlaine* in a strangely inappropriate way, he fills out his often very imperfect verse with phrases and passages suggested by his knowledge of Marlowe, and of Shakespeare; we cannot suppose Marlowe was in this matter borrowing from *The Troublesome Raigne*, and we can only suppose Shakespeare was doing so as long as we insist that Shakespeare only made his beginnings as a dramatist in 1591 or so. In spite, however, of the obvious *gaucherie* of the 1591 performance, this writer was able to lay out his action in a series of scenes so skilfully devised that Shakespeare had only to take over his arrangement with little alteration. Yet there is no known author in this early period who can match let alone compare with Shakespeare in his 'masterly development of the scenes', the one skill Tolstoy, a good judge in this technical matter, was willing to allow Shakespeare. How poorly Marlowe compared with Shakespeare in powers of construction Granville Barker's comparison of the plot of *Edward II* with *Richard II* is sufficient demonstration. Yet we are asked to regard the author of *The Troublesome Raigne* as capable of giving Shakespeare a lesson almost in his own speciality.

The assertion that in 1596 or 1597 Shakespeare followed *The Troublesome Raigne* so closely that he had no need to refer to Holinshed or any other chronicler

is equally surprising, as it is generally admitted that Shakespeare was well acquainted not only with Hall and Holinshed but frequently consulted other chroniclers as well. Professor Dover Wilson who regarded *The Troublesome Raigne* as Shakespeare's sole source finds himself in difficulties when he comes to *Richard II*. There is incorporated historical material taken not merely from English chronicles but directly, as Professor Dover Wilson thinks, from French sources which the English chroniclers themselves had used. To allow Shakespeare to have been so diligent a reader of history for *Richard II* and to confine him in *King John* to one eccentric source was, Professor Dover Wilson realized, hardly consistent or reasonable; he therefore postulates a source for *Richard II* similar to that for *King John*, and supposes that 'a "book" of King Richard the Second, by the same author as the learned historian, but very indifferent poet, who wrote the *Troublesome Reign of King John*, formed the basis of Shakespeare's play [*Richard II*]'. Here again, Professor Dover Wilson continues, speaking of *Richard II*, we have to ask 'Was Shakespeare a profound historical scholar or merely the reviser of such a scholar's play?' This question, however, conceals an assumption that makes any direct answer impossible, for even were *The Troublesome Raigne* an original work, its author was not a profound historical scholar. He had certainly done some reading in the Chronicles for himself, and he had a thesis to maintain as his address 'To The Gentlemen Readers' warns us; but it is crudely done. A profound historian need not show in dealing with beliefs and practices he cannot sympathize with the wit or irony of a Gibbon, but the scene in the monastery with the nun concealed in the chest and the friar in the press is conducted in a

M

style that hardly suggests the type of historian en-
visaged by Professor Dover Wilson:

How goes this geere? the Friers chest filde with a fausen
    Nunne.
The Nunne again locks Frier up, to keep him from the
    Sun.
Belike the presse is purgatorie, or penance passing
    grievous:
The Friers chest a hel for Nuns. How do these dolts
    deceive us!

To imagine what a play on Richard II from such a pen
would be like is to overtax our powers of conjecture.
To have to suppose that Shakespeare needed such an
intermediary between the chroniclers and his own
treatment of history seems a kind of *reductio ad absur-
dum* of Professor Dover Wilson's whole contention.

   As Mr Honigmann has argued, *King John* contains
historical points that cannot be found in *The Troublesome Raigne*, nor attributed to Shakespeare's invention.
The relationship between *King John* and *The Troublesome Raigne* is very like that between *King Lear* and
Leir. As long as commentators were satisfied that
Shakespeare spent his early years botching, as it used
to be called, the works of other dramatists, it was easy
to suppose that here too Shakespeare was the borrower.
Now, however, this cannot be taken for granted. On
the publication of *Lear* Shakespeare and his company
expressed their right to that piece in terms so explicit
that one may think they were indicating that *Leir* was
not the source of their production. For *King John* there
is no entry of any kind in the Stationers' Register before
its inclusion in the First Folio. Heminge and Condell
treated the publication of *The Troublesome Raigne* as

authorizing the printing of *King John*, a claim which could hardly have been maintained had *The Troublesome Raigne* been an original play by an author other than Shakespeare.

The answer to the relationship between the plays on John, as well as to that between those on Lear, seems to call for a knowledge of Shakespeare's early activities with the Queen's men that at present must remain conjecture only. Meantime it is not contrary to the evidence available to regard *The Troublesome Raigne* along with *Leir* as productions by imitators of Shakespeare, and not his sources. *The Troublesome Raigne* is not a bad quarto in the style of those put together by actors; it is the work of a man with a mission as well as an interest in the theatre, and one of his aims was to emphasize the patriotic note in Shakespeare's play by underlining in the crudest fashion the anti-Papal element that is inevitably present in any popular Elizabethan treatment of John's reign.

Shakespeare's play is not based on a profound historical knowledge of John's reign but made its contemporary appeal to two convictions commonly entertained at that time by intelligent Englishmen: the need for unity in face of foreign invasion; the danger of allowing Papal claims and policies to endanger national interests and security.

There is no mention of *Magna Carta*; that event in John's reign was to become a popular talking-point only when national independence having been securely established men could turn their minds to the difficult questions of enlarging civil liberty. Here again the appeal was not to any deep historical knowledge of the Charter but to what it was thought to stand for in the nation's social development.

King John becomes a protestant before the Reformation and a champion of England before the emergence of the idea of nationality in John Bale's *King Johan*. This historical morality was conceived in the reign of Henry VIII by a churchman who had become a determined opponent of Papal claims and a fierce critic of Rome's clerical representatives in England. In his play the King is poisoned by the monk Dissimulation; Nobility returns to its true allegiance, and Civil Order rejoices at the execution of Sedition by Imperial Majesty.

Shakespeare found it difficult to treat John as the representative figure later controversy had made him; he had therefore to create the character of the Bastard to support the national honour in spite of John's scheme to murder Arthur and his surrender to Pandulf. It is possible that *King John* was first drafted in the Armada years. It has no prose, little rhyme, and goes with a blank-verse group of pieces that belong to Shakespeare's early years; later touches may have been added but its political tone as well as its versification do not rule out a date before 1591 for its conception.

The first part of *Henry VI* treats of a series of events from the funeral of Henry V in November 1422 to the defeat and death of Talbot at Châtillon in July 1453, the encounter that ended the Hundred Years War.

Shakespeare, however, rearranges events within this period, and imagines others, entirely in the interest of his dramatic scheme. He represents Joan of Arc as present at the death of Talbot and indeed as one of the principal factors in his defeat, as no doubt she was, although she had been put to death in 1431 more than twenty years before Talbot's defeat. This free treatment of historical events is required by Shakespeare's theme,

which has at its heart the heroic struggles of Talbot, who can be overcome only by an enemy who is half a sorceress; and even against such metaphysical odds Talbot would have made headway but for the disgraceful rivalry between Somerset and York, who fail to provide the reinforcements he calls for. The feud of York and Somerset merely reflects the state of confusion and jealousy in England where Beaufort and Gloster quarrel over the custody of the child king.

That there was a highly popular play with Talbot as a central figure playing just before the plague closed the London theatres in the summer of 1592 is shown by a passage in Thomas Nashe's *Pierce Peniless His Supplication to the Devil* published about September 1592. Discussing and satirizing the various sins of mankind, Nashe defends in his section on Sloth the value of play-going as a form of recreation that may save a man from gambling or drabbing or drinking. It is the least harmful way of spending an idle afternoon. But this comparison, Nashe feels, does not do justice to the theatre, which he has been defending against its critics, and he continues:

Nay, what if I proove Playes to be no extreame; but a rare exercise of vertue? First, for the subject of them (for the most part) it is borrowed out of our English Chronicles, wherein our forefathers valiant acts (that have lain long buried in rustic brasse and worme-eaten bookes) are revived; and they themselves raised from the Grave of Oblivion, and brought to pleade their aged Honours in open presence: than which, what can be a sharper reproofe to these degenerate effeminate dayes of ours?

How would it have joyed brave *Talbot* (the Terror of the French) to thinke that after he had lyne two hundred yeares in his Tombe, hee should triumphe againe on the Stage, and have his bones newe embalmed with the

teares of ten thousand spectators at least (at severall times), who, in the Tragedian that represents his person, imagine they behold him fresh bleeding.

About the time Nashe was writing this note on a play with Talbot as its hero, there was playing at the Rose a piece described in Henslowe's *Diary* as 'harey the VI'. Its first performance there took place on 3 March 1592 and is marked by Henslowe as 'ne', that is a new or newly acquired piece; the takings were high on that occasion and the subsequent performances drew good houses; it was obviously a very popular play. The performers were Lord Strange's men reinforced by Edward Alleyn. As Shakespeare was at this time with Pembroke's men, and as the second and third parts of *Henry VI* belonged to that company, either 'harey the VI' was not by Shakespeare or Shakespeare had written it before he joined Pembroke's men, and a copy had passed from Shakespeare's earlier company to Strange's men. We know that after the failure of Pembroke's men in 1593 one of Shakespeare's plays, *Titus Andronicus*, was secured somehow for performance at the Rose; it is quite possible that 'harey the VI' had been written for the Queen's men, for there is some evidence that Shakespeare was connected with them before joining Pembroke's company. As Strange's men formed part of the Chamberlain's company that came together in 1594, 'harey the VI', if it was indeed Shakespeare's *1 Henry VI*, would be united with the second and third parts Shakespeare brought with him. It never appears in Henslowe's *Diary* after Strange's men left the Rose.

In *1 Henry VI* Shakespeare not merely emphasizes the rivalry between the English peers that leads to the loss of English possessions in France, he prepares for

the civil war in England that he is going to represent in his next play as following on the French disasters.

In the opening scene the funeral procession of Henry V is marred by the quarrelling of Gloster and Winchester; this is immediately followed by the successive entry of three messengers, the first announcing the loss of Paris and Rouen, the second the crowning of the Dauphin at Rheims, the third the defeat of Talbot at Patay, with the cowardice of Sir John Falstaff, and the capture of Talbot by the French. This is a sort of summary of the events of the next thirty years, some of which are re-enacted in later scenes of the play.

The Wars of the Roses that occupy the second and third parts of *Henry VI* are prepared for in the Temple Garden scene, where York and Somerset ask those listening to their dispute to signify their attitude either by plucking a white rose with York or a red rose with Somerset. This scene is immediately followed by one in which York's claim to the crown is foreshadowed: York's father had married Anne Mortimer, and the Mortimers were, through the marriage of Edmund Mortimer third Earl of March to Philippa daughter of the Duke of Clarence, descended from the third son of Edward III, while Henry VI was descended only from the fourth son, John of Gaunt Duke of Lancaster. In a later scene the King at his coronation in Paris has to deal with a dispute between adherents of York and Somerset; he takes the red rose from one of the disputants and to show the folly of quarrelling over such a trifle, and to demonstrate his own impartiality, wears it himself; York, however, feels that the King has taken a part against him.

Although at the end the French are supposed to be subdued, the whim that moves Henry to accept

Suffolk's advice and marry Margaret daughter of
Reignier, Duke of Anjou, prepares for the next part in
which the dissension that had brought about the death
of Talbot and the loss of France now leads to civil war.

That *1 Henry VI* as we now have it contains additions and alterations to bring it more closely into accord
with the two later parts of *Henry VI* is possible. From
the first, however, Shakespeare had in mind the effect
of baronial intrigue and selfishness not only in the
French field but in the affairs of England itself. *2 Henry
VI* begins with Queen Margaret's arrival in England
(1445) and ends with York's victory at the first battle
of St Albans (1455); while *3 Henry VI* carries on the
Wars of the Roses to the murder of Henry VI in the
Tower, after the rout of the Lancastrians at Tewkesbury (1471).

In *2 Henry VI* York is successful in depriving the
King of the services of the Protector, Humphrey Duke
of Gloucester, by 'winking at' the practices by which
the Queen, Suffolk, and their allies, deprive the 'good'
Duke of his power and then of his life. This murder is
followed by the banishment of Suffolk, who is slain on
his way to France, and the death of Cardinal Beaufort.
York having been given command in Ireland returns
with his forces to defeat the Queen and her allies in the
opening battle of the civil war. The main lines of the
action are laid out with the utmost clarity, from York's
detailed claim through the Mortimers to be the heir of
Lionel the third son of Edward III, to the clever exploitation of the opportunities provided by the conduct
of his opponents.

Of the numerous episodes fitted into the dynastic
struggle the Jack Cade rebellion is the most extended
and vivid. Cade has been encouraged by York, and the

behaviour of the rebels allows the dramatist to emphasize another aspect of the violence and destruction that is inevitable when those responsible for law and order are weak or indifferent. This episode is complemented by the scene in *3 Henry VI* in which during the battle of Towton a father finds he has slain his son, and a son discovers that the man he has killed and intends to plunder is his father. As R. W. Chambers has shown in his masterly discussion of the 147 lines in the manuscript of *Sir Thomas More*, which describe More's pacification of the May-day rioters, the treatment of the humours of insurrection, and the unhappy consequences for the humble citizen of disorder and riot in *2* and *3 Henry VI*, has on it the unmistakable impress of Shakespeare's hand. If the emphasis in *1 Henry VI* was on the destruction of the nation's power by faction and jealousy among its leaders, in *2* and *3 Henry VI* the same causes are seen as equally destructive of individual happiness. And the King who should maintain the peace can only look on at the sufferings of his subjects and weep.

Towards the conclusion of *2 Henry VI* and notably at the battle of St Albans York's son Richard, the future Richard III, makes a characteristic appearance, his sentiments and his actions anticipating his later style. Richard was at the time of the battle of St Albans not yet three years of age; Shakespeare, however, is looking forward to the part he is already planning for Richard in the sequel.

With the death of York at Wakefield early in *3 Henry VI* his son Richard, who had been his father's determined supporter, now follows a course somewhat similar to his father's in eliminating those who stand between himself and the crown; in his comments on

his eldest brother Edward's decision to marry Lady Grey (III. ii. 124–95) he muses on his prospects and his ability to 'set the murderous Machiavel to school'. With the dispatch of Prince Edward after Tewkesbury, and the murder of Henry VI in the Tower, the ground is partially cleared; and before the end of *3 Henry VI* Clarence is already marked down for removal.

From the first part of *Henry VI* Shakespeare had a clear idea of the scheme he intended to develop; and in the second and third parts dealing with the affairs of that reign the dramatist had obviously in mind the sequel that was to take shape in *Richard III*. The pirated versions of *2* and *3 Henry VI* put together by actors after the break-up of Pembroke's company in 1593, although recognized by Johnson as 'surreptitiously obtained' and proved so by Thomas Kenny in 1864, continued for long to be regarded, owing to the weight attached to Malone's opinion, as original versions by Greene and his associates that Shakespeare had revised. Yet the very scene in which York expounds his claim to the crown, *2 Henry VI*, II. ii, is so ill-reported in *The Contention*, the surreptitious version of 1594, that the pirate completely misrepresents the case on which the Yorkist claim to the crown was based. Such a misconception of the very facts that provide the key to the subsequent complications could not be attributed to the author designing the whole scheme. E. K. Chambers latterly recognized that *The Contention* and its sequel *The True Tragedy of Richard Duke of York* (1595) were stolen and surreptitious versions, too late, however, to allow him to revise a chronology that had been based on Malone's unhappy adoption of Farmer's misrepresentations. Professor Dover Wilson, however, while satisfied that *The Contention* and *The*

True Tragedy are imperfect reports of *2* and *3 Henry VI* still accepts one part of Malone's argument. Malone had treated what are now regarded as the bad quartos of *2* and *3 Henry VI* as original compositions by Greene and his associates; Professor Dover Wilson now transposes this suggestion, no longer tenable for *The Contention* and *The True Tragedy*, to *2* and *3 Henry VI*, and treats the whole scheme as developed in the three parts of *Henry VI* as largely designed by Greene, with Nashe, Peele, and latterly Shakespeare, filling in or developing the plot thus sketched for them. Professor Dover Wilson finds what may be called external support for his opinion in Greene's attack on Shakespeare, although the most obvious feature of that attack is Greene's scornful reference to a line from *3 Henry VI* as typical of Shakespeare's bombastic manner.

Even, however, if the interpretation of Greene's words advanced in an earlier chapter is accepted as supporting the attribution by Heminge and Condell of the *Henry VI* plays to Shakespeare, there still remains, Professor Dover Wilson insists, a passage in a volume issued less than eighteen months after Greene's death entitled *Greenes Funeralls* that may have some bearing on the question. This contains fourteen 'Sonnets', although the term here means no more than short pieces of verse; xiii and xiv are from the Psalms in classical metre added by the learned Richard Stanyhurst to his somewhat grotesque version of Virgil, the excuse for their inclusion among the 'Sonnets' being their use by Greene on his death-bed, a statement for which one might wish some confirmation. *The Repentance of Robert Greene* published in 1592 provides a different set of petitions. The other twelve pieces are attributed to '*R.B. Gent.*', who unfortunately cannot be

identified with any certainty. R.B.'s contribution is a strange gallimaufry or hotchpotch of sentiments. In the first sonnet we are told

> Nor Mouth, nor Minde, nor Muse can halfe declare
> His Life, his Love, his Laude, so excellent they were.

Yet in the twelfth Greene is called a 'sinfull offender', and his age here on earth described as a loathsome

> Puddle of filthynes, inly poluted
> With all abuse.

The stanza cited as supporting Greene's part in *Henry VI* opens sonnet ix:

> Greene, is the pleasing Obiect of an eie:
> Greene, pleasde the eies of all that lookt uppon him.
> Greene, is the ground of everie Painters die:
> Greene, gave the ground to all that wrote upon him.
> Nay more the men, that so Eclipst his fame:
> Purloynde his Plumes, can they deny the same?

Who are the men that 'eclipst' Greene's fame?—other dramatists or the actors? To say this is a contemporary's interpretation of Greene's attack does not give it any authority; R.B. is clearly a muddle-headed sort, and his interpretation, if it is so, of what Nashe called a lying pamphlet, itself needs interpretation. Only those who have satisfied themselves on other grounds that Shakespeare was in the *Henry VI* plays rewriting or revising Greene's work can regard R.B. as referring to Shakespeare.

The evidence for Shakespeare's authorship of the *Henry VI* plays lies not merely in the assertion by his colleagues Heminge and Condell that these were among Shakespeare's works; their testimony alone would be

sufficient to let us dismiss R.B.'s statements as in-applicable to Shakespeare, although we know from Nashe that Greene did plan pieces he wrote in colla-boration with his associates. The testimony of Heminge and Condell is, however, confirmed by the structure of the pieces themselves; there is nothing in any play that can be attributed to Greene of the coherence and drive with which Shakespeare makes his way through the events of the reign. In these pieces there is, as Professor Hereward Price has emphasized in his *Con-struction in Shakespeare*, not merely a series of happen-ings but an idea that gives the work a design and shape. Compared with his later masterpieces the *Henry VI* parts are no doubt less closely organized, but one can already feel the grip on his material that gives *Richard III* into which the *Henry VI* parts naturally lead so clear and forcible an appeal.

Two minor points confirm the Folio editors' attribu-tion to Shakespeare of these pieces. Shakespeare's use of the Chronicles, Hall, Holinshed, and others from time to time, continues throughout his life as a drama-tist and can be illustrated in *Henry VIII*, the last play he wrote. In *Henry VI* we have an early but charac-teristic handling of this material that cannot be matched by any contemporary who dramatized English history. The assertion sometimes made that, since Talbot is not mentioned in *2* and *3 Henry VI*, although he was alive and active till 1453, while the historical time of the opening scene of *2 Henry VI* with Margaret's arrival in England is 1445, these later parts cannot be by the author of the Talbot play, is to ignore Shakespeare's dramatic strategy. He disposes of affairs in France in *1 Henry VI*; to recall Talbot as he leads into the Wars of the Roses would merely confuse the minds of

spectators who had already witnessed his death in
1 Henry VI, and any attempt to explain the true historical sequence would have distracted attention from
the immediate issue, the civil strife in England. To
say nothing about Talbot in this connexion was a wise
stroke of dramatic economy. That *2* and *3 Henry VI*
were plays written for Pembroke's company, as the
pirated versions indicate, rules out Greene and the
collaborators associated with him, for there is nothing
to connect them with that company.

Richard III opens on a note already prominent in
2 Henry VI with Richard's determination to set about
disposing of Clarence before the death of Edward IV,
which is represented as imminent. By the end of Act I
Clarence is dead, his body thrown into a malmsey-
butt in the Tower; by the end of Act II—Edward IV
having died—the Queen's kindred have been arrested
and sent to Pomfret for execution; by the end of Act
III Hastings who refused to put aside the right to the
throne of Edward IV's son is disposed of, and Richard
accepts the invitation, engineered by Buckingham, to
receive the crown; by the end of Act IV Buckingham
who would not agree to the murder of the young
princes, sons of Edward IV, is a prisoner waiting execution. Meantime the princes have been murdered in
the Tower. Act V takes us to the battle at Bosworth,
the defeat and death of Richard, and the crowning on
the field of Richmond as Henry VII.

With the end at Bosworth and the establishment of
the Tudors as the inevitable conclusion that must have
been in the minds of his audience, however vaguely,
Shakespeare could exploit without restraint the clever
moves of a ruthless intriguer. Shakespeare is careful not to present the princes in the Tower and their

murder in the direct and open manner in which he puts the imprisonment and death of Clarence before us. To have dwelt on the death of the children except indirectly would have darkened overmuch the figure on which the interest is focused. Richard is the cynical, ironic realist, who sees the vulnerable side of those who would thwart him and finds a keen satisfaction in overreaching them and making them the objects of his sardonic mirth. As with the exception of the young princes and Lady Anne, those on whom Richard practises are themselves intriguers for place and power, their defeat appeals to us more as examples of Richard's dexterous timing than as instances of his victims' personal misfortune. There is just something, in our reaction to Richard's brutalities, of the way we witness the crimes of Punch in the Punch and Judy show, knowing Jack Ketch is waiting his turn to play his part in the performance. As children can watch without dismay the career and fate of the hunch-backed puppet, so audiences follow with interest the doings of Richard Crook-back, knowing as they do that in the end he will himself be brought to justice.

Shakespeare's portrait of Richard was in part suggested to him by the account of Richard left by Sir Thomas More; this is found in a Latin as well as an English version, both by More himself. Holinshed incorporated the English version as printed by John Rastell, More's nephew, in 1557; to the English text, however, Rastell had added short passages translated from the Latin version. Hall had earlier printed the English version but in an imperfect form. More had in his youth been attached to the household of Cardinal Morton. Morton, made Archbishop of Canterbury by Henry VII, was Bishop of Ely in Richard's reign and is

so represented in Shakespeare's play. Although More
was only seven years old or so at Richard's death he
would learn from Morton, as well as from his father
and his father's London contemporaries, what they
believed about Richard's rule. From Morton must
come the incident in III. iv where Richard asks Morton
to send for some strawberries from his garden in
Holborn. Later Richard appears at the Council and,
displaying his withered arm, attributes its condition to
the witchcraft of Jane Shore, and accuses Hastings,
who since the death of King Edward had kept Shore's
wife, of treason. The suggestion now is that what
Richard must have done was to eat the strawberries
knowing he was liable to strawberry rash, and that it
was this condition he showed to the Council as his
excuse for ordering the execution of Hastings. As everyone knew Richard's arm was deformed from birth,
some new condition would surely have been required.
The ironic and grimly humorous tone which More gives
his narrative, Shakespeare transfers to Richard himself,
and does not hesitate to add what may be regarded as
a comic setting to some of the Protector's most shameless devices.

There is an amusing passage in III. v in which
Gloucester, about to deceive the Lord Mayor, asks
Buckingham, who is to play a part in the deception,
about his capacity to act the role of one threatened by
sudden danger. Buckingham answers in the same vein,

> Tut, I can counterfeit the deep tragedian;
> Speak and look back, and pry on every side,
> Tremble and start at wagging of a straw,
> Intending deep suspicion.

Not, as Lamb observed, that the player impersonating

Richard is to act throughout in any such exaggerated fashion. Instead he should show 'the silent confidence, and steady self-command of the *experienced politician*' as well as the habitual jocularity that accompanies his amused contempt for the victims of his machinations. His very deformities provide him with the satisfaction of having turned them into advantages. Shakespeare was presenting his audience with a murderer, but as Lamb insisted, a 'man of vast capacity,—the profound, the witty, accomplished Richard'.

With *Richard II* Shakespeare opens a new cycle of Histories. Harking back to the event that made a breach in the established order of government, the deposition of Richard II, and that eventually allowed the entry of the tide of civil war in which Henry VI perished, Shakespeare in *Richard II*, *1* and *2 Henry IV*, and *Henry V*, covers the historical events that lie between Richard's disposal of his uncle Gloucester and the accession of Henry VI.

The theatrical representation of events that might be regarded as reflecting unfavourably on the continuance or stability of established government was naturally discouraged by the Master of the Revels. The publication in 1593 of Marlowe's *Edward II* did not seem to disturb the licensing authority, but when a quarto edition of *Richard II* was issued in 1597, the abdication scene, IV. i. 154–318, was omitted, and not restored till the reign of James I, when the question of the succession that so troubled the last years of Elizabeth's reign was answered. Yet this scene seems to have been allowed on the stage, for partisans of Essex had the play performed at the Globe on 7 February 1601, the day before Essex made his attempt to raise London against the government. The players were unwilling

N

to produce the piece, not because they suspected it was to be used to encourage the people to support a rebellion, but because it was an old play dating at least from 1595 and unlikely to attract a good audience. Only the offer of forty shillings above the takings at the doors had induced the company to substitute *Richard II* for the play they had intended to perform. So Augustine Phillips, who represented his fellows, explained to the Court that was investigating the circumstances of the rising of 8 February. The play performed on 7 February must have included the abdication scene, one would think, if the conspirators were to get value for their money. While the Court accepted the explanation offered by Phillips, the Queen no doubt to remind the actors of their indiscretion had the Chamberlain's men perform before her on 24 February, the evening before the execution of Essex.

Not only was the performance of 7 February cited at the trial of Essex as evidence of his treasonable intentions, the Queen herself spoke of it later in the year in the same strain to William Lambarde. Not long after his appointment as custodian of the records kept in the Tower, Lambarde, in August 1601, was giving to the Queen at Greenwich an account of the documents in his charge. When they came to those dealing with the reign of Richard II, the Queen exclaimed 'I am Richard II, know ye not that'. Lambarde understood the reference to Essex and his attempt to raise London, and to the comment on the Earl's ingratitude that this reference drew from Lambarde the Queen added: 'He that will forget God, will also forget his benefactors; this tragedy was played forty times in open streets and houses.'

Yet the play has been regarded in recent years as

evidence of Shakespeare's belief in, or at least favourable attitude towards, the doctrine of the divine right of kings. When the Queen talked of Essex forgetting God she may have been thinking of the ruler as God's deputy. Hooker in his *Ecclesiastical Polity* expressed the position in these words: 'Unto Kings by human right, Honour by divine right, is due; man's Ordinances are many times proposed as grounds in the Statutes of God.' That Shakespeare would have subscribed to Hooker's position many references in his works suggest; but Hooker is not an advocate of 'divine right' in the extreme sense in which it was to be interpreted by James. Nor need we regard Shakespeare as of that persuasion either, because he gives the Bishop of Carlisle, as he protests in IV. i. against Bolingbroke's action, words implying that the King is in no way accountable for his actions to his subjects. That we should take the Bishop's words as expressing Shakespeare's own views, because the prophecy that civil war will follow any violation of the King's authority is in fact fulfilled, will not, however, bear examination. Antony in *Julius Caesar* makes a similar prophecy over the dead body of Caesar without our attributing divine right to Caesar. The removal of authority inevitably endangers the conduct of affairs in a state, whatever the origin of that authority; and Richard as the last direct descendant from the Conqueror had a very special claim on the allegiance of his subjects. It was natural that such a break in the continuity of rule should have a more than ordinary sequel.

Yet however special Richard's personal claim on the spectator's sympathies, there was another claim even more paramount in the mind of the dramatist and his audience. This is illustrated in the discussion between

the gardeners in III. iv. The man who will not cultivate his garden, who allows it to go unweeded, and leaves its wholesome herbs swarming with caterpillars, must expect to be replaced. And this, like one of those every-day illustrations with which Socrates used to bring home to his hearers the vital aspects of human conduct, is an obvious corollary to the dying Gaunt's exhortation to Richard to remember his responsibility to England.

Like Clarence's dream in *Richard III*, Gaunt's descant on the theme of king and country is a very special episode in the development of the idea informing the play. The seizure of Gaunt's estate is the characteristic response Richard makes to such exhortation. Here is one of those mistakes that is in material consequences worse than a crime. As York reminds the King, this act is an injury to his own rights,

> for how art thou a King
> But by fair sequence and succession?

Richard is with his own hands, as it were, destroying the very bonds that entitle him to inherit the estate of his ancestors. He challenges his own claims at the same time as he provokes a protest from Bolingbroke that he cannot answer. It is useless for the man who has taken by force the estates of Bolingbroke to complain when he himself is deprived of his ancestral inheritance. There is no such thing as divine right to do wrong.

Yet although we cannot take this play as Shakespeare's subscription to the doctrine of divine right, Essex and his partisans, and those to whom Elizabeth herself referred, were as ill-advised in regarding it as a precedent for rebellion. Even in *Richard II* itself Bolingbroke feels he has acted, in part at least, as one

driven by circumstances. By the time of the Essex
rising, Shakespeare had further emphasized the unhappy aspects of the deposition of Richard, not only
in both parts of *Henry IV*, but even in *Henry V* just
before the return of Essex from Ireland in 1599. In the
hour of suspense before the battle Henry prays that his
father's act may not be visited on his forces.

In his study of Richard, the dramatist found a theme
that exists in a special form in a ruler with the King's
responsibilities: the contrast or harmony between what
may be called the public and the private life of the individual, a contrast that is almost baffling in the fate
of this gifted but unhappy man. Shakespeare especially
in the Roman plays was to find his interest in a somewhat similar contrast; but although the dramatist did
his best to hold the balance fair between the contending
forces in Richard's soul, and drew, either indirectly
through Holinshed, or even directly, as Professor
Dover Wilson has argued, on French sources, where
Richard is presented as a saint and martyr, there remains an impediment to a completely disinterested
treatment of his acts. Richard was a martyr, if one will,
to his own temperament, but he was not as a king a
blessing to his country.

Shakespeare followed the progress of Bolingbroke
into *Henry IV*, but the dramatist's style and interests
were developing rapidly, and there is a freer treatment
of the historical material in the interest of a new motif.
Bolingbroke while admirable as a foil to the more
passionate Richard was not himself a promising protagonist. He could hardly now provide the cause for the
movement and change from one state to another, without which there can be no drama; this was to be the
part assigned to the Prince of Wales, who would in

carrying forward the action through this reign be pro-
gressing towards the triumphant conclusion of his own
rule as king.

Holinshed, following earlier writers, touches briefly
on the King's displeasure with the conduct of the
Prince, who is reported as associating with 'misrulie
mates of dissolute order and life'; and Holinshed also
mentions the story of how the Prince at the trial of one
of his minions struck the Chief Justice on the bench
and was himself committed to prison. At his coronation, however, Henry determines 'to put on him the
shape of a new man' and banish (suitable financial provision having been made) his former companions. This
is the change on which the action of the two parts of
Henry IV turns.

The reform of the prodigal is naturally a popular
theme, but the Prince's change of heart has been treated
by some modern commentators as a heartless example
of expediency, and his after-the-coronation lecture to
Falstaff on the need for good behaviour worthy of
Machiavelli's Prince. Macaulay's comparison of Frederic the Great's conduct on his accession to that of
Shakespeare's Henry V might be used to illustrate
Wilde's jest about Life imitating Art:

The disappointment of Falstaff at his old boon-com-
panion's coronation was not more bitter than that which
awaited some of the inmates of Rheinsberg. They had
long looked forward to the accession of their patron, as
to the event from which their own prosperity and greatness was to date. They had at last reached the promised
land, the land which they had figured to themselves as
flowing with milk and honey; and they found it a desert.
'No more of these fooleries', was the short, sharp admonition given by Frederic to one of them.

No one doubts that Frederic had long meditated, even as he played the intellectual voluptuary at Rheinsberg, the life of industry and aggression that marked his rule as king. Shakespeare, it has been argued, saw the same dissimulation in Henry, for the first scene in which he appears contains his assurance that he is merely amusing himself with Falstaff and the others, so that his emergence as the true prince may be the more spectacular and arresting:

> I'll so offend to make offence a skill
> Redeeming time when men think least I will.

Nothing could be less like the prodigal son of the parable, or resemble more nearly the attitude of Frederic to his unsuspecting associates.

Yet to treat the Prince's soliloquy as Shakespeare's notion of the art of preparing for the dénouement he was planning is to suppose him as ignorant of his business as Rymer and those of his persuasion have argued. 'The art of preparation,' as Mr Percy Lubbock observes,

is no art if it betrays itself at the outset, calling attention to its purpose. By definition it is unrecognizable until it attains its end; it is the art of rendering an impression that is found to have been made later on, but that evades detection at the moment.

To illustrate this art from Shakespeare would be simple. At the opening of *Henry IV*, however, Shakespeare found himself with an assignment that made any attempt to untie, however cleverly, the knot of the complications in which he was to involve the Prince beyond even his skill; in this emergency he indicates baldly how the knot is to be cut. This liberty, however lacking in art, was made possible by Shakespeare's confidence

that his audience would be ready to interpret the
Prince's acts for the best. Yeats's remark that the
Elizabethans had the admiration for Henry 'that school-
boys have for the sailor or soldier hero of a romance in
some boys' paper' requires to be qualified by the fact
that the Elizabethans were adult enough to know that
Henry was indeed the victor of Agincourt. To make
sure that the Prince's enjoyment of the irregular
humorists would not be considered derogatory to his
dignity Shakespeare disclosed his plan. The public enjoyed the comedy unreservedly, and even the Queen
herself, who was not indifferent in matters of decorum,
could command, if tradition can be trusted, the further
appearance of Falstaff. Shakespeare, however, was careful to confine Falstaff in *The Merry Wives of Windsor*
to less exalted society than that in which royal personages moved.

The two parts of *Henry IV* are not then to be judged
by the same canons as *Coriolanus* or *Macbeth*. The
national prejudices of his audience were part of Shakespeare's context here; in a later generation Yeats may
regard Henry's successes as the result of his common-
place vices, but such a point of view would hardly have
been intelligible to the Elizabethans, not because they
were obtuse or without humane feelings but because
Henry was the kind of man they felt their country
needed. They could not help enjoying Falstaff; yet like
Mistress Quickly, even while their hearts went out to
Falstaff, they felt with her 'The King is a good king'.

Mistress Quickly's feelings may be those of a somewhat simple soul, but all efforts to resolve the contra-
dictions of her verdict end in confusion. The attempt
to write down Falstaff is as damaging to the dramatic
interest as to treat the Prince as a blackguard. To play

down Falstaff or represent the Prince as an unwilling or half-hearted partner in their goings-on is to deprive the Prince of half of his vitality. As Maurice Morgann observes: 'the Prince is supposed to possess a high relish of humour and to have a temper and a force about him which, whatever his pursuit, delighted in excess.'

If in Falstaff Shakespeare found for the Prince a companion who provided one form of excess in which he could find delight, Hotspur embodied another extreme form of activity in which the Prince also excels.

As a portrait of a fearless irascible fighting man Hotspur is hard to match. His hearty dislike of the lord who turned up after the battle fresh as a bridegroom to demand the prisoners is as characteristic as his impatience with Glendower's calling 'spirits from the vasty deep'. His reply 'But will they come when you do call for them?' shows the touch of dry wit men of his kind often have. His scheme to divide up the country with Mortimer and Glendower is as irresponsible and more dangerous than any of Falstaff's pranks. Almost inevitably he finds himself at Shrewsbury unsupported by his father and Glendower. Though even the Douglas feels their absence serious Hotspur is his sanguine self: 'Doomsday is near; die all, die merrily.'

By the end of the first part the Prince has redeemed his promise to his father and made his reputation as a soldier.

Shakespeare had no doubt planned his second series of Histories more or less on the lines of the *Henry VI–Richard III* cycle. How far when he was writing one part he foresaw the next is a question suggested by the relation of the two parts of *Henry IV*. Some feel they should be taken together as one play, and certainly the Prince's promise to give up Falstaff and his hangers-on

is not fulfilled till the very end of part two. On the other hand the Prince and his father seem fully reconciled at Shrewsbury. The renewed differences in part two leave the impression that they are revived merely for the dramatist's convenience; in spite of the King's assurance of his son's devotion, the dramatist requires continued doubts and fears to make the closing stages effective, otherwise the scene between the Prince and his dying father would lack motive. Again the campaigning episodes seem like feebler copies of the earlier incidents, except that the preliminaries give us a closer view of Falstaff's practices. At Shrewsbury Falstaff turned up with a set of recruits that the Prince described as 'pitiful rascals'. In the second part we see Falstaff in the very act of raising a new company, and the dishonesty that was only hinted at before is now exposed in detail, as Falstaff allows those who can pay to buy their exemption and presses only those too poor to bribe him. His relations with Mistress Quickly in the second part are also more unhappy and disreputable than before. Indeed the second part is largely given up to the affairs of Falstaff and the doings that may persuade us to accept his banishment from the new king's entourage as not merely reasonable but necessary. To enforce this aspect of Falstaff's fortunes Shakespeare shows his dealings with a new set of characters, on one side Justice Shallow and his cousin Silence to provide fresh victims for Falstaff's bag, and on the other the Lord Chief Justice to deal with an individual who had come to think the laws of England were at his commandment. It is the fortune of Falstaff that provides the feeling of continuity in the second part; the historical material is adjusted somewhat perfunctorily to give this a plausible setting.

The wonderful party in Justice Shallow's orchard that is brought to a sudden and hectic end by the arrival of Pistol and his news of the death of Henry IV, the spectator has been able to view with the knowledge that the King is dead; so that when Falstaff exclaims 'Woe to my Lord Chief Justice', we are reminded of the previous scene in which the new king has confirmed the appointment of that officer, although this was the judge who had committed him as Prince of Wales to prison. By this act Shakespeare leaves us to understand for ourselves what Burke said of Cromwell's choice of Hale for his Chief Justice. That great lawyer refused to acknowledge the legality of Cromwell's government, but in reply Cromwell merely required that he administer in accordance with his wisdom and character that justice without which human society cannot subsist. With this example of the new king's zeal for civil order, the optimistic words with which Pistol, at the end of Shallow's party, welcomes the future

'Where is the life that late I led?' say they.
Why here it is; welcome these pleasant days.

naturally leave us wondering about the days ahead. And we are not surprised when the Lord Chief Justice shapes the future on somewhat different lines from those contemplated by the tipplers in Shallow's orchard, and the party from Gloucestershire ends up in the Fleet.

In the Epilogue to 2 *Henry IV* Shakespeare refers obliquely to the substitution of the name Falstaff for that of Oldcastle; as Sir John Oldcastle was a Lollard and had suffered death in the reign of Henry V, Shakespeare could refer to him as a martyr. Oldcastle

had married a Cobham, and that family had doubtless
protested about the abuse of their ancestor's name.
William Brooke, the seventh Lord Cobham, was Lord
Chamberlain from July 1596 to his death in March
1597, and it may have been during his period of office
that the change was made.

In *Henry V* Shakespeare reaches the triumphant
conclusion to the story he had begun in *Richard II*; yet
few if any of his pieces have met with such severe
condemnation—it has even been described as the worst
in the canon. The reasons are not far to seek: it is the
most English of the Histories and might well seem to
a Frenchman on a level with *1 Henry VI*, where Talbot
plays the part of the terror of the French. Yet many
English critics share this disapproval and the ground
of their displeasure is perhaps best indicated by Bernard Shaw, who, though Irish, speaks here as a dramatist. The characters, Shaw feels, 'are labelled and
described and insisted on with the roughest directness',
so much so that this directness defeats its purpose. As
Tolstoy said: 'Every one knows the feeling of distrust
and resistance always evoked by an author's evident
predetermination. A narrator need only say in advance,
"Prepare to cry", or "to laugh", and you are sure
neither to cry nor to laugh.' The order 'Prepare to be
patriotic' is doubless no less stultifying. Even in *Henry
IV* the Prince's conduct has to be seen from a specially
selected standpoint, if he is not to appear more than
something of a Philistine; but it was because Shakespeare could judge just where his audience would stand
that he showed them the Prince as he did. As *Henry V*
taxes even further the prejudices, prejudice being
understood as Burke defined it, of his countrymen,
Shakespeare gave his piece a special form, introducing

each Act with a chorus, and shaping the action in some respects more like a pageant than a play. In a pageant local and patriotic sentiment may find direct and blameless expression. Just as the man who dropped in France by parachute in the small hours of D Day could quote Henry's remark on 'gentlemen in England now-a-bed', as he thought of what they were missing, without being treated as a Jingo. Few will dispute the right of the Elizabethans to enjoy this presentation of a ruler who seemed to them 'a paterne in princehood, a lode-starre in honour and mirror of magnificence'. The Chronicles speak of Henry in terms resembling those in which Shakespeare himself in his last History, and indeed in his last play of all, was to speak of the Queen in whose reign he himself was born and grew to manhood: 'faithful to his friends, and fierce to his enemies, towards God most devout, and to his realm a very father.'

The play is generally dated by the expression in the Prologue to Act V of the hope that Essex will be successful in his Irish campaign and return to enjoy the welcome with which London would receive him. Essex left for Ireland in March 1599 amid the cheering citizenry and returned secretly and in defiance of the Queen's instructions in September of the same year, having made no headway against Tyrone.

An anonymous publication called *The Famous Victories of Henry the Fifth* is dated 1598. This was entered to Thomas Creede in the Stationers' Register on 14 May 1594, but no edition is known earlier than that dated 1598, which attributes it to the old Queen's company. It treats in most uncouth form events that are also found in Shakespeare's *Henry IV* and *Henry V*, and is generally considered a debased version of pieces

that may go back as far as Tarlton's day. *Tarlton's Jests* describes Tarlton's part in the scene in which Henry gives the Chief Justice a box on the ear; this scene is presented in *The Famous Victories*. Tarlton died in 1588; any version of *Henry V* he played in must therefore be early; the earliest extant edition of the *Jests*, however, is dated 1638. The relationship between *The Famous Victories* and Shakespeare's *Henry IV* and *Henry V*, though *The Famous Victories* is generally regarded as one of Shakespeare's sources, remains a puzzling one. *The Famous Victories* goes with the other source pieces that are associated with the Queen's company and that still present a problem alike to the historian of the drama and to the textual scholar.

The earliest references to *Henry VIII* are found in letters written not because Shakespeare after two years' silence had produced a new play, but because at a performance of *Henry VIII* at the Globe on 29 June 1613 the theatre was burnt to the ground. Writing to Sir Edmund Bacon on 2 July 1613 Sir Henry Wotton describes the disaster in easy and humorous fashion:

Now to let matters of state sleep, I will entertain you at the present with what has happened this week at the Bank's side. The King's players had a new play called *All is True*, representing some principal pieces of the reign of Henry VIII, which was set forth with many extraordinary circumstances of pomp and majesty, even to the matting of the stage; the Knights of the Order with their Georges and garter, the Guards with their embroidered coats, and the like: sufficient in truth within a while to make greatness very familiar, if not ridiculous. Now, King Henry making a masque at the Cardinal Wolsey's house, and certain chambers being shot off at his entry, some of the paper, or other stuff, wherewith one of them was stopped, did light on the thatch, where

being thought at first but an idle smoke, and their eyes more attentive to the show, it kindled inwardly, and ran round like a train, consuming within less than an hour the whole house to the very grounds.

This was the fatal period of that virtuous fabric, wherein yet nothing did perish but wood and straw, and a few forsaken cloaks; only one man had his breeches set on fire, that would perhaps have broiled him, if he had not by the benefit of a provident wit put it out with bottle ale.

That this was Shakespeare's *Henry VIII* other references to the event make clear, and in the Prologue itself the phrase 'our chosen truth' supports the conclusion that *All is True* was the alternative or sub-title. That what Wotton regarded as the almost offensive extravagance of the production would be natural, if Shakespeare had been persuaded to return to take yet another farewell, is also evident.

At a time when less respect was paid to the statement by Heminge and Condell that they were editing Shakespeare's plays, and when what E. K. Chambers called the disintegration of Shakespeare was the fashion, there were those who felt that Shakespeare, had he been indeed the author, would have written *Henry VIII* on very different lines from those we find in the First Folio version. Some found it difficult to believe Shakespeare could have allowed the praise of Elizabeth to be expressed so fervently in the reign of a successor who cherished no love for her memory; some could not understand how the dramatist who treated Catherine's misfortune so sympathetically looked upon the birth of Elizabeth as a blessing to her country; and Spedding ventured to think that, had Shakespeare written the play, 'the final separation of the English from the

Romish Church . . . would naturally be chosen as the focus of poetic interest'. Such opinions, telling Shakespeare how it should be done, of which those mentioned here are merely random samples, have no critical value; and the commonly accepted division of the play between Shakespeare and Fletcher must rest on the metrical and linguistic evidence by which the division is effected.

It is impossible to discuss in detail the material evidence; the opposing views may be found in the respective editions by Mr J. C. Maxwell and Mr R. A. Foakes. One illustration only of the manner in which the evidence is so regularly interpreted on an assumption that is taken for granted may suffice. Examining the ratio of final monosyllables to the total of feminine endings, Mr Maxwell gives the following percentages, after Mr Ants Oras: *Cymbeline* 18, *Winter's Tale* 20, *Tempest* 23, *Valentinian* 32, *Bonduca* 30, *Monsieur Thomas* 42. He then finds that in *Henry VIII* for the whole play the percentage is 24. That would seem to agree with the gradual progression from 18 in *Cymbeline* to 23 in *The Tempest*, and to differ decisively from the figures for Fletcher. But Mr Maxwell argues that we can divide *Henry VIII* into two parts in which the percentages are 14 and 29 respectively, and so assign the lower percentage to Shakespeare, the higher to Fletcher. This, however, rests on the assumption that ratios of this sort will be uniform throughout a play, although he goes on to point out that Shakespeare may use such a device for a special purpose, even to distinguish a particular character. In short Mr Oras' figures do not rule out Shakespeare's sole authorship.

Mr Maxwell puts the matter comprehensively in one question: Assuming that Fletcher did write as much of

the play as Shakespeare, what do we think Heminge and Condell would have done with it? The answer is simple: they would have omitted it, as they omitted *Pericles*, and *The Two Noble Kinsmen*, as well as other pieces in which Shakespeare may have had only a share.

The evidence of Shakespeare's hand in the very passages that are denied him is obvious. The Prologue begins: 'I come no more to make you laugh.' This according to Mr Maxwell merely indicates that the last play was a comedy, an explanation that hardly explains the phrase 'no more', for we cannot suppose that an anonymous Prologue was promising no more comedies. Yet Shakespeare, in spite of his fame in tragedy, was regarded even by his father, if the report of what he said in his shop is true, as a wit, though his father felt he could cope with him; and the very well instructed writer of the remarks prefixed to the second issue of *Troilus and Cressida* insists on Shakespeare's supremacy in comedy. As Henry VIII had already been treated farcically on the stage, Shakespeare was warning his audience not to expect, as they might well have done, a characteristically comic effort. The Epilogue, also assigned to Fletcher, contains the invitation to the ladies in the audience to lead the applause, almost a formula with Shakespeare, as the Epilogues to *As You Like It* and *2 Henry IV* show. Cranmer's prophecy at the christening of Elizabeth:

She shall be loved and feared. Her own shall bless her;
Her foes shake like a field of beaten corn,
And hang their heads in sorrow. Good grows with her;
In her days every man shall eat in safety
Under his own vine what he plants, and sing
The merry songs of peace to all his neighbours.

o

God shall be truly known, and those about her
From her shall read the perfect ways of honour
And by those claim their greatness, not by blood.

gives to the Queen under whom Shakespeare had
grown to manhood those qualities that are treated elsewhere in his Histories as so necessary for the country's
welfare. The compliment to James that had necessarily
to follow so heart-felt a tribute to Elizabeth emphasizes
a topic that we know from *The Tempest* Shakespeare
was much interested in. There he drew freely on
documents dealing with the affairs of the Virginia company; now Shakespeare refers to the colonial ventures
under James's patronage and the 'new nations' that he,
so prophetically, foresees in the vision he allows to
Cranmer.

Why, it may be asked, did Shakespeare vary the style
of blank verse, alternating between a form that is not
without precedent in some earlier plays, but that does
have affinities with Fletcher's verse, and a type that
employs less frequently double endings, the hepthe-
mimeral caesura, and the inverted accent, to use the
terms employed by Roderick in his early examination
of the metre of *Henry VIII*. The answer is that here
as elsewhere Shakespeare felt the need of variation in
his medium; he wished to set off different aspects of the
action against one another in forms of verse in keeping
with the changes of emotional key. He has only some
seventy lines of prose in 2,800 lines or so, thus dis-
pensing with this form of contrast; nor is there sufficient comedy to provide the light and shade without
which force and definition are unobtainable. The variation in the handling of the blank verse is Shakespeare's
means here of maintaining within the tonality appropriate to his subject the necessary contrast and variety.

In *Henry VIII* Shakespeare at the end brings the story of his country that he had followed through its many vicissitudes to the happier and more spacious days of Elizabeth. Nor does he fear to look into the future with the hope and confidence given him by his study of his country's history, his knowledge of his countrymen, and his own vital spirit.

Chapter Five

THE TRAGEDIES

THE Tragedies are of all Shakespeare's works the most subject to philosophic discussion and interpretation; this is no doubt inevitable as tragedy by its very subject-matter raises in extreme form the question of the nature of dramatic entertainment; but as Shakespeare's tragedies, with two exceptions, belong to his maturity and were his main concern from his thirty-fifth to his forty-fifth year (1599–1608), any effort to see Shakespeare's art in its wholeness must give special attention to what is the most sustained and intense phase of his development as a dramatist.

The attempt to attribute this development to some episode in Shakespeare's private life—to make the fickleness of a dark lady or the fall of Essex the cause of the despair and disillusion that pseudo-biographical commentators always find in the Tragedies—ignores not only Shakespeare's earlier productions but misrepresents the very nature of tragedy itself. Shakespeare had not lived till 1599 in a dream world that excluded the strife in the individual's own nature or in society at large; even were one to put aside *Titus Andronicus* and *Romeo and Juliet* as somehow deficient in tragic power, the early Histories provide a record of strife, revenge, and murder, that shows Shakespeare's familiarity with the ambitions and passions of men. *Henry VI*, *Richard II*, and *Richard III*, though Histories, are full of tragic matter, and cannot be put aside as unrelated to the later development in the Tragedies.

The basic error, however, of the biographical explanation of the Tragedies is the supposition that tragedy is the expression of despair and disillusion and so of a neurotic condition in the dramatist himself. Were such an interpretation of tragedy true, the poets themselves must have been strangely mistaken in their comments on this particular form. Milton regarded it as 'the gravest, moralest, and most profitable of all other Poems'; and although he added the qualification 'Tragedy as it was anciently composed', not being an admirer of Elizabethan or Jacobean drama generally, he included Shakespeare's plays among those productions of a later age, however rare, that had ennobled the tragic scene. And it was *King Lear*, a play often regarded as presenting its author's pessimism in its most naked condition, that Keats chose to illustrate what he took to be the function of art:

The excellence of every art is its intensity, capable of making all disagreeables evaporate, from their being in close relationship with Beauty and Truth. Examine 'King Lear' and you will find this exemplified throughout.

Keats is here explaining in his own way to his brother what Aristotle had taught his students some two thousand years earlier: that tragedy deals with incidents arousing pity and fear, not that fear and pity may be the emotions that finally possess the heart but only a phase in the realization of what makes fear and pity an utterly inadequate response to the action before us. The paradox that Keats like Aristotle finds in tragedy is the paradox at the heart of any moral or religious response to life itself. And this the reader can test for himself by answering a simple question. Does he agree or not with Hall's definition of the Faithful man: in common

opinion miserable; but in true judgement more than a man? Those who answer no must find some explanation of tragedy very different from that proposed by Aristotle and Keats; those who answer yes need have no difficulty in understanding how what Hall calls common opinion may be corrected and transformed and pass into true judgement. This transformation was for Plato the task of philosophy; Aristotle saw the same process as the justification of art. And this initiation into a truer judgement of conduct was, Wilde held, the significance of Aristotle's term *katharsis*. The dramatist asking apparently no more from us than the fear and pity with which common opinion reacts to his episodes yet submits the spectators' whole response to an intensity of treatment—for in Greek *katharsis* can mean purification by fire—that refines and clarifies it.

It is perhaps not too misleading to compare the view of tragedy in Plato's *Republic*, as a form of self-indulgence in emotion, and Aristotle's defence of the form, as a discipline for our common reactions, with the earlier and later interpretations of certain types of dream offered by Freud. For Freud became aware towards the end of his life that dreams in which are re-enacted some terrible experience from the dreamer's past are not wish-fulfilments but a struggle on the part of the sufferer to free his mind and will from disabling memories; in short to regain by such a catharsis of his fears and self-pity normality and health. Freud never seems to have developed this new category in his discussion of art, which remained for him a narcotic or form of day-dreaming. It is clear, however, there lies at the core of any study of life the disturbing thought that virtue, so far from ensuring victory and triumph for its possessor, may be the cause of his destruction, by

exposing him to dangers from which the more selfish shrink, or offering him as an easy target for the malice of those whose only law is their own immediate interest. This is the dreadful thought that informs all tragedy, yet tragedy is, like the sufferer's dream, a reaction against this threat to man's moral freedom. It was because Rymer found the danger of virtue so vividly presented in Shakespeare's tragedies that he denounced them as unchristian and a scandal to Divine Providence; the poet, Rymer felt, must silence any complaints or murmurings against God Almighty by showing that obviously fair distribution of rewards and punishments he so inappropriately named Poetical Justice. Rymer would have tragedy gratify common opinion by ignoring the challenge to which all that dignifies man is exposed.

The notion of tragedy as an exhibition of retribution human or divine is no doubt anchored on Aristotle's expression *hamartia*, and his insistence that the perfect tragic plot will show the cause of the change from happiness to misery to lie not in depravity but in some great error on the protagonist's part. Yet the trouble here is that what may seem a great error when viewed from the standpoint of mere expediency may be morally deserving of praise. Even Bradley, who insists on some form of just retribution as the basis of tragedy, feels compelled to regard the protagonist as in some sense superior to the world. He talks of the world *as it is presented*, and this provokes the question 'presented to common opinion or to true judgement', for these it was agreed may put very different valuations on the actions of men.

It is true that in some tragedies the protagonist can be held to have been guilty of much more than mere

error: Brutus might be regarded as an assassin, Hamlet as a homicide, and Othello as a murderer. Yet moral issues can be judged only from a consideration of the context in all its complexity. It would clearly be wrong to regard Brutus, or Hamlet, or Othello, as guilty of murder in the sense that Macbeth is guilty of murder. The man who kills his trusting sovereign and goes on to murder women and children cannot call himself an honourable murderer. Yet even in *Macbeth* the tragic aspect of the action is not found merely in the vengeance that overtakes a tyrant and murderer. Had Macbeth rejoiced in his wickedness as does Shakespeare's Richard III his fate would not be tragic; but the man whom Macduff kills knows he has already lived too long; the voice he heard saying 'Sleep no more' was that of his own prophetic soul which he struggles vainly to deny. There is something, if one may borrow Lamb's phrase for this type of sinner, of a right line even in his obliquity. Sympathy with the protagonist, even if accompanied by condemnation of his conduct, is an essential element in our sense of the tragic.

Titus Andronicus, the earliest of Shakespeare's tragedies, had belonged to Pembroke's company. They returned to London in August 1593 in a bankrupt condition and had to pawn their costumes; they also parted with their play-books. Sussex' men performed *Titus Andronicus* at the Rose, under Henslowe's management, on 24 January 1594; on 6 February 1594 it was entered in the Stationers' Register and described on the title-page as having been performed by 'the Earl of Derby, the Earl of Pembroke, and Earl of Sussex their Servants'. The title-page of the second quarto (1600) gives more accurately the order in which these companies played in it, as Pembroke's, Derby's, Sussex's, and adds

the latest owners, the Chamberlain's men. As Henslowe's *Diary* gives a very complete record of the pieces performed by Strange's men (Lord Strange becoming Earl of Derby on 25 September 1593) before the closing of the theatres on 23 June 1592, and there is no mention of *Titus Andronicus* in their repertory, the conclusion that they acquired it from the bankrupt Pembroke's men is unavoidable. Henslowe may have acquired it for them, and when Sussex's men performed it at his theatre he put against it in his *Diary* the mark he used to indicate a new or a newly acquired piece.

The reference to Titus and the Goths in *A Knacke to Know a Knave*, performed at the Rose on 10 June 1592, indicates that *Titus Andronicus* was already a well-known piece, and Jonson in the Induction to *Bartholomew Fair* (1614) links it with Kyd's *Spanish Tragedy* as a long out-moded type of Revenge play: 'He that will swear *Ieronimo* or *Andronicus* are the best plays yet shall pass unexcepted at here as a man whose Judgement shows it is constant and hath stood still these five and twenty or thirty years.'

The play opens with a dispute about the election of the new Emperor; Titus arrives in triumph from his conquest of the Goths, declines to accept the Senate's offer of the Imperial title, and secures it for the elder son of the late Emperor, only to find that his pious and patriotic intentions entangle him in a deadly intrigue that involves all the leading characters. Already Shakespeare shows the dynamic power of exposition that sets the action in motion right away, and already he gets the structural centre of his action firmly placed in the third act, with the transformation of the loyal and unselfish servant of his country into the obsessed and determined but half-crazed avenger. The finale in which Titus

serves to the Emperor and his ruthless consort a pie
in which are baked her sons, the villainous Demetrius
and Chiron, has seemed to many too outrageous to be
attributed to Shakespeare, although the device is taken
directly from the *Thyestes* of Seneca, the dramatist then
regarded by scholarly opinion as the model for writers
of tragedy. The resemblance between the type of
revenge practised by Atreus on his brother Thyestes
and that by which Procne punished her husband Tereus
for the rape and mutilation of her sister Philomela
prompted Shakespeare to decorate his Senecan theme
with motifs from Ovid. Add to this such echoes from
Roman story as the slaying of his defiant son by Titus,
and his delivery by his own hand of his daughter
from the dishonour of her rape and mutilation, and
even then the list of classical embellishments is incom-
plete.

To attribute to the author of *Julius Caesar* and
Coriolanus so unrestrained a treatment of classical
themes as is displayed in *Titus Andronicus* has seemed
to many commentators impossible. Yet the construction
of the action in its firmness and clarity is like that of his
early comedies unmatched by any contemporary of
Shakespeare's early years; and for the unchastened
treatment of the material that now seems so un-Roman,
this treatment, as Professor Terence Spencer has so
convincingly shown, was suggested to Shakespeare by
his early excursions in Roman history, before the
discipline of his art and his study of Plutarch had
enabled him to develop a profounder and more human
conception of the Roman scene.

In the imagination of the sixteenth century the
Romans, as Professor Spencer has pointed out, were
Suetonian and Tacitan rather than Plutarchan. Of the

twelve Caesars of Suetonius at least seven, if not nine, died by poison or the sword; and even the calm and classical Augustus could on the capture of Perugia offer as human sacrifices on the Ides of March at the altar of the deified Julius three hundred prisoners of equestrian and senatorial rank. In Guevara's account of the next ten Caesars, translated by Edward Hellowes in 1577, one could read how the Emperor Bassianus, known even in history by his nickname Caracalla, murdered his brother in his mother's arms, slew half the Vestal Virgins because he insisted they were no longer virgin, and then slew the other half because they were. Lack of historical perspective, Professor Spencer concludes, is what allows us to see *Titus* and its horrors as a mere phantasmagoria of Shakespeare's own invention without precedent in classical literature and history. It is the attempt of the youthful schoolmaster turned dramatist to write a Roman tragedy; it was obviously popular in Elizabethan and Jacobean days as Jonson's censure indicates; and it is so well put together that it can still be taken on a successful continental tour by the Stratford company. That Shakespeare was to proceed from this Senecan beginning to a conception of tragedy that challenges, as Jonson admitted, the supremacy of the Greek masters in that kind is evidence of that power of self-development which is the prerogative of supreme genius in drama as in the other arts.

Titus Andronicus is the only formal tragedy of the first period; *Romeo and Juliet* occupies a similar position in the second period and belongs to that group of lyrical plays that come early in Shakespeare's association with the Chamberlain's men, a group that includes *Richard II* and *Midsummer-Night's Dream*.

How Shakespeare's dexterity as a theatrical craftsman

develops to sustain his maturing sense of the dramatic is well illustrated in *Romeo and Juliet*.

Many of the motifs in the story have a long literary history behind them, but it was Luigi da Porto in his novella *Giulietta e Romeo* (1530) who first gave the lovers and their families the names and the local habitation adopted by Shakespeare. Although not the first to set his love story against a background of family rivalry da Porto remembered Dante's denunciation of civil strife in the *Purgatorio* vi, 106–8, and named his warring families the Montecchi and the Cappelletti after factions mentioned by Dante.

Shakespeare may have known da Porto's version, for there are a number of points exclusive to Shakespeare and da Porto, but Shakespeare's most immediate source was Arthur Brooke's *The Tragicall Historye of Romeus and Iuliet*, the title-page of which goes on to say, *written first in Italian by Bandell, and now in Englishe by Ar. Br.* Matteo Bandello's *Romeo e Giulietta* was published in 1554; this version follows da Porto with variations in detail and some additions from cognate versions. It was not Bandello, however, that Brooke did into metre but Pierre Boaistuau's *Histoire* (1559), another version that retains the main features of the story with details from more than one earlier account.

Almost all the main episodes of Shakespeare's play are found in some form in Brooke's poem; yet Shakespeare has completely redesigned the mechanism of the action, if one may use such an expression, to give the love theme its full force and life. The reduction of the months of Brooke's story to days is only an index of this transformation.

It has been objected, however, that the origin of the family feud against which the lovers' parts stand in such

sharp relief is never explained to us and that Shakespeare's general design is as a consequence too weak to carry the burden of the calamity. Yet the very opposite is true: it is the absence of a cause that allows us to see the quarrel in its futility and deadly folly. There is an instructive parallel in Marbot's Memoirs, so admired by Henry James, of how a feud may provide those who know nothing of its origin with a pretext for manslaughter. Two French regiments, who for some unknown reason shared a mutual hatred, found themselves encamped together again for the first time for fifty years; no one now remembered the cause of the quarrel, but arrangements were at once made, the senior officers affecting ignorance of the intention, for a meeting between a representative swordsman from each party. In the encounter the youthful Augereau, later the Duke of Castiglione, disposed of his opponent, a professional duellist who expected to kill his man as easily as he had till then dispatched the many earlier victims of his expertise.

The wanton nature of the feud in Verona is clear from the opening scene in which idle retainers find it an excuse for mischief and Tybalt makes it an occasion for gratifying his quarrelsome humour. The part Tybalt has in the tragedy may illustrate the manner Shakespeare transforms Brooke's story into a drama. In Brooke we are told, incidentally as it were, of a fatal encounter between Romeo and Tybalt; as this is the turning point in the action Shakespeare prepares for it in a way for which there is no hint in Brooke. The first scene shows us Tybalt and Romeo in contrasting attitudes. Their opposition becomes clearer as they are brought closer to each other at Capulet's feast, when Romeo's exchanges with Juliet are all but interrupted

by Tybalt's fury, a fury quite uncalled for as the host himself old Capulet, never a very patient man, insists. The feast is the prelude to the marriage, but also the occasion of the interlude that brings Romeo and Tybalt face to face. Insulted publicly in the presence of his friends by an arrogant bully Romeo acts with a restraint completely incomprehensible to Mercutio, who feels he must cover up his friend's dishonourable submission by his own intervention. Romeo's attempt to separate the combatants gives Tybalt the chance to deliver the fatal thrust. Tybalt's return in his zest for more mischief forces on Romeo the duty, if only in self-defence, of disposing of this incorrigible homicide. The blood of Tybalt gives new life to the expiring quarrel, and the Prince feels bound to banish the man who both by word and deed did his utmost, even at the cost of his reputation with his friends, to keep the peace.

Those who censure Augereau for taking the place of a married man on whom the lot of representing his regiment had fallen and whose chances of survival were poor, like those who think Romeo should have allowed Tybalt to continue to behave as outrageously as he wished, are generally inhabitants of a locality where the police are on the telephone.

Tybalt's death leads to Juliet's ordeal, for it prompts her father to force on her a marriage about which reasoned denial is not possible. The objection that chance now plays too decisive a part in the catastrophe ignores the precise timing required by the Friar's plan. Any delay is naturally fatal. Critics allow Sophocles to let Haemon arrive just too late to save Antigone and to spare his own life. The struggle with Creon has left them both desperate but resolute. Romeo too is a desperate man and his encounter with Paris at the

tomb quickens his despair and his resolution to join
Juliet in death. Those who find Shakespeare's plot lacking in what they regard as tragic inevitability should
explain why the *Antigone* is not equally faulty.

The denial of tragic status to *Romeo and Juliet* cannot
be justified by emphasizing features of the plot that are
not without parallel in plays admittedly tragic. Indeed
the criticism comes from the surprising strength of a
feeling that contributes in some measure to the response
to all tragedy but that may assume unexpected force
when the victims of tragedy are devoted lovers—the
feeling Henry James could formulate as a conviction,
even as he concluded the story of one of his frustrated
heroines, that any passion so great, so complete is, in
spite of fortune and the stars, a life.

The years immediately following the production of
Romeo and Juliet were given by Shakespeare to History
and Comedy; on the opening of the Globe, however, he
began the series of tragedies that make the years 1599
to 1608 the most important in the history of English
drama. *Julius Caesar* must have been produced very
shortly after the opening of the new house, for a Swiss
traveller Thomas Platter, who left some account of his
travels in England, saw it performed there on 21 September 1599:

After lunch, about two o'clock I and my party crossed
the water, and there in the house with the thatched roof
witnessed an excellent performance of the tragedy of the
first Emperor Julius Caesar with a cast of some fifteen
people; when the play was over, they danced very mar-
vellously and gracefully together as is their wont, two
dressed as men and two as women.

The dance Platter admired was the jig, the after-piece
to tragedy as well as comedy at the public theatres.

That it was Shakespeare's play at the Globe and not
some piece on a similar subject at the Rose or the
Swan, both on the South Bank, is confirmed by
references of about this date to Shakespeare's *Julius
Caesar*, by Weever and Ben Jonson, as a new and
popular play in that year.

Shakespeare had already been a borrower from
North's translation of Plutarch as the names of Theseus'
various loves in *Midsummer-Night's Dream*, II. i. 77–80,
indicate; now in *Julius Caesar*, as in the later Roman
tragedies, Shakespeare finds almost all his material in
North, drawing in the present instance on the *Lives* of
Julius Caesar and Mark Antony but above all on that of
Marcus Brutus. For although Shakespeare called his
play *Julius Caesar*, and Caesar may be said to survive in
spirit to be revenged on his assassins, the note on which
the play ends 'This was a man' refers not to Caesar, or
to any ghostly embodiment of the dictator, but to
Brutus. Shakespeare's invariable practice is to bring the
tragic action to a close on the key that is basic in his
design and the foundation of its tonality. Unless, therefore, Shakespeare's treatment in *Julius Caesar* is exceptional, Brutus is the protagonist, and 'the general honest
thought' that moves him the idea that is developed in
the action.

That Brutus acted honestly need not imply that he
acted wisely. Bernard Shaw's complaint that Shakespeare in his ignorance had glorified one of the greatest
political blunders in history comes not from superior
historical knowledge but merely from neglect of Shakespeare's text. Shakespeare took over the situation
described by Plutarch, who for all his republican sympathies does not shrink from saying that the state of
Rome had come to such a pass, owing to the fury and

madness of the people, that the only hope of salvation lay in the rule of a dictator. Accordingly from the opening scene to the murder of Cinna the poet by the irresponsible populace we see the unstable foundation on which Brutus was building his hopes of republican virtue.

In his dream of turning back the current of affairs in Rome Brutus is persuaded to join the conspirators. Cassius knows they must enlist the moral authority of Brutus, yet he lacks the insight to see that such a leader will be their undoing. In the hour of what seems their triumph Brutus commits two errors or faults, as Plutarch describes them, in insisting that the conspirators spare Antony and that they allow him to make the funeral oration that turns their success into defeat. To Cassius the danger is only too apparent, but having surrendered the moral initiative to Brutus, without whose authority the conspiracy could not have found expression in action, Cassius finds himself baffled by considerations in which mere expediency has no part. Cassius when next we see him is making an effort in the critical situation in which the faction finds itself to recover the initiative, yet he is again confronted by a choice between honesty and expediency. Brutus insists on putting a matter of peculation by a subordinate before all other questions, however precarious the position of their forces; and Cassius in the end cannot deny the assertion that those who stabbed Caesar in the cause of freedom and honour would stand as self-confessed murderers should they resort to robbery and oppression.

The quarrel scene has from Shakespeare's own day to the present been regarded as one of the great moments of the play; yet critics have found difficulty in assigning

to it a comparable importance in the structure of the action. Bradley describes it as 'an episode the removal of which would not affect the natural sequence of events', unless, he adds, it explains why Cassius allows Brutus to have his way about fighting at Philippi. This it certainly does and it cannot be treated as an unnecessary though arresting interpolation. For what Bradley calls the natural sequence of events cannot be dissociated in Shakespeare's tragedies from the moral issues from which the events derive their dramatic significance. In the quarrel scene the conflict between honesty and expediency that has smouldered so far now bursts into full view, and we realize how it determines the time and place of the decisive battle.

There is in Plutarch's Life of Timoleon an episode that reduces to its simplest terms the idea that informs Shakespeare's play. Timoleon of Corinth 'was naturally inclined to love his country and common weale; and was always gentle and courteous to all men, saving that he mortally hated tyrants and wicked men'. Unhappily his brother Timophanes was of a contrary disposition, sparing none in his progress to tyrannical power. In a fierce dispute with Timoleon and his friends Timophanes was slain. Although all acknowledged that no selfish motive had prompted Timoleon, fratricide was a deed hardly to be condoned. Cast off by his mother and in retirement Timoleon was unexpectedly called to help the Syracusans whose mother city was Corinth. At the embarkation ceremony the chief magistrate in wishing Timoleon success added these words: 'If you handle yourself well, we will think you have killed a tyrant; but if you do order yourself otherwise than well, we will judge you have killed your brother.' The challenge Timoleon met not because he was to prove, as

he did, successful, but because he conducted himself in all his adventures with courage and humanity. In forgoing the advantages that the murder of Antony might have given him, Brutus behaves very differently from the triumvirs as they prick down those that are to be, in totalitarian parlance, liquidated, and his financial integrity contrasts with their dishonest treatment of Caesar's will. It is this forbearance and integrity that justifies Antony's final tribute to a man honest even in killing, however unwisely, the man he feared would prove a tyrant.

Shakespeare's *Hamlet*, as we have it in the second Quarto of 1604–5 and the First Folio of 1623, may be dated about 1600. In a 1598 edition of Speght's *Chaucer* its owner Gabriel Harvey wrote: 'The younger sort takes much delight in Shakespeares Venus and Adonis: but his Lucrece, and his tragedie of Hamlet, Prince of Denmarke, have it in them to please the wiser sort.' In another part of the same note Harvey says, 'The Earle of Essex much commends Albions England.' One would hardly expect Harvey to use the present tense 'commends' after 25 February 1601, the date of the Earl's execution. The note therefore suggests a date about 1600 for the version of *Hamlet* that is now known.

There was, however, a *Hamlet* on the stage as early as 1589. Nashe in his Epistle prefixed to Greene's *Menaphon*, in some satirical references to theatrical productions, writes: 'English *Seneca* read by Candle light yeelds many good sentences . . . and if you intreate him faire in a frostie morning, hee will afford you whole *Hamlets*, I should say handfuls of Tragicall speeches.' As there is also a reference that points to Kyd as one of the dramatists Nashe is jeering at, the suggestion has been made that Kyd was the author of this early

Hamlet. For this there is warrant neither in Nashe's remarks nor in the subsequent history, as far as it can be traced, of the piece. It was played when the newly formed Chamberlain's men opened after the plague of 1592-4 at Newington Butts with two other pieces by Shakespeare, and later at the Theatre, as a reference in Lodge's *Wits Miserie* (1596) indicates. There is no evidence that any of Kyd's plays went to the Chamberlain's men. The ascription to Kyd seemed plausible only because of the oft-repeated but wholly unwarranted notion that Shakespeare came to London only in 1590, and that he then set about rewriting the work of well-established dramatists, because he was too illiterate to do otherwise.

It may be that Shakespeare's naming his son Hamnet or Hamlet, for the forms were interchangeable, after the friend Hamlet Sadler mentioned in Shakespeare's will, and that a Katherine Hamlet's drowning in the Avon, an event that stirred some local interest in 1580 when Shakespeare was sixteen or so, have no connexion with Shakespeare's first interest in the Hamlet story. Yet they are as suggestive pointers to the authorship of the early *Hamlet* as Nashe's reference. For Nashe is being deliberately vague in his attack on a rival group of dramatists, and leaves the contemporary theatre-goer to identify, as he easily would, the individuals glanced at.

It would be difficult to find in any of the arts a better illustration of the original use of old material than *Hamlet*. Many of the leading characters and important episodes are found in the *Historia Danica* written in Latin about 1200 by Saxo Grammaticus. Yet everything is informed with a new idea, and embodies a conception very different from that found in Saxo's

treatment of the story, or in the French version made by Belleforest in 1576, the fifth volume of his *Histoires Tragiques*. Not only is what may be called the general intention of Shakespeare's play entirely his own, the subordinate intentions, to borrow Henry James's phrase, bring the episodes that have obvious parallels in the source into keeping with the new design.

The opening scene makes us aware of the heroic figure Hamlet's father appeared in life. Saxo's first nine Books are full of the combats and duels between the parties and factions in the earlier years of his story, and the killing in single combat of the King of Norway by Hamlet's father is one of the outstanding feats in this chronicle of famous fighters. The Ghost's appearance to the watch draws from the astonished and puzzled Horatio an account of the duel with Norway, and Shakespeare has established in our minds one of the elements that go to form the idea or general intention of his drama. The other and opposing element that is needed to complete the idea is introduced in the second scene when we learn that the dead King's son is the student from Wittenberg.

In Saxo's story Wittenberg could have no place. His hero belongs to the same tradition as his father; he needs no exhortation to drive him to revenge; he differs from his father only in the subtle and penetrating intelligence with which he baffles and then surprises the uncle who has killed his father and seduced his mother. Wittenberg is the token of the new element introduced by Shakespeare, the *humanitas*, that has somehow to be combined with the ancient valour.

By the end of the first Act father and son have met on the battlements, and the student from Wittenberg has received the command to kill his father's murderer.

The opposing aspects of the idea, the imperative duty of seeing the wild justice done that only a cowardly and disloyal son could shirk and the compunction that a humaner tradition imposes, are now at war in Hamlet's soul; these are the elements that engage in the kind of fighting that will not let Hamlet rest.

Commentators usually belong to one of two groups, some stressing with the older critics such as Goethe the Prince's duty, others of a later persuasion the claims of compunction. Both groups pronounce Hamlet unequal to the situation.

The older critics tended to stress what they regarded as the Prince's delay in performing the command from the other world and the almost accidental nature of the retribution that overtakes Claudius. For Goethe the Prince is a most noble and moral nature but lacks the nerve required of a hero. Yet the man who follows the Ghost, leads the boarding party in the grapple with the pirate ship, kills the man behind the arras, and turns the tables on Rosencrantz and Guildenstern, can hardly be called even by Weimar standards destitute of nerve. Yet a little learning in psychiatric lore has persuaded some later commentators that Hamlet is the first neurotic in literature.

Opposed to those who censure the delay are those who regard Hamlet's whole conduct as merely brutal and his readiness to listen to the Ghost the root of his offending. To Miss Rebecca West it is not Hamlet's delay that is censurable but his will to act that is corrupt and damnable. Miss West seems to regard Goethe as at fault in failing to understand that the effort to avoid sin is a form of sinful self-assertion, a discovery of the New Theology she shares with some of Goethe's later compatriots.

For the conflicting attitudes Hamlet himself may be said to provide the evidence, at one moment describing himself as too cowardly to do his duty, at another declaring himself too brutal to stab a villain at prayer and give him the chance of salvation.

The prayer-scene as it is called is often misunderstood. To ask heaven to forgive you and at the same time to allow you to enjoy the fruits of wickedness is not to pray. Even the priestess at Delphi, as Herodotus reports, could tell the Spartan who asked the oracle if he might safely retain the money he had stolen that to ask the god's approval of a wicked deed was as heinous as the crime itself. And Claudius rises from his knees to put in motion the murder of Hamlet in England.

As the use of the vocabulary of repentance combined with the determination to secure his gains by another murder cannot be regarded even by the most charitable as evidence of the King's contrite heart, so the brutal words of Hamlet as he spares his defenceless enemy should not mislead us into accepting Johnson's judgement that his speech is 'too horrible to be read or uttered'. Yet the thought that he was too decent to stab the kneeling King in the back, let alone the expression of such a sentiment, would have seemed to Hamlet the basest disloyalty to his father. His self-respect requires him to see his compunction as his determination to make his task complete. It is not Claudius who is the Christian here but Hamlet, who, to borrow Bernard Shaw's description of him, is a Christian without knowing it.

The entangled moral issues of the action may be seen reflected in simplified form in the remarks of Johnson on a case of murder that had been before the Court of Session a short time before his arrival in Edinburgh.

Callum Macgregor, indicted for murder, had successfully pleaded that the lapse of twenty years since the
event at issue barred proceedings against him. On this
Johnson observed:

If the son of the murdered man should kill the murderer
who got off merely by prescription, I would help him to
escape; though were I upon his jury, I would not acquit
him . . . the young man, though politically wrong, would
not be morally wrong. He would have to say, 'Here I
am amongst barbarians, who not only refuse to do justice,
but encourage the greatest of all crimes. I am therefore
in a state of nature; for, so far as there is no law, it is a
state of nature: and consequently, upon the eternal and
immutable law of justice, which requires that he who
sheds man's blood should have his blood shed, I will
stab the murderer of my father.'

What Johnson thought the son of the murdered man
would have to say can be said with even more justification for Hamlet. There is no court before which Hamlet
can bring his case. His moral right on Johnson's
premises is clear. To Saxo's Prince the challenge of
villainy is accepted with a zest that has no misgivings:
to the student from Wittenberg it presents a bitter task
to which he has to sacrifice his studies, his love, and his
life. This is what justifies Pasternak in regarding *Hamlet*
as a drama of duty and self-denial, a self-denial far
beyond that demanded of Saxo's Prince, and no less
heroic.

Where Shakespeare found the name Othello no one
yet knows. In Cinthio's *Hecatommithi* III. 7, the story
that formed the basis of Shakespeare's plot, the only
named character is Disdemona; the others are referred
to merely as the Moor, the Captain, the Ensign.

Cinthio offered his story as an illustration of the

dangers of marriage between those of different race and different social background. The danger of such a marriage is an important element in Shakespeare's plot, but it is subordinate to the love that united Desdemona and Othello. For the danger here comes not from any incompatability in the minds and hearts of husband and wife, but from the possibility that the very strength of feeling that enabled them to make their way through all the impediments to their union could be turned to their destruction. In Cinthio the Moor is merely the gull of the Ensign. Shakespeare, however, gives the deception a human and tragic interest by showing how the very qualities that give Othello his ardour and nobility and Desdemona her devotion and loyalty, though perverted and misrepresented by the wickedness that preys on their ignorance, are never more manifest to us than in the moments just before their deaths.

What may be called the psychology of Shakespeare's development of a situation suggested to him by Cinthio's narrative is outlined for us by Keats in some observations he made on the balance of feeling and knowledge in conduct. Without knowledge high sensations exposed their possessor, Keats felt, to the danger he described as 'falling continually ten thousand fathoms deep and being blown up again, without wings, with all the horror of a bare-shouldered creature'. Shakespeare's later tragic protagonists, Othello, Macbeth, Lear, and Coriolanus, all exhibit a disproportion in their natures between what Keats described as high sensations and the knowledge required as a counterpoise. As a soldier the force and impetuosity of Othello's nature are tempered by his service and experience in war. His natural and prompt alacrity, however, expose him in an unknown terrain to a danger he

has never even suspected. There is a somewhat comparable failure in Coriolanus to adjust himself to peace as to war, in 'moving From the casque to the cushion'; and yet the very words with which Aufidius concludes the censure of his rival's conduct, 'he has a merit To choke it in the uttrance', are as applicable to the worst that can be said of Othello as they are to Coriolanus himself. For had Othello's love for Desdemona been of his life a thing apart and not as much his whole existence as Desdemona's love for him was hers, Iago's slanders would not have proved so fatal a poison to his happiness. His crime is not the evidence of a base and brutal nature, but the corruption of what is recognized by a soul as heroic as his own as his true and noble mind.

Othello might be used to illustrate Shakespeare's complete comprehension of a truth that Burke urged on the apprehension of his countrymen: 'All men that are ruined, are ruined on the side of their natural propensities. There they are unguarded. Above all, good men do not suspect that their destruction is attempted through their virtues.' Iago, however, was aware of the vulnerable nature of virtue as he plans to destroy Desdemona and her husband:

> So will I turn her virtue into pitch
> And out of her own goodness make the net
> That shall enmesh them all.

Desdemona's innocence and compassion, Cassio's courtesy and very devotion to the general and his wife that seems to sanction the extra drink that cashiers him, like Othello's own simplicity, provide the occasions that Iago exploits so cunningly.

Shakespeare followed Cinthio in making his prota-

gonist a Moor, for he saw that this enabled him to make intelligible a blindness in Othello that would have seemed improbable in a Venetian. The notion, however, that Shakespeare did not understand the difference between a Moor and a Negro cannot be maintained. In *Titus Andronicus* Aaron the Moor is a Negro; in *Merchant of Venice* Morocco is a tawny Moor. The distinction was familiar: 'For they make the river Senega to divide and bound the Moors, so that on the South side they are black, on the other only tawny.' In 1600 a mission from the King of Barbary visited England. The portrait of the ambassador that headed the mission, Abd el-Ouaked, now hangs in the Shakespeare Institute at Stratford and the subject is clearly not a Negro. Like the painter the Londoners, many of whom must have seen the visitors from Barbary, for they remained some six months in England, would be familiar with the difference between a Negro and Shakespeare's Morocco.

As is usual there is evidence of Shakespeare's reading round his subject. When Brabantio at I. i. 83 talks of raising 'some special officers of night', the dramatist is drawing on the translation of Cardinal Contareno's *The Commonwealth and Government of Venice* by Sir Lewes Lewkenor; there are also borrowings from Pliny's *Natural History* in Philemon Holland's translation—the Pontic sea image, as well as the references to chrysolite, mandragora, and the coloquintida, can all be found there.

Passages from *Othello* are embedded in the bad quarto of *Hamlet* printed in 1603, so that the performance at Court on 1 November 1604 was of an already established play.

No external evidence that would determine the

chronological position among the Tragedies of *Timon
of Athens* has yet been found. To give some colour to
his notion that Shakespeare's concentration on this
form of drama ended in a nervous breakdown, E. K.
Chambers persuaded himself that *Timon* was the last
of the Tragedies and left in its unfinished state by the
dramatist exhausted by his efforts to give expression to
his despair. Timon, however, has little resemblance to
Coriolanus, a very late, if not the last, of the Tragedies;
while with *Lear* it has many affinities of theme and
style. The Alcibiades sub-plot echoing the main *Timon*
plot, recalls if it does not anticipate the purpose of the
Gloster episode in *Lear*.

Timon and Alcibiades react in different ways to what
they regard as the ingratitude of their fellow citizens. In
his effort to persuade the Senate to spare the life of a
soldier and friend, Alcibiades is driven to remind them
of his own claim to be heard with consideration,

> I cannot think but your age has forgot me . . .
> My wounds ache at you.

And he returns from the banishment now pronounced
against him for his importunity to enter Athens as a
conqueror. Timon in a similar key comments on the
Senate's age when they decline to help him, although he
has spared neither his person nor his estate on their
behalf:

> These old fellows
> Have their ingratitude in them hereditary . . .
> And nature, as it grows again towards earth,
> Is fashion'd for the journey dull and heavy.

Timon's indignation, however, takes a very different
course from that of Alcibiades; he withdraws from

human fellowship, and nothing can tempt him to re-turn. It is not the common spleen of disappointed ambition, an unmanly melancholy from change of for-tune, as Apemantus declares, that drives him to soli-tude; for just before Apemantus attributes to Timon his own beggarly spite, we have seen Timon discover enough gold to enjoy the fortunes of his former days, while later he rejects with derision the supreme authority the Senate in their distress come to bestow on him.

It has seemed to some commentators that the gener-ous host of the opening act and the recluse hungry for death at the end cannot be the same man; that while the contrasting and contending elements that go to the making of Shakespeare's tragic characters may have an artistic justification they have no foundation in human nature. Such an opinion, though it might seem more tenable in *Timon* than elsewhere in the Tragedies, mis-represents the nature of Shakespeare's art. Timon's is an exceptional case no doubt; but so was that of the man who crossing the field of Solferino was moved by his compassion for the wounded and dying to think of establishing the organization that carries the Red Cross through a stricken world; for Henri Dunant seems to have spent his last days shut off from society, a recluse to whom the face of man or woman or child was as unwelcome, as disturbing to his solitude, as were the Athenians to Timon in his cave.

It is difficult to see how the second part of *Timon*, which consists of a series of exchanges between Timon and the visitors to his cave, could have held the public stage. Further the study here of the reactions ingrati-tude may provoke is so much more elementary and negative than in *Lear* that only the desire to find

evidence of a neurotic condition, induced in a play-
wright of genius by dramatic composition, would without other evidence regard *Timon* as later than *Lear*, or
associate it with *Coriolanus*.

Henslowe's *Diary* records a performance of *King
Leare* by the Queen's men at the Rose on 6 April 1594.
Soon after, on 14 May 1594, there was entered in the
Stationers' Register *The moste famous Chronicle historye of Leire kinge of England and his Three Daughters*,
but no publication is known to have followed. Not till the
entry in the S.R. of 8 May 1605 is there a corresponding quarto, *The True Chronicle History of King Leir
and his three daughters, Gonorill, Ragan, and Cordella*.

It is generally taken for granted that the *Leir* of the
1605 quarto is substantially the same as the piece mentioned some ten years earlier in Henslowe's *Diary*; and
that this *Leir* is the chief source of Shakespeare's *Lear*
entered in the S.R. on 26 November 1607 in a form that
gives in unusual detail the author, the date of its performance before the King (26 December 1606), and the
company that performed the piece. The quarto dated
1608 was issued with a title-page repeating the detail
given in the S.R. but giving the further information
that Edgar son of the Earl of Gloster is a prominent
character in the play. Crompton Rhodes argued that all
this detail was to distinguish Shakespeare's piece from
the *Leir* published in 1605. No doubt this was one of
the reasons, but although the endings of the *Leir* of
1605 and Shakespeare's *Lear* are very different, and
only in *Lear* is there any part for Edgar and Gloster,
there still remains the question of Shakespeare's right
to appropriate so much of another dramatist's work. As
long as the notion that Shakespeare was in the habit of
rewriting the plays of other dramatists was generally

accepted no difficulty seemed to be raised by regarding
Lear as Shakespeare's revision of *Leir*. The assumption,
however, was based on evidence that is no longer
acceptable, and the relationship of the *Leir* of 1605 and
Shakespeare's *Lear* still requires detailed study. As
Professor Kenneth Muir observes in *Shakespeare's
Sources*: 'Too little is known about Shakespeare's early
career for us to be certain that he never belonged to the
company which owned the play.' Enough, however, is
known of Shakespeare's early career to assert that by
1594 he was an established dramatist with a considerable body of work to his name. That the Queen's men
who performed *King Leare* at the Rose may well have
been the company Shakespeare had served with before
joining Pembroke's men, and that *King Leare* may have
been his work, are admittedly conjectures, but so are
other views of the relationship of *Lear* and *Leir*. The
unusual detail in the Entry for the Quarto of *Lear* and
on its title-page suggest a determination on the part of
Shakespeare and his company to draw attention to their
right to be regarded as the possessors of the play, a
somewhat high-handed claim if *Lear* were no more
than a rehandling of a piece by another author and in
the possession of another company.

King Lear in the form found in the Quarto of 1608
cannot be earlier than Harsnett's *Declaration of Egre-
gious Popishe Impostures* (1603). In that work Dr Samuel
Harsnett, Chaplain to the Bishop of London, examined
certain Jesuit claims to have delivered from devils
that possessed them various afflicted individuals, including some servant girls. The five fiends that Edgar
as Poor Tom declared had been in him at one time are
all borrowed from Harsnett, including Flibbertigibbet
'who since possesses chamber-maids and waiting-

women'. Theobald pointed out the contribution to
Edgar's pretended lunacy that Shakespeare drew from
Harsnett; Professor Muir in a recent examination of
the Chaplain's work has shown how pervasive are its
phrases and words throughout *King Lear*.

In *Lear* as in *Timon* ingratitude provides the force
against which we can measure the reaction of the protagonist. In *Timon* ingratitude is associated with age;
both Timon and Alcibiades regard the Senate as composed of men whose

> blood is cak'd, 'tis cold, it seldom flows;
> 'Tis lack of kindly warmth they are not kind.

In *Lear* ingratitude is seen not merely as the inertia of
age but as an active principle that may animate the
young and harden even the hearts of children against
their parents. Ironically the action takes off from what
Lear feels is an act of ingratitude by his youngest and
best loved daughter; she will not pay the price, the
public proclamation of her love, he requires for his
ostentatious bounty.

Having decreed, as he thinks, that 'Nothing will come
of nothing', he soon discovers that Nothing may also
come from those who have been given everything.
There are not wanting commentators who think that
much can be said on behalf of the Senate who decline to
subsidize a man who gives away his money so freely as
Timon. In the same strain something might be said for
daughters of an imperious father, and that in spite of
the dues of gratitude, were Goneril and Regan not so
unashamedly selfish and wicked. Here Shakespeare
leaves no excuse for the casuistry that would justify the
Senate, a weakness in the structure of *Timon* that may
help to explain why Shakespeare left it unfinished.

Not only is ingratitude in *Lear* more wicked and unnatural than in *Timon*; the reaction is equally powerful.
In *Timon* ingratitude makes one victim a misanthrope,
the other a successful rebel. In *Lear* it stirs in the King
as he passes through the ordeal of flood and fire the
hidden strength in his nature, so that the bonds of age
and infirmity cannot subdue his heart as it goes out first
in compassion to humble sufferers and then in gratitude to Cordelia.

Shakespeare prepares this encounter of father and
child on lines quite contrary to those followed in *Leir*.
There the outcast King goes in search of the daughter
he has himself cast off. There is no sense in Leir of the
sovereign shame, that burning shame that detains
Shakespeare's Lear from Cordelia. Cordelia has to seek
and find her father; and then, and only after he fails to
persuade her to return evil for evil, does he surrender
to the miracle of love. *Lear* has been described as a
study of wrath in old age; this, however, is to omit
what gives the tempest in his mind its significance; it
is as if one described the earthquake and flood and fire
that confronted Elijah in the wilderness and forgot the
still small voice. That Lear can hear and respond so
passionately shows a strength of heart that Timon and
Alcibiades felt beyond the strength of nature at four-
score and upward.

Johnson complained that Shakespeare had in giving
the play so tragic an ending ignored his sources. Even
were *Leir* a source it is singular in offering a happy
ending; in Geoffrey of Monmouth, who is the first to
tell the story, Lear is restored to his kingdom but after
his death Cordelia is imprisoned by her sisters' children
and in despair takes her own life. Some later versions to
clear Cordelia of the sin of self-destruction have her

killed by her captors. Such an ending would not have
allowed Shakespeare to enforce the idea shaping the
play that finds its most explicit expression in the reunion of Lear and Cordelia; even in their deaths they
were not to be divided. In a last rally, as it were, Lear
kills her executioner, and in his anguish as he bends
over his child he cannot but think she lives, and in the
instant dies 'his hart . . . stretched so far beyond his
limits with this excesse of comfort, as it was able no
longer to keep safe his roial spirits'.

It is in these last words that Sidney in his *Arcadia*
describes the death of the blind King of Paphlagonia
who is delivered from the suffering inflicted on him by
his illegitimate son by the son he has himself grievously
wronged. In adapting Sidney's story as a sub-plot
Shakespeare retains the manner of the blind King's
death in the account of how Gloster's heart 'burst
smilingly'; and the Gloster sub-plot allows Shakespeare to offer us in Gloster's relations with his sons a
parallel to those of Lear with his daughters, and to prepare us to feel in the death of Lear what could not be
conveyed directly without violation of dramatic keeping, that Lear dies not in despair but from the excess of
joy, as he thinks Cordelia lives, that his frame can no
longer support.

The reference by the Porter in *Macbeth* (II. iii) to the
equivocator 'that could swear in both the scales against
either scale' is generally taken to refer to the defence of
equivocation by the Jesuit Henry Garnet at his trial on
28 March 1606 for his complicity in the Gunpowder
Plot. The doctrine of equivocation was not heard of for
the first time at this trial, but as there are other in-
dications that *Macbeth* was written in 1606, and as it
is strewn with what are obvious references to affairs

affecting King James, to look further than the Gunpowder Plot, which gave so startling a significance and
publicity to the doctrine defended by the Jesuit, seems
superfluous.

King James on his visit to Oxford in 1605 was met
before the North Gate by 'three Sibyls', who greet
James as a descendant of Banquo to whose issue the
weird sisters had promised *imperium sine fine*. That
Shakespeare may have heard or even witnessed this
declamation of Dr Matthew Gwinne's Latin verses by
the scholars of St John's is possible. The weird sisters,
however, figure so prominently in Holinshed's account
of Macbeth, and are introduced to so different an end
by Shakespeare, that a debt on his part to Gwinne's
pageant need not be insisted on.

The 'thre werd systrys' first appear in Andrew
Wintoun's metrical history in Scots. Macbeth dreams
that they meet him while hunting with Duncan, and
their prophecies spur him to the murder of the King.
In the Latin history by Hector Boece, the first Principal
of the University of Aberdeen, published in Paris in
1527, the sisters of the dream now pass for historical
figures who meet Macbeth and Banquo, who with
Fleance his son is another of Boece's inventions, no
doubt to provide the Stewarts with a suitably ancient
pedigree.

Shakespeare's weird sisters, though Holinshed calls
their counterparts in his story 'goddesses of destinie',
are in some aspects more like witches as Shakespeare's
contemporaries imagined them. Their greetings to
Macbeth do, as he admits to himself, suggest the
thought that he might become king by murdering
Duncan. In the historical context in which his story is
set by Holinshed, this thought is not surprising. As

Professor Dover Wilson reminds us, of the nine kings who reigned between 943 and 1040, the year Macbeth became king, all but two were killed either in feud or by their successors. The thoughts that Macbeth now puts aside as horrible imaginings and terrifying fancies start up again when Duncan proclaims his eldest son the Prince of Cumberland and his successor. At this point in Shakespeare as in Holinshed the thoughts that Macbeth described as fantastical assume a firmer outline. In Holinshed Shakespeare would read that Duncan was here ignoring 'the old lawes of the realme', the Celtic mode of tenure called Tanistry, that allowed the succession to continue in a family group but not necessarily from father to son. Shakespeare, however, does not stress as Holinshed does that Macbeth might feel in resenting Duncan's decision that he had justice on his side; having represented Macbeth as hitherto prepared to leave the promise of rule to be fulfilled by chance, Shakespeare presents Macbeth's reaction to the proclamation as a step on the way to murder. To argue the rights and wrongs of political murder was not here Shakespeare's purpose. He allows us to see how the thought might well occur to a man in Macbeth's position, and that although he was not by temperament without compunction. It is here that Lady Macbeth hurries him into taking what seems to present itself as the perfect opportunity for his half-formed purpose.

Shakespeare in handling Scottish story and legend had no need to observe the limitations, adaptable as these were, that English history imposed on him. In Holinshed the King is killed openly by Macbeth and his supporters among whom Banquo was chief. In the play Macbeth and his wife alone are responsible for the secret murder, Shakespeare adapting features from

Holinshed's account of the murder of King Duff by Donwald, who 'abhorred the act greatly in his heart' but was persuaded by his wife that it was easy to kill an un-suspecting guest. From another murder, that of Duff's son Malcolm, Shakespeare transfers the voice that dis-turbs the sleep of his assassin, the voice that Macbeth thought he heard saying 'Sleep no more'.

Macbeth, though Shakespeare adapted situations from history, is not a historical play; it is a creation of the historical imagination. Shakespeare realizes for us the temptations that might beset such a man as Mac-beth in the conditions prevailing in the Scotland of his day, and not merely the temptations but the hidden and humaner elements in his nature that might assert themselves in spite of himself, driving his wife to suicide and leaving him in the blankness of despair.

The sleep-walking scene belongs to that wonderful group of scenes that includes the reunion of Lear and Cordelia, and the quarrel scene in *Julius Caesar*, in which the moral issues of the storm and strife that have gone before are brought home to us. None, however, surpasses that in *Macbeth* in the skill with which Shakespeare with a few *sotto voce* and almost incoherent phrases not only recalls the whole murderous pageant that has passed before our fascinated eyes but enables us to look on it again, our eyes now open to the spirit and moral quality of the human actions that have held us in suspense.

The witches, the part given to Banquo that frees him from any part in Duncan's death, the show of Kings, the touching for the King's evil, all these features no doubt suggested themselves to the dramatist as likely to interest King James, but have been so exposed to the imaginative fire and pressures that went to the creation

of the fabric of the tragedy that they are now completely incorporated in its splendid design.

Antony and Cleopatra was entered in the Stationers'
Register in May 1608, and was on the stage at least as
early as 1607, if the additions that Daniel made to his
Cleopatra, when he published in 1607 a revised version
of his 1594 text, were, as seems probable, suggested to
him by Shakespeare's play. This date is supported by
the internal evidence of the versification.

As an example of Shakespeare's virtuosity *Antony and
Cleopatra* can hardly be surpassed. Musical critics have
admired the genius with which Bach has at times com-
pressed on to the four strings of the solo violin or cello a
harmonic design so spacious that its complete statement would require the resources of a full orchestra.
Shakespeare's five acts encompass an episode in history
that might seem to require for its proper development
much more than the resources available to a dramatist.
Shakespeare was fortunate in having Plutarch's account
of Antony's part in the story. From Plutarch and his
reading in Appian, and with hints from other treat-
ments of the affairs of the period, Shakespeare was able
to construct a drama that suggests to the imagination
not merely the full and ample range of the Roman
Empire across which Antony moved so powerfully, but
the intense attraction that could reduce for him this
world's 'vastidity' to 'a determin'd scope'.

The battle of Actium is at the centre of the action.
This turning point in the fortunes of the protagonist is,
as always with Shakespeare, in Act III. Here we have
the thematic development, the box which holds what
Pasternak has called the mainspring of the mechanism.
The absolute unity of these two aspects, the thematic
and the constructive by which the theme is given its

embodiment, could not be better illustrated than in Shakespeare's treatment of this phase of the action. Everything is carefully prepared for and we understand why Antony abandons his men so shamefully; and what follows on such a dereliction of duty is equally intelligible. Pasternak has criticized Shakespeare's handling of the middle scenes of his plays as artificial; yet it is impossible to see how Shakespeare could have adapted the historical account of the battle more naturally and powerfully to his purpose. Here in the central scene all that has threatened to draw Antony from the path to power and sovereignty is presented to us in one critical and fatal moment. It might seem unnatural for so proved a veteran as Antony to be represented as taking to flight at the very moment when his skill and valour were most urgently called for. But Shakespeare could appeal to history and had not neglected to give the act dramatic probability.

It is hardly necessary to insist on the stagecraft by which Shakespeare contrives to bring home to us in the agonized exclamations of Enobarbus and Scarus the full significance of the naval battle. The same device is used by Thucydides to enable us to feel how the last and decisive naval engagement in the harbour at Syracuse affected the Athenian forces on shore as they saw their hopes not only of victory but of survival perish in the encounter.

The central and thematic action, if one may use such an expression, here as in all Shakespeare's other tragedies, makes clear the tension between the contrary instincts in the character of the protagonist. No one supposes that Antony runs away because he is afraid, any more than anyone, except Mercutio, thinks Romeo declines Tybalt's challenge from fear; and it is only

commentators who can regard Hamlet's sparing his
kneeling uncle as evidence of some melancholic or mor-
bid hesitation. In every instance the choice is not only
characteristic of the man's nature but fatal to his fortunes. To wish Romeo like Mercutio, or Hamlet without compunction, though not explicitly recommended
to us by commentators, is yet implied in their describing these actions as faults, merely because the sequel is
unhappy. The conduct of Antony is clearly more open
to criticism. As a captain he has failed his men, as the
lover of Cleopatra he has placed her above his duty. In
the lines that bear the title *Which?* Browning, who
found the conflict of loyalties in such a position as confronted Antony a matter for debate, offered a justification of the feeling that seems to conflict with our
apparently more considered censure of Antony's conduct. It is true Antony may be described as a failure
politically, but to the tragic dramatist the terms success
and failure as current in the world have no significance;
they are the impostors that would hinder us from looking at the man himself. And even if we felt justified in
declaring Antony a bad man we should have to admit he
loved Cleopatra, that for her he left even the ranks in
which he had been proud to fight, and that it was not
weakness and mere dotage that made him her victim;
for the force and power of the passion that destroyed
him is itself the evidence of the strength that gives his
fate its tragic interest.

In Cleopatra the dramatist saw the perfect counter-
part of Antony. It was as if the myth Aristophanes told
the party at the banquet given by Agathon had come
true. That Antony and Cleopatra were like the halves
of one of those earlier beings, cut in two by the orders
of Zeus, who had at last discovered one another and

were determined to be made whole again. Cleopatra no more than Antony can be described as a model of domestic deportment; yet she has a place in Chaucer's *Legend of Good Women* and for qualities that Shakespeare in his turn did not fail to develop as he matches her with Antony.

The conflicting currents in the natures and conduct of the lovers are reflected in the comments of Enobarbus whose censure of their proceedings alternates with his recognition of the fascination they exercise over him; and this conflict is carried into his own struggle to escape from a service he can no longer regard as worth while, that yet ends in his death at the very thought of what he feels has been a shameful act of desertion.

A former dramatic critic of *The Times*, John Palmer, writing on 20 February 1934 of a then recent production of *Coriolanus* at the Comédie Française observed: 'Coriolanus, banished from Rome in 468 B.C. resumed his political career in Paris on December 9, 1933, and, incurring once again the wrath of the tribunes, has again departed into exile as an enemy of the people.' It has been said that one can do anything in Paris that does not incur the express disapproval of the Prefect of Police. The conduct of the audiences at the performances of *Coriolanus* became so riotous, even pistol shots being exchanged between boxes occupied by heated political partisans, that the Director suspended the production, for it was obvious that the Prefect would not tolerate for long such hooliganism even in the house of Molière.

The English do not perhaps take the theatre so seriously as do the French; yet English theatre critics can be found expressing themselves about Coriolanus in words, if not in deeds, loaded with disapproval as

strong as that discharged in Paris against his appearance there. 'A beef-witted, overweening patrician . . . a braggart boasting of his victories' is what one critic feels about him; to another he is 'this foul-mouthed, peevish, arrogant, cruel, insensitive, sarcastic Roman traitor'. To yet another Volumnia his mother seems even more defective in humanity, and responsible for her son's pride and vanity.

Were one to read such comment without knowing the play one might suppose that Coriolanus showed up so badly because Shakespeare had placed him against a background of public-spirited and intelligent citizens with no private axes to grind. The briefest examination of the play is sufficient to show that these critics have not been treating Coriolanus as a character in a drama, but as a man who fails to measure up to what the critics regard as their standard of public conduct.

The opening scene shows Marcius at his worst and at his best. He treats his turbulent fellow citizens with contempt: he is ready to take a subordinate place as long as he is allowed to serve in arms. The tribunes interpret his disinterestedness according to their own lights; they think he seeks reputation without responsibility. Act II opens with Rome awaiting the victorious return of Marcius. Menenius is reminding the tribunes that although as individuals their 'abilities are too infant-like for doing much alone', they make much of their importance among the many and are not without personal ambition. The Senate wish to make Marcius, now Coriolanus, consul, but the tribunes insist on his asking in proper form the suffrages of the people. Coriolanus certainly requests the votes of the citizens, as Sicinius foresaw he would, as if he were asking for something that he disdained to think was in their power

to give. Yet the plebs are not without some sense of what his rudeness obscures and give him their voices. Here the tribunes have to intervene to present the conduct of Coriolanus in another light; and they do not hesitate to ask the people, easily argued out of their first and instinctive reaction to the candidature of Coriolanus, to pretend that it was their tribunes who had persuaded them to support him. Underhand malice and cowardly pretence are not mentioned among the faults we have heard attributed to Coriolanus; the strategy of the tribunes should, however, be remembered when we examine a later phase in the debate.

The third act begins with the tribunes opposing the progress of Coriolanus, rousing his anger, and summoning the people to support them. In the disturbance Coriolanus and his supporters drive off the tribunes and their following. It is clear, however, that the multitude cannot be overcome by force, and the Senators and tribunes agree that Coriolanus shall appear before the people and answer for his conduct. In the next and central scene Volumnia points out to her son that all he has to do is to speak to the people as if he were their servant, not as their master, whatever his intentions when in office; but Coriolanus, astonished at his mother's attitude, does not hesitate to describe what she calls policy as deliberate lying and adds

> I will not do't
> Lest I surcease to honour mine own truth
> And by my body's action teach my mind
> A most inherent baseness.

This so angers his mother that he has to pacify her by promising to obey her injunctions.

Volumnia has been censured and Coriolanus denounced for showing 'a wanton disregard for the values

that form the moral basis of any decent society'. It is
clear, however, that in the society where Brutus and
Sicinius exert such political power Volumnia has proposed the correct answer, and one that might be forgiven a mother, to their lying and treachery, provided
we regard political victory at any price, as the tribunes
do, as the end of party politics. Nor is it true to say that
Coriolanus responds finally to his mother's persuasion;
there is nothing of the cogging and mountebanking,
for Coriolanus does not hesitate so to describe what
is required of him, in the scene that follows, at least
not on his part. The tribunes see to it, even were
Coriolanus capable of dissembling, that there will be
only one outcome from what was to be a judicial
assembly.

By the end of the fourth act the traitor, as the
tribunes described him to the approving multitude, is
again at the gate from which the people at their tribunes'
instigation had hooted him out. The tribunes, the
people, Rome itself, are at the mercy of Coriolanus.
One may fairly ask here who has betrayed the republic;
for one can do so without enlisting with the enemies of
one's country. To say that the tribunes are competent
in their management of affairs and show a cleverness
beyond the capacity of so beef-witted a fellow as Coriolanus is only true if competence and cleverness may be
used to describe manœuvres that lead directly to total
destruction; for that, all agree, is inevitable if Coriolanus
does not show a forbearance that was not extended to
him.

In the fifth act the issue is determined between
Volumnia and her son. To speak with one commentator
of 'Volumnia's denial of values essential to life' when
she saves the city at the price of the person she holds

most dear, is a strange assessment of the character who makes such a sacrifice for the common good, as well as in the cause of honesty. To talk with Wyndham Lewis about Coriolanus as a boy of tears is to look at him with the eyes of the man who was about to murder him, and that in circumstances that made the deed a specially cowardly one. We cannot expect Aufidius, a jealous rival for prestige, to see that in listening to his mother at the end, and forgoing revenge at the risk of his own life, Coriolanus reveals himself to us as her twice valiant son; one might, however, expect commentators to take a more dispassionate attitude. To say he brags as he reminds the cowards who are closing in on him, standing defenceless in an alien city, that they had in war fled before him is to misrepresent a gesture of defiance and contempt, in one impatient as ever, no doubt, but utterly fearless, a man who never spoke of his own prowess except when to do so was an act of reckless courage and a challenge not merely to his enemies, but to all who wonder how a character who has so alienated from himself the hearts of his critics can yet be the protagonist of what is admittedly the severest and most Roman of all Shakespeare's tragedies.

The audience at the Comédie Française unfortunately found it easier to indulge their political prejudices than to think and feel about the real debate Shakespeare has presented so starkly in this tragedy; nor have English critics always helped in disentangling from the claims of the contending parties in the drama the human issue in which Shakespeare found his interest and his inspiration.

Troilus and Cressida was entered in the Stationers' Register on 7 February 1603 by James Roberts, with

the note 'to print when he hath gotten sufficient
authority for it'. This was an entry to prevent unauthorized publication, as no edition followed till 1609,
when a Quarto was issued by Bonian and Wallcy,
seemingly in defiance of the wishes of the King's
men.

The title-page of the first issue of the 1609 Quarto
offers the play 'As it was acted by the Kings Maiesties
servants at the Globe'. This title-page was cancelled,
the reference to public performance omitted on the new
title-page, and there was added a short introduction
headed, 'A never writer to an ever reader. Newes.' This
refers to the piece as 'a new play, never stal'd with the
Stage, never clapper-clawd with the palms of the
vulger'. 'New' here must mean new to the reader, and
unfamiliar to theatre-goers, for the play had been
written six or seven years before it appeared in print.
The writer goes on to say 'Amongst all [his Comedies]
there is none more witty than this. . . . It deserves such
a labour [of comment], as well as the best Commedy in
Terence or Plautus.' And he adds that it is none the
worse 'for not being sullied with the smoaky breath of
the multitude', and that it is now printed contrary to
'the grand possessors wills'.

Bonian and Walley must have recognized the
authority of their informant before they expended time
and money on the changes suggested by him. Internal
evidence supports the conclusion that the play was
written for private performance, not, however, at
Court, for the epilogue spoken by Pandarus suggests
that there may be in the audience some with venereal
disease who may dislike further revelations. Shakespeare in his Epilogues, when he addresses the female
part of his audience, as he often does, always does so,

however jocularly, within the limits prescribed by the decorum of the age; it would seem, therefore, that the audience for *Troilus and Cressida* was a male one; for the 'maidens' addressed at the conclusion of III. ii are obviously male. Further, Professor Evans has pointed out in his analysis of the piece how it differs from plays written for normal production; there Shakespeare prepares his audience for every step in the argument, while in *Troilus* an acquaintance with the story is taken for granted. Where an audience sufficiently learned to enjoy Shakespeare's deliberately cynical treatment of classical material, and sufficiently sophisticated to be addressed in the terms used by Pandarus, could be found outside the Inns of Court it is difficult to guess. A special audience of this sort would allow one to discount any idea that the play reflects some deep-rooted cynicism in its author's attitude at this time; the satiric strain would be in part at least explained by the quality of persons in the audience and the time and place of the performance. The printing of the piece may have been made possible by a transcript passing to the publishers from private hands, for transcripts of a special piece for private collectors are not unknown in Jacobean times. Later in 1623 when Heminge and Condell were having their edition of Shakespeare's plays published, Walley made difficulties about their right to include *Troilus*, and his objections obliged the cancellation of the first attempt to print it immediately after *Romeo and Juliet*. Just before the publication of the First Folio, and too late to include *Troilus* in the Catalogue of contents, it was inserted in a kind of no-man's land between the Histories and the Tragedies. Heminge and Condell meant to put it among the Tragedies; yet the author of the *Newes* before the Quarto in

introducing *Troilus* as the wittiest of comedies was not doing so in ignorance of its nature. Ambiguous between comedy and tragedy the peculiarity of the piece is doubtless to be accounted for by the special occasion for which it was designed.

The Trojan war is treated as a foolish expenditure of life, all for a somewhat worthless woman. Achilles is a sulky unchivalrous but dangerous fellow, Ajax a blockhead, the gull of the cunning Ulysses; Paris and Helen in no way an attractive pair, with Hector and Troilus among the few heroic figures, Troilus, however, captivated by the wanton and heartless Cressida. Pandarus provides the chorus to the wooing as does Thersites in his scurrilous manner to the general situation.

There is no question here of Shakespeare's treatment being attributable to ignorance. As Professor Muir's summary of his borrowing shows, Shakespeare was familiar not merely with Chaucer's *Troilus*, but with the relevant work of Henryson, Lydgate, and Caxton. In 1598 Chapman published his translation of seven books of the *Iliad*; in addition to knowing this translation, Shakespeare had some knowledge of books yet untranslated by Chapman; Shakespeare's 'less Greek' may have been sufficient for this. For this play as for others Shakespeare obviously got up his subject, and his treatment of his material is deliberate and carefully considered.

The affairs of Troilus and Cressida are seen against the background of war, and this itself is given an added depth by what may be called the political considerations that govern its phases. Shakespeare anticipates here the brilliant development of the relations between politics and war in *Antony and Cleopatra*. Ulysses' famous

address on the importance and necessity in all enter-
prises of the observance of degree, priority, and place
is now as familiar as Antony's appeal to his 'Friends,
Romans, countrymen', although there is still a ten-
dency to take the argument of the politic Ulysses as an
explicit statement of Shakespeare's own political creed.
At the other extreme we have Thersites telling Achilles
and Ajax that 'Ulysses and old Nestor, whose wit was
mouldy ere your grandsires had nails on their toes,
yoke you like draught-oxen, and make you plough up
the wars'.

This is the world in which Troilus sets his heart on
Cressida, and finds himself as unfortunate in love as
Troy and her children are to prove in war. No doubt
there is something unusual in the passion and devotion
Troilus feels for Cressida that lays him open to the
laughter or at least the amused comment of the world,
and in beleaguered Troy to the malice of chance and
accident. But though those with an eye for incon-
gruities have amused mankind with the contrast that
Troilus himself feels between a desire that is boundless
and the act that is a slave to limit, and have given an
added zest to the discomfiture of the idealist by the
response he often receives from the object of his passion, the cool scrutiny that an Alceste may receive from
a Célimène, or the cynical treatment that Troilus meets
with, yet the foundation of the jest is the sincere and
compulsive nature of their passion. Were it in any way
a mere pretence or fashionable affectation or simple
selfishness their situation would not seem so ridiculous.
While, therefore, *Troilus and Cressida* cannot be placed
in the same category as the straight tragedies, and its
protagonist regarded as among the accepted tragic
heroes, it is equally mistaken to treat Troilus as a

R

purely satiric or merely comic character; if a term must be found for his peculiar role, one might perhaps borrow a title from Meredith and describe Troilus as Shakespeare's tragic comedian.

EPILOGUE

THE monument to Shakespeare that now stands within the chancel rail of the church of the Holy Trinity at Stratford was erected by his family shortly before 1623, as it is referred to by Leonard Digges in the memorial verses he contributed to the First Folio. As the son of the former Mrs Digges, now married to Thomas Russel who lived near Stratford and had acted as supervisor of Shakespeare's will, Leonard Digges no doubt spoke of the monument from personal inspection. It was the work of Gerard and Nicholas Johnson, or Janssen, of a family from Amsterdam, whose yard stood on the Bankside next to the Globe theatre.

The chief feature of the monument is the half-length effigy of the poet himself in the act of composition. Above his coat-of-arms is in bas-relief and below are cut a Latin and an English epitaph:

Iudicio Pylium, genio Socratem, arte Maronem,
Terra tegit, populus maeret, Olympus habet.

Stay Passenger, why goest thou by so fast?
Read if thou canst, whom envious Death hath plast
Within this monument, Shakspeare, with whome
Quick nature dide, whose name doth deck this Tombe
Far more than cost; sith all that He hath writt
Leaves living art but page to serve his witt.
  Obiit Año. Do¹. 1616
  Ætatis 53 Die 23 Apʳ.

If those at Stratford who cherished Shakespeare's memory had no doubts about his genius and his lasting fame, his colleagues in London who collected his plays

for the delight of after times felt they did so not merely because of the excellence of his wit, but because, as the last of the inner circle of the company that Shakespeare had joined some thirty years before, they felt they had a duty 'to keepe the memory of so worthy a Friend, and Fellow alive, as was our Shakespeare'. In addition to their dedication to the Lord Chamberlain the Earl of Pembroke, and to his brother the Earl of Montgomery, Heminge and Condell explained in a note 'To the great Variety of Readers' the effort they had made to give the public an authentic version of the plays, and the means at their disposal for doing so. As further tributes to Shakespeare they included Ben Jonson's lines 'To the memory of my beloved, The Author Mr William Shakespeare', as well as contributions from two Oxford scholars, Leonard Digges and his friend James Mabbe, and one from Hugh Holland of Cambridge.

Heminge and Condell included thirty-six plays in the volume they gave the public in 1623 as *Mr. William Shakespeares Comedies, Histories, and Tragedies*. This is now known as the First Folio, to distinguish it from the later editions in this format in 1623, 1663, and 1685, known respectively as the Second, Third, and Fourth Folios. Sixteen of the thirty-six pieces were being printed in 1623 for the first time. The authority for their publication is recorded in the Stationers' Register as follows:

8th November 1623. Master Blounte. Isaak Jaggard. Entred for their Copie under the hands of Master Doctor Worrall and Master Cole warden Master William Shak-speers Comedyes Histories, and Tragedyes soe manie of the said Copies as are not formerly entred to other men. vizt. Comedyes. The Tempest. The two gentlemen of Verona. Measure for Measure. The Comedye of Errors.

As you like it. All's well that ends Well. Twelfe night.
The winters tale. Histories. The thirde parte of Henry ye
sixt. Henry the Eight. Tragedies. Coriolanus. Timon of
Athens. Julius Caesar. Mackbeth, Anthonie and Cleopatra. Cymbeline.

Of the other twenty plays in the First Folio, all had
already appeared singly in quarto format, some, however, in pirated and imperfect versions. All twenty,
however, with the exception of *King John*, had been
entered in the Stationers' Register, although not in all
instances before their first printing.

Since copyright as now understood did not then
exist, and as entry in the Register secured for the
member of the Stationers' Company who made it the
printing rights of the piece entered to him, Blount and
Jaggard had to associate with themselves in the publication of the First Folio other members of the company who already possessed printing rights in certain
of the quarto pieces.

For the sixteen plays entered to Blount and Jaggard,
Blount being a stationer and Jaggard the printer, the
printers had to work from manuscripts supplied by
Heminge and Condell. For the other twenty the
printers used, whenever possible, quarto texts with any
corrections or alterations, suggested by the corresponding manuscripts, set out in the margins or between the
lines of print. That there would be errors in the process
is to be expected, and as neither the proofs of the Folio
text nor those for the earlier Quarto texts were read
except by someone in the printer's shop, it is perhaps
surprising that there are not even more errors and confusions in the text than those so far detected. The
printers, however, in part because their manuscript
material was more adapted for use in the theatre than

for their convenience, in part because they preferred to work from printed copy even if heavily corrected from manuscript, left throughout their texts a sufficient scattering of error to tax the patience and ingenuity of a long line of editors who are not likely to lack successors in the years yet to come.

In modern editions of the text *Pericles* is generally added to the thirty-six plays attributed to Shakespeare by Heminge and Condell. As *Pericles* was entered in the Stationers' Register to Blount as early as May 1608, it cannot have been excluded from the First Folio for want of authority to print. Although the second half of the play is clearly by Shakespeare, the first two acts can hardly be from his hand, and we may presume that Heminge and Condell omitted it, though a popular piece, as only in part by Shakespeare. It had been printed in very imperfect form in quarto in 1609 and attributed to Shakespeare on the title-page. In 1664 it was added to the second issue of the Third Folio with a number of other pieces not by Shakespeare; its addition to the canon at that late date gives no authority to its attribution even in part to Shakespeare, which must rest on the evidence of the style and temper of those acts that link it with the last group of comedies known as the Romances.

FURTHER READING

THE discussion of Shakespeare's work by such critics as Maurice Morgann, Johnson, Coleridge, and Lamb, hardly needs mentioning; its importance is so generally recognized. Of modern works, the best brief introduction to a study of Shakespeare's Life and Times is *Shakespeare Truth and Tradition* by J. S. Smart; although regarded by A. W. Pollard as 'a new landmark in Shakespeare scholarship' it has long been out of print. *A Life of William Shakespeare* by J. Q. Adams, though out-of-date on some points, is still a very useful account of Shakespeare's theatrical connexions. The student should then be able to use E. K. Chambers's *William Shakespeare*, especially useful for the Appendices in Vol. II. In 1911 E. K. Chambers held that 'The Shakespeare drama is magnificent and incoherent; it belongs to the adolescence of literature, to a period before the instrument had been sharpened and polished, and made unerring in its touch upon the sources of laughter and tears'. This and his Academy lecture of 1924, *The Disintegration of Shakespeare*, show the assumptions Chambers was struggling by 1930 to escape from, an effort that makes his discussion difficult, except to those who come to it with some understanding of his problems. *Shakespeare's England*, by various authorities, provides a guide to many important features of the age.

Among literary and dramatic studies Granville-Barker's *Prefaces to Shakespeare* have the interest that attaches to the interpretation of one who was not only an actor and producer but also a dramatist. A. C. Bradley's *Shakespearean Tragedy* has been for a period out of fashion; but as Miss Lascelles has recently observed, 'for all the perils of misunderstanding with which it is beset, the study of the characters in their relation with

one another . . . remains the right approach; and its alternative, a pursuit of phantoms'. Dr Helen Gardner's *The Business of Criticism* and Professor Alfred Harbage's *As They Liked It* have much that is pertinent to the study of Shakespeare.

Of studies devoted to special aspects one may mention *Shakespeare's Globe Play-house* by J. C. Adams, *Shakespeare's Audience* by A. Harbage, Shakespeare's *Sources* (Comedies and Tragedies) by Kenneth Muir, *Narrative and Dramatic Sources of Shakespeare* (to be completed in six volumes) by Geoffrey Bullough, and Dr Leslie Hotson's *I, William Shakespeare*, as well as his other important discoveries.

The introductions by Professor Dover Wilson to *The New Shakespeare* published by the Cambridge University Press and those by various scholars to the *Arden* edition published by Methuen are full and scholarly. *The Shakespeare Survey* edited by Professor Allardyce Nicoll provides in addition to special articles a review of the year's work on Shakespeare.

INDEX

R*

THE HOME UNIVERSITY LIBRARY
OF MODERN KNOWLEDGE

252

SHAKESPEARE